Advance Praise

"I love this book. The first time I read it I was bowled over, and each time I return to it, I find some new wonder. It's a book about a culture—and a way of being—that seems almost fantastical, although it was just a few decades ago. It's a book about manners, about putting on a brave front, about brilliant women trapped in a moment that expected everything and nothing from them. Set in Los Angeles over a period ranging from the 1970's to the present day Haldeman locates a great story within a girl's life, and her eye for the exquisite detail—of clothes, of decor, of catered food served in silver chafing dishes—has a precision reminiscent of Didion writing at the height of her powers. Funny, sly, open-hearted and beautifully written, it's a winner from the first page to the last."

> —Caitlin Flanagan, staff writer, *The Atlantic;* author of *Girl Land*

"Old time, moneyed Los Angeles. Women whose lives are dictated by the men they're married to, and a child narrator who sees it all. *Kids and Cocktails Don't Mix* is the tender yet quick-witted story of Heatherbean, an overweight girl trying to make sense of world that doesn't and shouldn't make sense, and Marilyn, her starstruck mother who yearns for the glamour and ease life has told her to expect. Haldeman has crafted an enthralling tale that mixes the allure of rubbing shoulders with the glitterati with the harrowing grit underneath the sparkle. Reading this story, I cheered for Heatherbean and Marilyn, wanted to take a two-by-four after Heather's father, and felt my heart break again and again, set off by bouts of laughter."

> —Bernadette Murphy, author of *Harley and Me*

"In *Kids and Cocktails Don't Mix* we meet the Eaton family—observant Heather, her self-assured older sister April, their unreliable father, and larger-than-life mother, the unsinkable Marilyn. They enjoy a glamorous lifestyle in an exclusive Hancock Park neighborhood, but when the marriage collapses and funds run out, Marilyn, trained for no work outside the home, must seek a new breadwinner. Heather, the youngest, overlooked in a fractious blended family, finds ways to console herself. The author has an eye for telling detail, a compelling, honest voice and a sly sense of humor, viewing the often tragic occurrences with accuracy but also love. A fascinating and entertaining memoir of tribulations and survival."

—Marjorie Tesser, Editor, *Mom Egg Review*

Kids and Cocktails Don't Mix

Enjoy!

Heather Holdener

Kids and Cocktails Don't Mix

A Memoir

Heather Haldeman

Apprentice House Press
Loyola University Maryland

First Edition

Hardcover ISBN: 978-1-62720-335-7
Paperback ISBN: 978-1-62720-336-4
Ebook ISBN: 978-1-62720-337-1

Printed in the United States of America

Design: Sarah Thompson
Promotion plan: Peyton Skeels
Managing editor: Danielle Como

Published by Apprentice House Press

Apprentice House Press
Loyola University Maryland
4501 N. Charles Street
Baltimore, MD 21210
410.617.5265
www.ApprenticeHouse.com
info@ApprenticeHouse.com

For all those who, as children of divorce,
felt fat, ugly, and dumb, I see you.
And for my mother Marilyn, who in the end, saw me.

This memoir is faithful to how I recall actual events in my life. Though I recreated some conversations, they remain true to the timbre of those events. To respect the privacy of individuals, I have changed some names.

Chapter One

1964: 127 Fremont Place

Kids and cocktails don't mix.
—Mom

"Damn it," Mom shook her finger, looking at the orange-painted fingernail she'd just broken. The manicure was brand new, and now, look at it. Ruined.

Balanced on a stepstool, a hammer in one hand, a nail in the other, and a scowl on her face, she was decorating the house for that night's party. She let go of the offending fish net, which fell to a heap on the back porch.

"Your father should be here doing this. Not playing golf at the goddamn Wilshire Country Club."

"But you love to decorate for parties." I dangled my chubby legs from a patio chair, breathing in the buttery smells coming from the kitchen. Josephine, the caterer, was making cheese-puff hors d'oeuvres.

Two men from Abbey Rents, meanwhile, lined Tiki torches along the perimeter of the landscaping that framed the large pool. When the sun went down, those torches would light up the yard, casting an enchanted glow. The pool lights would be turned on, flowers floating on the surface.

"Hand me the net, Heatherbean," Mom said, using the nickname she'd given me because I looked like a bean when I was born. A lima bean, I always assumed. I'd entered the world two weeks overdue with a nice layer of fat to get me started.

Mom pounded the edge of the netting into the pillar. Dressed in stovepipe capris with a white blouse tied at the waist, she was a fashion plate for 1964. She stepped down and dragged the stepladder over to the other pillar. I trailed behind with the netting.

"Ma'am, where do you want this?" A man appeared, pushing a thatch-covered cocktail bar on a dolly.

"Over there." She pointed the broken-nailed finger to an open area by the pool. "Front and center where everyone can get to it."

Why everything was a Hawaiian theme when we lived in Los Angeles I never understood. But it was beautiful, enchanted and dreamlike.

Mom stepped down, the hammer next to the top of her slim thighs, and surveyed the blue glass balls on the ground awaiting their artful arrangement in the net. She waved her arms to take in all the magical décor. "This is what sets the scene."

••

With Hollywood names like Jack Lemmon and Blake Edwards as clients, my father's law practice was thriving. The money was flowing and Dad had decided a year earlier that we should move from our modest home to a more impressive one. I was eight when we moved into 127 Fremont Place.

One of the few gated communities in Los Angeles, Fremont Place was a well-known and sought-after address in LA at the time. The entrance, at the intersection of Rossmore and Wilshire, was impressive, with large stone gates and a security guard named Hank. The reality, though, wasn't what it seemed. Hank was a retiree and spent most of his time asleep, sitting up in his dated parked patrol car. Even the car was a pretense, unable to reach speeds in excess of 10 mph, parked only as a deterrent to intruders. Like much on Fremont Place, it was just for show.

Most of the 73 homes in this private park—mansions, really— were over fifty years old, each with its own grand style. The silent film star Mary Pickford had once rented number 56. During our time on Fremont, the musician Lou Rawls, the California Secretary of State, Marge Fong Eu, and the world-heavy boxing champion Mohammed Ali all became our neighbors.

Ours was a beautiful white colonial with a center-hall floor plan, spanning 4,500 square feet. The purchase price in 1963 was $67,500.

••

On another night, a cold winter one, Mom set the scene with a roaring blaze in the fireplace of the spacious living room. Candlesticks of varying sizes held green-ridged candles, color-co-ordinated with the throw pillows on the white sectional. Placed on side tables, the coffee table, and just about every surface, they lit the rooms with their flickers. Fancy people wearing cocktail dresses and dark suits stood around talking, smoking, and drinking in the ethereal, dim glow.

By the mantle, my maternal and paternal grandfathers were deep in conversation. My mother's father, Goodwin J. Knight, whom we called Papa, was the former Republican Governor of California. He'd left office in 1959. Cal, my paternal grandfather, was the boxing promoter at the Olympic Auditorium in downtown LA.

Cal stood a few inches shorter than Papa, who always seemed larger than life. Amazingly, Cal was not bitter about the time Papa Goodwin had lifted the lid on dirty dealings in the boxing business back in 1956. Now, the two men clinked his Scotch glasses, deep in conversation. Papa's second wife Virginia, my mother's step-mother, stood next to her husband, while Dad's stepmother, next to Cal, was draped in pearls and still wearing her fur coat. She wore her hair in a bubble 'do that matched my mother's exactly, only Aileen's was flaming red and Mom's a frosted yellow blonde.

Cal and Aileen had only stopped by the party for a quick visit. She put her arm through Cal's. "It's time to go," she said. "We'll be late for Chasen's."

Papa, though, stayed for the whole party. His presence was a must at any of the soirees, not so much because he was family. "Your father likes to surround himself with important people," Mom said. "It makes him feel like a big man."

Meanwhile, Josephine was in the kitchen, heating up the cheese-puffs. Winter or summer, tiki torches or roaring fires, there would always be cocktails and cheese-puffs.

I was eight, of average height and thirty pounds overweight. Those puffs were my favorite. Mom, who counted her calories to stay thin, had recently begun monitoring my food. Having a fat daughter didn't fly with her. My sister April, five years older, balked whenever Mom handed me cookies and treats to shut me up. "Don't keep feeding her like that! It's not right, Mom." And now, I was overweight.

I snuck into the kitchen and ate fistfuls of the piping hot, bite-size treats, fresh out of the oven, burning the roof of my mouth. My chubby hand was quick. I barely had time to savor the cheesy taste. I didn't want Mom to catch me eating them. If she saw me, a flash of anger would appear in her clear, light-blue eyes, outlined in false lashes. "Quit that!"

Dinner at these parties was dished up in the dining room buffet-style in large silver chafing dishes lit with Sterno. Every time the swinging door opened from the dining room to the butler's pantry, the purplish flames waved violently and then settled back

4

down. Josephine favored recipes like Beef Stroganoff and Turkey Tetrazzini. The main course always covered a heap of thick egg noodles.

Parties were the only time our house smelled like a real home. Mom's meals, workaday dishes like stew and hash, were okay, but there was something comforting about the aroma of Josephine's cooking.

After I'd had my fill of cheese-puffs, I crouched behind the antique wooden cradle in the hall that Mom had filled with fake ferns and rubbery Philodendron to spy on the guests. The waxy leaves provided the perfect coverage. On this night, Connie and Richard Rossi, my parent's best friends, were bragging about Connie's latest piece of jewelry, a gift from her husband.

"Richard won another case," Connie crowed.

Like my father, Richard was a successful attorney. They spoke with Aunt Carolyn, my Mom's younger and only sibling. Connie stretched out her arm, twirling at the wrist to show off her latest shiny bangle. Aunt Carolyn didn't pay much notice. She looked bored, puffing on a cigarette, and sipping her vodka. She wasn't interested in trappings. Mom said Carolyn was a really a Beatnik disguised in a shirt-maker dress and blonde ponytail.

Back by the mantle, Virginia took her third glass of wine from the server's tray, replacing it with an empty one. Papa and Virginia had married ten years earlier while he was still Governor. His former wife, Arvella, had died back in 1952. It was the first time a sitting Governor of California had married at the Governor's Mansion. I'd seen the picture. Papa, with his compact physique and distinguished grey hair, was barely visible carrying Virginia over the threshold. She wore a wide smile, her shapely legs spilling out of a big petticoat.

"Did you notice? Hank was asleep in his patrol car again in front of Cardinal McIntyre's house," Papa was talking to Uncle Charlie, Aunt Carolyn's husband.

Charlie puffed his chest and took a sip of his drink. "Well, Governor, as a lawyer…"

"Hey, good buddy," Dad interrupted, putting a hand on Charlie's shoulder.

Papa ignored my father. "Go on, Charlie."

Charlie gave a weak smile to Dad and continued. "As I was saying, I think they need more than one guy patrolling Fremont. There are 73 homes in here. Important people live here." He paused to take a sip of his drink. "These people are rich, and lousy wrought iron gates at the end of the street are not going to deter the criminal faction."

My father nodded in agreement. He creased his forehead, his bushy dark eyebrows meeting as one.

"Not to mention," Uncle Charlie said, "that patrol car is next to useless."

"Lot of good he does protecting Fremont Place," Papa laughed. "People can get away with driving through those front gates at all hours of the night. Hank would never have made my detail up in Sacramento."

My father looked uneasy. "If you'll excuse me, I need to refill my drink."

••

Papa didn't trust Dad, even though it was Papa himself who was responsible for my parents getting together in the first place.

When Papa had been Lieutenant Governor, he'd disapproved of my mother's desire to become an actress and wanted her to settle down. He learned that his friend and campaign contributor, Cal

Eaton, was likewise unhappy with his son's taste in women. "He only dates showgirls," Cal had complained to Papa.

"Let's set them up on a blind date," Papa suggested.

"Friday night fights at The Olympic. I'll arrange it," said Cal. "Let's hope they can like each other. If they do, we'll be in fat city."

Mom and Dad's first date had been a middle-weight boxing match surrounded by other well-dressed spectators in front row seats.

After that date, Mom reported back to her parents. "He's slim and not that tall. But, he's fur-on-a-bear, full of action and life. Bob can open up a room; he's got that way about him. He's fun and games, and I'm hooked."

They met in April, were engaged by July, and married five months later on a rainy evening in December. Just before the wedding day, Mom's little teenage sister, Carolyn, provoked Mom, teasing her about being a blushing bride. Just as my mother lifted a hand to playfully hit her, Carolyn jumped out of the way. Instead of hitting Carolyn, Mom hit one of the glass panes in the French doors leading to the backyard.

Mom walked down the aisle two days later with a plaster cast on her right arm covered up with a cascade of white spray roses. "I should have known then," Mom would say later.

••

When Mom was pregnant with me, her second child, eight years after the wedding, Papa suspected that my father was cheating on her. He stayed out late too many nights, always with flimsy excuses. Mom must have complained to Papa, because he hired a private investigator to trail Dad. Papa showed up one day with the photographs of Dad on two separate occasions at Perino's with different women, proof that Dad had other women.

Eight months pregnant, Mom kicked Dad out. But a month later, just before I was born, she took him back.

"What the hell else am I going to do?" she told Papa. Her mother, Arvella, was no longer around to offer advice. She'd died of a heart attack.

••

As I crouched behind the plastic foliage, Dad walked by to refill his J & B from the bar in the butler's pantry.

"Bob, *I'll* get you your drink." My mother followed him, nervously fluffing her hair. "I don't know where the damn serving-girl is."

My father turned and planted a perfunctory kiss on her lips. His hazel eyes held her gaze. "You just keep the party going, Marilyn. You're good at that."

Meanwhile, glasses clinked, table lighters lit cigarettes, and small talk continued as Freddy Karger, Dad's best friend, played Cole Porter on our big white piano in the corner of the living room. He was the bandleader at the Star on the Roof at the Beverly Hilton, and, even though tonight was his night off, my mother had coaxed him to play.

"Music keeps a party going, Freddy. You should know that!"

••

I looked up from behind the plants to see Molly, our new Irish maid, stalking down the hall, looking for me. "Heather, don't be bold, now. Where are you?"

My parents had recently fired Shirley, our old maid, when they suspected she had ties to the mob. The day she took me out for a ride in her boyfriend's Cadillac without telling my mother had been the last straw. When we'd arrived home that day, Mom had been frantic, twisting the end of her hair with her index finger. She would have fired Shirley on the spot, she told my father later, except that she needed somebody to watch April and me so they could go out that night.

So far, Mom wasn't thrilled with Molly, either. Her Irish brogue got on Mom's nerves. "She hangs on the 'e' too damn long. Mrs. Eeeeeton. Mrs. Eeeeton."

A lot of things made Mom nervous. Mostly, though, it was my father. "I have to be 'on' all the time. 'Over-alert,'" she told her best friend, Connie, on the phone one day. "No matter what is happening, I can't upset the husband."

But Molly was a more fitting housekeeper for the nicer house we now lived in; she dressed in a maid's uniform, all white and crisp with pockets. Her thick, flesh-colored stockings on her shapeless legs went swish-swish when she walked. Molly even made friends with Martha, the Scottish maid, who worked for my friend, Mary Jo Duque, down the street.

Now, Molly looked past the cradle and peered left into the dining room. Josephine was stacking the china dinner plates with the gold edges that Mom used for parties. "You seen the little one, Heather?" Molly asked in her Irish lilt.

Josephine looked up. "Hmmm... She was just in the kitchen not long ago stealing my cheese puffs. But, don't you go telling her mother, now."

That was my chance to escape up the front stairs. I checked to see if the hallway was clear and made a mad dash up to my bedroom. I needed to get ready.

I pulled the pink tulle nightgown over my head. The lace on the sleeves itched and the waistline felt tight as I tugged it down. I slipped on the sheer pink matching robe with the scratchy ruffled cuffs. My mother dressed April and me up for these parties.

9

We actually had separate sets of nightclothes we wore when guests came over.

April walked out of her room looking like a fairy princess, thin and lithe, her waist-length honey blonde hair covering the back of her matching lavender robe and nightgown. On the edge of adolescence, she was granted sophisticated colors like blue or lavender. My nightgown sets were bubble-gum pink. A baby sister color.

"I hate showing off for Mom," April said to Molly who corralled us. "Heath, you go first."

"No," I protested. "You're the oldest and Mom likes to show you off."

"Malarkey," Molly snapped. "Go on, you two. Together now."

Resigned, April and I made our way down the carpeted front stairway. Just as we reached the bottom and were ready to make our entrance, a loud scream erupted from the dining room. We headed in to find one of Josephine's servers teetering on the seat of a purple velvet dining-room chair. Dressed in a maid's uniform, complete with a ruffled apron tied around her thick waist, she wailed at the gathered crowd. "There's a rat! I swear I saw a rat!"

My parents stayed calm. Dad helped her down and Mom handed her a drink. "Not to worry, honey," she said. "The eyes can play tricks when the room's lit by candles. We've never had a rat in this house."

April and I stood there, not knowing what to do. "Should we go back upstairs?" April whispered.

Mom caught us out of the corner of her eye, relieved for the diversion.

"Look. Look!" She called out. "It's April and Heather, come to say good night before we eat."

Somewhere in the crowd I heard one of the men say: "Screw the food. Let's just keep drinking."

We positioned ourselves on the second step to be seen by the guests. "Good night, everyone," we said in unison. After the formality, we were whisked upstairs by Molly.

Mom had a cardinal rule: "Kids and cocktails don't mix."

After I changed into more comfortable nightclothes, I had trouble falling asleep. I always did on these nights. Mom kept the party going until way past midnight. The music got louder after Mom sidled up to the piano. With Freddy to accompany her, it was her opportunity to sing. The party stragglers encouraged her, drunk and ready to be entertained, as she belted the words out in a throaty and sultry vibrato.

"Fly me to the moon."

Off to the side, Aunt Carolyn would be playing the bongos, drumming to her own beat.

Chapter Two

Playing party pretend.

—Mom

I took in the hushed atmosphere and the soft lighting as we passed through the foyer of Perino's Restaurant on Wilshire. A Los Angeles hallmark, Perino's was famed for its celebrity clientele—Cary Grant, Marilyn Monroe, Alfred Hitchcock, Dean Martin, Joe DiMaggio, and Elizabeth Taylor regularly dined there—though I didn't know any of that. All I knew was that being at Perino's made me feel rich.

John, the maître 'd, led us to the same velvety banquette to the right where we always dined. According to Mom, my father liked to bring us here so that he could look like a big man with his family. It was also convenient. Dad's legal office was just across the street, and the restaurant was a five-minute drive from our home on Fremont Place. It was my father's favorite watering hole, where he ate lunch every day and had drinks every night after work.

I ran my hands along the thick, white tablecloth as I sat down. Dad took a seat soon after having been pulled aside by John, the maître 'd. The waiter never looked my mother in the eye.

My sister, April, confident in her beauty, wearing a yellow mini-dress, smiled across the table at Dad while Mom opened the clasp of her beaded clutch and pulled out her cigarettes. I was only interested in the specialty of the house, a thin crispy Pumpernickel toast topped with melted Parmesan cheese. When the waiter served me, I took as many slices as I could pile on my butter plate. It didn't take long to finish those and I reached for more from the cloth-lined basket, aware of the watchful eye of my mother. I knew she wouldn't risk making a scene by scolding me at Perino's over a few pieces of toast. Still, I felt a little guilty taking advantage of the situation.

Dad didn't notice my overeating. His mind was elsewhere as he fixated on centering his monogram—RAE—on the cuff of his white dress shirt.

Mom was carefree and animated now that Dad was with us, different from how frantic she got when Dad wasn't around, which was happening more often these days.

"What are you having?" I asked April.

She fiddled with her St. Christopher necklace as she looked at the menu. "Hmmm. Maybe the squab. You?"

"Fried scallops with tartar sauce."

Mom held her lit cigarette to the left, dipped her chin slightly to the right, and lowered her false lashes with a coy look.

"Thank you, Bob, for taking me to this beautiful place. I can't get enough of it." She pulled at her neckline, lowering the already deep V-neck of her black cocktail dress. "Do you like my outfit tonight?"

Dad reached for his Scotch and soda. His star sapphire pinky-ring clinked against the glass. "I'd tell you if I didn't."

Mom nodded with a painted smile on her frosted lips and reached for her vodka on the rocks. April rolled her eyes. I fished out the maraschino cherry from my Shirley Temple and popped it in my mouth, letting the sweetness of the waxy syrup linger before swallowing.

Soon, our dinner plates arrived with a soft whoosh as they were set down.

••

A few days later, Mom was asleep as I got up and ready for school. I have no memories of her ever being awake before nine. Back in third grade, I'd decided to take charge of waking myself, setting the alarm on my clock radio the night before. Now, dressed in my wool plaid uniform jumper, I headed for the kitchen. April was usually behind me on the linoleum back stairs that had the noisy metal ridge on each step.

Molly was up early, but not much of a cook. "Irish," my mother would say. "Have you ever eaten good Irish food?" Molly loved her tea and didn't mind my taking a quick sip of her brew as I headed out the door. She handed me my favorite, a packet of cinnamon Pop Tarts, to eat on the school bus.

The bus stop was at the corner, across the street. April refused to take the bus, claiming that as an eighth grader, she was too mature for such indignation. Instead, she went with the Brandlin's two blocks up at 108 Fremont. Five of their eight children attended our same parochial school, Cathedral Chapel.

I wasn't wild about riding the school bus, either. But none of the Brandlin kids were my age, so I couldn't tag along. Besides, I felt much more comfortable with my friend, Anne Woodward, who lived around the block at 76 Fremont. So that's where I headed.

The wonderful aroma of bacon, sausage, and toast hit me as soon as I opened the back door of the Woodward's house. As usual, the breakfast room was well lit, and the large round wooden table in the center was littered with breakfast plates, newspapers, schoolbooks, and half-filled juice glasses. Five school lunches, in little brown bags with names on them, lined the kitchen counter.

No one packed lunches for me. So I always made sure to sit next to Margaret O'Connor on the benches out in the playground lunch area. A mere toothpick in size, Margaret chose the carrot sticks, apple slices, and Oreo cookies from her lunch over the Oscar Mayer bologna sandwich with rubbery American cheese and yellow

French's mustard on soft, white Wonder Bread. It tasted great. I sat next to her knowing she'd always offer me at least half. My mother nagged me so much about my overeating yet she never bothered to ask Molly to pack me a healthy lunch with all that weird diet food she bought at Mrs. Hannibal's Health Food Store on Larchmont.

Now, with their own lunches in hand, Anne and her four siblings piled with me into Mrs. Woodward's Ford Country Squire station wagon for the ten-minute ride to school. Anne and I clamored for the back seat that faced out the rear window so that we could make faces and wave at the other drivers behind us.

"I keep wondering, since your mother's paying for the bus," Mrs. Woodward said, pulling out of the driveway. "Is this okay with her that you go with us to school?"

"Oh, sure," I lied. My mother had no clue I got a ride from the Woodward's. I think Mrs. Woodward was onto me, though. But, she was a good Catholic and didn't ask questions.

••

Saturday mornings were different. When my mother finally got up on a Saturday, the first thing she did was to slip downstairs to the kitchen and fill a ceramic mug with lukewarm water and two scoops of Taster's Choice freeze-dried instant coffee. Then, she went back to bed for at least an hour with the coffee cup and the telephone. Like clockwork, she'd pull the powder blue phone (to match the bedspread and carpet) and place it next to her on the king-size bed. Her morning dialing would begin.

My parents' room was directly across the hall from mine and I was able to tell by the tempo of the rotary dial whom she was calling. A long sound would be a nine, a short sound, a three. A medium sound, a four. She was calling Aunt Carolyn. WEbster 4-5421.

"I found lipstick on his collar." She paused, and then took a long slurp of her coffee. In a husky voice with a slight hitch, she added: "And, it wasn't mine."

I didn't eavesdrop. I didn't have to. Mom's voice carried straight into my room.

I ignored the talk. Mom was dramatic, and it was easier to move into my world of Barbie dolls and create my own little family in the corner of my bedroom.

I spent hours sitting on the hardwood floor dressing Barbie, fussing with her hair, changing her outfits, things that my mother did with herself. But, the imitation stopped there. Barbie and Ken had four children. Four seemed like the right number of children to me, like my best friend Mary Jo Duque's family down the block at 122, not the scanty two in our family.

My Barbie was calm, just like Mrs. Duque. My Barbie never minded the background noise of the TV, like Mrs. Duque, who let Mary Jo and I sit for hours on the beige shag rug in front of the large console watching TV in the Duque's master bedroom.

My Barbie played paddle tennis and wore only lipstick, no fancy eyelashes. She belonged to fancy charities and wore Pique shifts in the summer.

I connected the metal snaps in back of Barbie's rosebud pink garden dress and smoothed the eyelet lace in front.

"He didn't get home until two," Mom's voice drifted to my room.

Picking up a little plastic comb, I worked on Barbie's blonde bubble, starting slowly with the side curls, moving to the crown of her head.

"He's got another broad. I know it."

I moved to the cardboard Barbie house that Molly and I had assembled, taking a full day to put it all together. I positioned Barbie at the front door. It was time to call her children in for dinner. "Mary Jooooo, Tooooom, Mark and Martha, time to come in for dinner!" Barbie called cheerfully.

Day in day out, my mother spent hours on the phone with her friends. At 5:30 every evening, she took a Bufferin tablet to ease the tension of waiting for my father to show up.

•••

"Are you coming home on time?" Mom asked hopefully one morning when he was leaving for work. It was two weeks after our family dinner at Perino's.

"Marilyn, don't start the nagging."

That night, when April, Molly, and I finished eating dinner in the Green Room off of the porch—Mom names all the rooms in the house by their color or décor—April went upstairs. I wandered to find Mom, carrying my schoolbooks into the Music Room (named for the Hi-Fi and an odd assortment of musical instruments—a set of bongos, a tall African drum, and an Indian ankle bracelet with the tiny bells).

She was sitting on the couch under the two large windows that looked out on the backyard, nursing a single vodka and water in an old fashioned glass. She sipped it slowly to make it last. Little drops of condensation dripped from the glass onto the cocktail napkin underneath. By night's end, I knew that the napkin would be a soggy mess.

As she talked on the yellow phone (to match the window shades), her manicured right hand held up the mustard-colored receiver, leaving her left hand free to twist the ends of her short frosted hair, always the signal that she was anxious. Occasionally, she reached for the smoldering cigarette in the crystal ashtray next to her drink. One drag, then her hand would be back to the hair. After a few hours of twisting, a stiff curl would form and stick out from her bubble hairdo, looking out of place. Mom didn't mind if I hung around on the floor by her feet.

"The maître 'd, he told Bob the other night that his signature wasn't good until he paid up his tab," she said into the receiver.

She listened to the other end of the phone, then responded. "I gulped down my drink and we left. When I brought it up on the way home, he got hostile. Said that John was a liar. And, of course, I just agreed with him. I didn't want to rile him up."

I made a half-hearted attempt to do my schoolwork. After hearing this, though, I had bigger things to worry about other than stupid geography and what three countries are in North America.

As soon as my father pulled in the driveway, Mom rushed to hang up, ending the phone conversation the same way every time with her friend on the other end of the line: "Don't say a word."

At the door, Mom greeted Dad as if it was nothing that he was hours late. *I didn't want to rile him...*

He didn't look happy to be home, more resigned. His narrow shoulders slumped slightly under his custom-made suit. He attempted a grin for me: "Hi Smiley!"

"Get me a scotch, Marilyn," he said, heading into the living room.

I went upstairs to my room and shut the door where I could go back to my latest Nancy Drew and escape into her world of sleuth and an adoring father. That year, in 5th grade, I was getting C's and F's in Math and Geography. More often than not, I didn't hand in my homework.

Later, long after I'd gone to bed, Dad opened the door and peeked his head through the doorway of my darkened bedroom. The light from the hallway sliced across the wood floor and my blanket.

"Good night, Smiley."

"Nite, Dad," I mumbled. The smell of Scotch and Cezanne aftershave lingered long after the door closed.

Chapter Three

If wishes were horses, we'd all ride.

—Mom

It was 1966. I was 9 and my sister, at 14, had the body of a 22-year-old—a very sexy 22-year-old. Though barely 5'2", everything from her C-cup breasts, to her 22-inch waist, down to her shapely legs, was in perfect proportion. My sister even had pretty feet.

Her grey-blue eyes were small, her lashes were short, her nose was slightly long, and she had a crooked smile. But, her bone structure was flawless, so all put together, the combination made for a beautiful face. And she knew it.

Naturally, April was popular with the boys. They called her "the Bod," because of her voluptuous figure. Most afternoons that summer, she held court on the brick steps leading up to the front porch of our home.

From the balcony outside my second-story bedroom, I spied on her and her entourage. The scene reminded me of the opening of *Gone with the Wind,* where Scarlett O'Hara is at the Wilkes barbeque, flanked on either side by admiring young men. Like Scarlett, my sister craved attention from the boys. Also like Scarlett, she led them all on.

Some took turns showing off. "Hey, April, look!" Steve said, popping a wheelie on his Sting Ray bike. I moved downstairs to a dining room window at the front of the house, peering through the broken shutter on the left side of the room. Then, boldly, I moved to the two rectangular windows on either side of the front door.

Danny, jerking his head back to get his thick auburn hair out of his eyes, saw me through the glass and coaxed me to come outside. "This your little sister?" he asked April. "What's her name?"

"Heather," she answered, her eyes focused on Bobby Sproul, the neighborhood heartthrob.

I slowly opened the front door and peaked my head out. "You guys are so silly when you show off for my sister."

"Come on out here," Danny said. All eyes turned to me, except my sister and Bobby who only had eyes for each other.

"It's Heather Eat-a-ton," said, Brian, making a play on my last name.

"How do you know?" I laughed. "You can't even see though all that blonde hair in your face."

The other boys laughed. "She got'cha, Brian!"

I started to hang around April's boyfriends and she never seemed to mind. I was hardly a threat. The boys joked with me about being fat. The more familiar with me they became, the more they joked. It became a game. One afternoon, one of the boys asked me what my favorite food was. I suspected that this was a ploy to tease me about my weight. When I answered "hot dogs," they switched my nickname from "Heather Eat-a-ton" to "Hot Dog Heather."

They'd call me that name whenever I came outside.

"And there you are, you dopey boys!" I laughed along with them. Even though deep down it hurt to be teased, part of me loved the attention and I always came back for more.

••

My mother idolized glamour. Hollywood was her god and her heaven. When not on the phone, she spent countless hours reading

Photoplay magazine and the biographies of famous movie stars and filmmakers. Mom saw great star potential in my sister's looks.

She bought April low-slung hip-huggers in the latest mod prints, thick patent leather belts and clingy poor boy tops to show off her ample cleavage. April was allowed to wear the shortest mini skirts and the smallest bikinis held together with thin, little strings. Mom took pride in my sister's appearance, encouraging her to wear provocative outfits.

"Stop!" April scolded Mom when she pulled down the ring on the front zipper of her top to show more cleavage.

"You won't get Bobby's attention all zipped up to the neck."

April pulled the zipper up to reveal just her clavicle. "Don't say that!"

Mom shrugged. "I give up. You do it your way."

"I will!" April headed downstairs to greet the adoring group of boys on the front porch.

Mom was always trying to push April to get into show business, a career Mom aspired to, though she claimed she was just too lazy to get up that early in the morning. My sister had no interest in my mother's fantasy. An avid animal lover, April's dream was to raise and ride horses.

••

Still, April spent countless hours grooming herself in her lavender bedroom. She straightened her persistent curl by using empty orange juice cans as rollers, securing them with long, black bobby pins, and sleeping on them every night.

She was putting on her contacts in the bathroom we shared between our bedrooms when she said I could hang out in her room and listen to albums while she put on her make-up if I didn't bug her.

Her thick-lensed cat-eye glasses lay on the sink. It was all I could do not to try them on. While my sister hated wearing glasses, I wished I needed them.

"Glasses," Mom said, "make people look smart."

April played "I'll Cry If I Want To" by Leslie Gore and Dionne Warwick's "Walk On By" on the orange-and-white Motorola record player.

I followed the lyrics printed on the back of the albums and mouthed along with her as she sang into the mirror over her antique walnut bureau. "I wan-na be Bo-obbie's girl, I wan-na be Bo-obbie's girl." Leslie Gore's music made her emotional and her eyes became glassy. "It's my party and I'll cry if I want to, cry if I want to."

The tears interfered with the makeup application so she switched to Dionne Warwick and began belting out the tunes on the scratchy, overplayed record. April turned from emotional to gutsy, rocking her hips back and forth with her generous chest thrust forward. To the beat of Dionne, she gave off an air of confidence with every beat of the song. "Do- you- know- the- way- to- San- Jose."

My sister wore a lot of make-up for a fourteen-year-old. I watched her expertly draw black liquid eyeliner on her upper eyelid. Next, the swift brushing of blue eye shadow followed by black mascara and the finishing touch, her new tube of Slicker frosted lipstick.

"The last is the hair," she said, reaching to release the orange juice cans. Down came her golden hair, smooth and silky. Facing the mirror, April cocked her head to one side, then, scrutinizing the finished result.

"Good enough," she said to herself.

Standing next to her, I avoided my reflection in the mirror. My mousy brown hair round face and chubby body were nowhere "good enough" by anyone's standards, especially my own.

••

My mother's dressing room separated my bedroom from my parents' room with a door on each side. Both doors were slightly ajar as I sat at my desk struggling to write a book report for fifth grade on *The Box Car Children*, a book I hadn't read. The rise and fall of my mother's voice on the phone in her bedroom distracted me.

"It's chicken one day, feathers the next," Mom said to Connie. "One week, he gives me $150 for the household expenses. The next week, it's $75. Last week, it was $100, always in cash. He doesn't give me a check anymore."

At home, things had been steadily changing. My parents had stopped giving parties. They never traveled anymore. The last time Dad gave Mom an expensive gift was on her birthday six months ago, last June.

"It's beautiful!" Mom had exclaimed when she'd opened the black velvet box after dinner. They hadn't gone out to celebrate. Mom's birthday dinner was in the dining room with April and me, a celebratory dinner of *coq au vin* that Mom had cooked herself.

Dad, seated at the head of the table, smiled tight, his lips making one thin line.

"Look, girls," she said showing us the pearl and sapphire dome ring still in the velvet box.

"Why don't you take it out of the box, Marilyn?" Dad put his fork on the side of his plate and reached for his scotch.

Mom tried to slide it onto her right ring finger but it was too small, even for her thin graceful fingers. She quickly slipped it on her right pinkie. "There. Perfect!"

Mom always claimed her hands were her best feature, proudly displaying them whenever she could. On this night, she barely glanced at them as she reached for her glass to sip vodka. Then, quickly, she brought her hands back down in her lap out of sight.

"Guilt gift," she told Connie on the phone the following morning.

Two nights later, Dad came stumbling in at 2:30 in the morning. My mother turned on the hallway light, sending a stream of light under my bedroom door that woke me.

"Who is she?" Mom accused through tears, just outside my door. "You reek of another woman's perfume."

"There's no one. Goddamn it, Marilyn. I told you. I fell asleep in the car!"

"Until 2:30?"

I covered my head with the pillow.

The money situation had been gradual, debt creeping into our lives like a fungus. My father's philandering and heavy drinking took a toll on his law practice. According to Mom, his business was hanging by a stem.

She did what she could to help drum up business for him, even called her rich childhood friend, Louise, who'd recently separated from her husband. "Bob would be a great attorney for you with the divorce," she promoted. "And besides, he needs the business," she told Louise.

Mom also fielded phone calls at home when clients couldn't find him at the office during regular hours. Ruth, Dad's secretary, covered for him as well.

"It's all I can do not to tell them to check Perino's," she told April.

Mom's form of self-care included a daily Dexamil to help her "stay thin for Bob." Still, the slightest disruption set her off. "Keep the noise down in the pool," she'd scream from the second-story balcony, bringing our loud "Marco! Polo!" game to heavy whispers. My friends became scared of Mom. Anne had stopped wanting to spend the night, and I could hardly blame her. Besides, it was more fun over at the Woodward's with all of her siblings, and her mom's big spaghetti dinners on the weekends.

Mom's rattled nerves were even worse in the car. If we were out doing errands on Larchmont, the quaint half-square-mile old-town shopping street in the heart of Los Angeles, and she couldn't find a parking space right away, she'd lose patience. First, she'd tap at the wooden steering wheel of her blue Mustang convertible (another guilt gift from Dad) making a "clink, clink" with her rings as they hit the silver, indented studs on the sporty wheel. Then she'd lunge the car forward (her right foot on the gas), then stop abruptly (her left foot on the brake, the way she always drove), the car moving like an excited rabbit as she searched for an empty spot. By the time she came to a screeching halt in one of the angled spaces, I was mortified.

"Finally!" she said. "Christ, it's just *not* my day." I was used to her recent outbursts. But, inside, I cringed, scanning the sidewalk to make sure that no one on the street had noticed her dramatic parking job or her language.

She regularly made the round of calls to all Dad's gin mills.

"It's Mrs. Eaton. Is my husband, Bob, there? How long ago did he leave?"

Her ashtrays were all over the house, full of lipstick-stained Larks smoked down to the filter.

Then, Molly was let go.

"Mom told me you're leaving," I said to Molly as I entered her room. She was stacking her white uniforms in her big faded yellow suitcase with brown stitching on the edges.

"I'm going back to Ireland." She reached for a folded pile of slips.

"Why?"

Molly stopped to look at me. She ran a knobby hand through her curly grey hair and sighed. "Your mother says," she paused to calculate her words. "Well... it costs too much to keep me."

"We can't afford you?"

She smoothed my hair. "You'll have to ask your mother about that."

My eyes filled. "Who's going to look after me?"

Molly drew me closer, my tears wetting the slippery sleeve of her white nylon uniform. "You'll be fine," she said. "You'll be fine."

The following week, Lupe, a forty-three-year-old Mexican woman, was hired for half Molly's salary. The maid's room took on a whole new look. Gone were Molly's crocheted doilies draped over the top of the dark wood dresser and on the arms of the old stuffed chair in the corner. The faded rose prints above the single bed had been packed along with the rest of her belongings, and replaced with a single large crucifix, Lupe's treasured possession.

A devout Catholic, Lupe turned the top of the dresser into an altar, complete with candles painted with the Virgin Mary, a heavy rosary (the kind that the nuns wore around their waists at my school), and a Holy Bible. Mom wasn't wild about all the candle lighting for fear that she'd burn the house down, but she figured Lupe's prayers were much needed in the house.

I was relieved to have Lupe. Molly would have scolded Dad for how he treated Mom if she'd had the chance. Lupe just quietly emptied Mom's dirty ashtrays in the morning. No questions asked.

Chapter Four

Christmas, 1966

Hiding behind the fan.
—Mom

School had never been a priority for me, and I was lucky to get C's. My mind wandered each morning as soon as the class began to recite the Pledge of Allegiance. Standing next to my desk, I placed my hand over my heart and faced the flag at the front of the classroom.

"I pledge allegiance to the flag..." *Hmm, Susan got some new cable knit knee socks. Boy, I wish I had her legs. My legs would look huge wrapped in cable knit.* "Of the United States of America..." *Ann Marie got a haircut.* "And to the Republic for which it stands..." *I liked it better long.* "One nation..."

Daydreaming continued throughout the day. Either I stared outside through the thick Venetian blinds onto busy Cochran Avenue...*there's the mailman*... or I watched the clock...*twenty more minutes 'til recess and lunch.*

I was still struggling in fifth grade at Cathedral Chapel where the nuns were far from relaxed. One false move, such as talking in class, and you were kneeling at the statue of the Virgin Mary in the "grotto" outside the nuns' residence next to school. I hated being sent there. I can still hear the steady drops of water in the tiny waterfall and feel the statue of Mary staring down on me with what I knew must be disdain.

I cheated to get by and became a master of the side stare. I knew exactly from whom to cheat. Eric was the smartest, but he was long-limbed and left-handed, which posed a problem. His work was always partially covered up by his left arm when he scrawled the pencil across the paper. Brice was good, but his handwriting was too small. It took too long to decipher his writing and made me nervous. It was too easy to get caught. If I was seated across from Margaret or Melinda, it was perfect. Not only were they both smart, they sat up straight offering easy access to their work with large, flowery handwriting.

Trouble was that today's test was on *The Box Car Children*. I hadn't read the book and hadn't turned in the book report. I looked at the questions on the page. My heart raced. I scanned my surroundings as if hunting for prey. Eric was to my left. For once his being left-handed offered me a bird's-eye view. A side-glance to his paper and I was in business.

No matter where the nuns moved my desk in the classroom, I found a way, and I was never caught. They must have known about my cheating from my incomplete answers and homework, but a word was never said. I was always promoted to the next grade level.

Meanwhile, our home began showing more noticeable signs of neglect. The once spotless white colonial exterior had begun to peel on the left side of the house where the sun hit the strongest and above the second-story windows just under the rain gutters. The giant sycamore on the front lawn was thick with leaves. "Pruning that tree is the last thing on the list," Mom told Henry, the gardener. "The Birds of Paradise next to the driveway and the roses on the other side of the lawn are much more important."

Inside the 4,600-square-foot house, Mom had hired a cheap painter named Mo who cut corners by painting over wallpaper, light switches, and heating grates. But she hadn't found a cheap way to refinish the dull hardwood floors in April's and my bedrooms. Some of the slats in the white shutters inside the dining room windows had started to come out of the grooves. "Leave 'em open," she told me when I tried to close them one Sunday night. "That way the broken parts won't show."

••

"Charlotte feels uncomfortable coming over here," Freddy told Dad by the pool. Lighting his last cigarette, Freddy crumpled the empty packet and stuck it in one of Mom's abalone shell ashtrays. "It's because she knows you have other women. And, you know, she likes Marilyn, feels bad for her, Buddy."

Mom and Freddy's girlfriend, Charlotte, were inside making dinner.

Dad paused for a minute. Looking down at his hands, he checked his buffed nails and fiddled with his gold and onyx pinky ring. "Well, then I guess we'll have to get together at Perino's," he said.

They kept their voices low so I wouldn't hear their conversation as I floated in the pool on my turquoise rubber raft. I lay on my back, hands dipped in the pool, water trickling through my fingers as if I hadn't a care in the world as it all sank in. Mom's morning phone calls to Connie and Aunt Carolyn about Dad being out late, her frantic calls at night looking for him at Wilshire Country Club and Perino's. *You sure he isn't there?*

Freddy stopped coming over after that.

••

At 6:45, April and I waited patiently at the rickety card table while Mom busied herself in the kitchen on this Christmas Eve night. Mom wanted to do something special. "Give him incentive to be home," she'd told Aunt Carolyn over the phone.

Mom had set up the folding chairs and card table in front of the fireplace in the living room, making the scene festive with a green tablecloth, red cloth napkins, and the silver candelabra from the dining room table. She set the table for four with our best china and made sure the fire was lit to give a cozy feeling.

I was beginning to sweat from the warmth of the blazing fire. My green velvet dress, a holdover from last Christmas, was too tight and left no room to breath. As the flames grew hotter, I wanted to run upstairs and change into something comfortable. But Mom wanted us to look nice for Dad, so I endured the heat. He was 45 minutes late.

April looked fresh in her thin white blouse and green plaid taffeta skirt. She wasn't bothered by the heat.

"Check on Mom," she said, inspecting the ends of her long blond hair by the light from the candles on the table. "She said that we were eating at 6:30. I told Bobby to call me at 7:00." She went upstairs.

By 7:30, I could no longer sit there at the table by myself. I was hungry and tired of waiting. But the sound of Mom's voice on the phone stopped me short as I started to push through the swinging door that led from the dining room to the kitchen.

"Is he there?" she asked. A long silence. "Are you sure? Have you checked the bar?"

Leaving the door cracked, I watched her stir her special meal: "nail soup"—a vegetable and beef concoction that starts with a real nail at the bottom of the pot. My stomach was rumbling. "He loves my nail soup," she'd told Aunt Carolyn. "It's a recipe from an old folk tale and not Christmassy, but he's always happy when I serve it to him."

••

She hadn't bothered to put on an apron. Soup was splattered on the front of her white low-cut chiffon blouse. My mother loved to cook, but refused to wear aprons. "Dowdy," she called them. "I'd rather have spots on my clothes and send them to the cleaners than look like I stand behind a stove all day."

April came up behind me. "What're you doing?"

"Shhhh. Mom's on the phone looking for Dad."

"It's nearly 8:00," she whispered. "Tell Mom, I'll be back upstairs. Just call me when dinner's on the table."

I nodded, never taking my eyes off of my mother. She was rubbing the spots on her blouse with a wet dishtowel.

"Is this Carter?" she asked, after dialing the Wilshire Country Club. "Yes, it's Marilyn Eaton." She threw the dishtowel on the counter and focused on the phone call.

More silence. Then, her voice lifted. "Oh, how long ago did he leave?" Tapping the receiver with her index finger. "Three hours ago?"

I pushed through the door slowly. "Mom, let's wait for Dad. It's no big deal. Really. April's on the phone with Bobby, anyway."

"The bastard," she said, putting the receiver back on the hook.

Finally, at nine o'clock, the three of us sat down in front of the fireplace to eat Mom's "amusing" meal. Thankfully, the fire had died down to a few smoldering ashes. I took away Dad's place setting so it wouldn't look so pathetic. Before we started the meal, Mom raised her wine glass. "Let's toast."

Obediently, we raised our crystal water glasses.

33

"Merry Christmas to April and Heather," she said, forcing a smile. "The two reasons I'm glad I married your father."

Later, in bed, I listened hard for the purr of Dad's Lincoln Continental. The engine barely made a sound when he drove in the driveway, so I waited for the noise of the heavy driver's-side door closing. I got sleepy after a while and decided instead to concentrate on Santa coming down the chimney, even though I knew that there was no such thing.

My father appeared in the living room the next morning dressed in pajamas. In the middle of the night, I'd heard his voice in the hallway outside my door.

"Merry Christmas, Marilyn," he'd slurred.

April got a new record player and a score of new record albums, her favorite was The Turtle's "Happy Together." She pretended to be surprised. Only I knew that she'd opened every present the week before and rewrapped them. "I can't stand the wait.," she'd told me.

My parents and April made a big deal about Santa bringing me a giant dollhouse. I fingered the cheery wallpaper on the walls of the tiny rooms, the miniature furniture arranged in each room, so pristine and inviting. I wanted to shrink down and crawl in.

But, the big present that morning was to Mom from Dad.

"Close your eyes," Dad said, leading Mom out the front door after the last under-the-tree gift had been opened.

It was sunny outside and the air was crisp. Mom moved tentatively in her nightgown, measuring each step in bare feet.

"Open your eyes!" Dad said with what sounded like faked enthusiasm. His voice rose. "Hope you like it!"

"It's a station wagon," Mom's voice was flat, disbelieving. It was a used Mercury Meteor. Quickly, she shifted gears. "I love it!"

"He's hardly Santa Claus," Mom said to April and me as we stood on the porch watching Dad, now dressed in the navy mechanic-style belted jumpsuit he wore when he relaxed at home (or was hung-over), attempt to untie the big red ribbon from the roof rack. "It's just another damn guilt gift." She crossed her hands across her chest with a sigh. "He could have saved some money and just bought me an apron. Same thing as this damn wood-paneled station wagon."

That afternoon, we piled into the Mercury to visit Dad's father, Cal, who was sick in the hospital. Dad said Cal's heart was giving out. "The boozing didn't help," Mom said about Cal when Dad was out of earshot.

I climbed in the very back of the wagon. There was no stow-away seat, so I settled myself on the ridged vinyl surface. It didn't take long to notice a long line of dried greenish-yellow snot on the wheel well. I imagined some boy around my age picking his nose and swiping it there to leave his disgusting mark.

Up front, Mom called back to me. "You alright back there, Heatherbean?" Her voice seemed strained and I didn't want to make a scene.

"Everything's great back here." I resisted the urge to move into the middle seat with April.

Dad, at the wheel, said nothing.

For me, the station wagon made up for Dad's absence. He'd bought us a family car. Now, Mom could leave the flashy blue Mustang in the garage. She'd be like all the other mothers in the neighborhood who drove station wagons.

Chapter Five

If she doesn't stop eating, she'll be the size of Guam.

—Mom

It was Indian summer that Saturday in late January 1967, with unseasonably warm weather from the Santa Ana winds. Mary Jo and I had hopped on the new bikes we got for Christmas for a mile and a half ride to the stores on Larchmont, my third such unsupervised outing since I'd turned eleven on November 22nd.

Mary Jo, more athletic and lithe, was normally way ahead of me whenever we rode our bikes. But this time I took the lead. The heat of the day only fueled my mission. I couldn't wait to eat a big cold turkey sandwich from Jurgensen's.

Jurgensen's, a fancy grocery store situated in the heart of Larchmont, sold the finest meats, the freshest produce, and the best made-to-order sandwiches. The small store was all about service and convenience to its upscale customers who could afford the luxury of over-priced, home delivered groceries and "house charges" that were paid in full at the end of every month.

I loved Jurgensen's sandwiches. There was something comforting about the soft sourdough bread, bathed in mayonnaise and mingled with shaved iceberg lettuce and thin slices of tomato. The turkey was incidental.

I pedaled hard, leaving Mary Jo at a stoplight. "Wait up!" she yelled across Third Street. "Why are you going so fast?"

Dare I admit to my friend, who had no interest in food, that my speed was about the pursuit of a turkey sandwich?

From the butcher counter, I watched Mary Jo finish locking her bike out in front of the store. I had already ordered my sandwich, keeping tabs on the butcher, eyeing him to make sure that he spread on the extra mayonnaise I'd requested. As she passed through the double glass doors, I saw her reach in her back shorts pocket and pull out her little pink plastic wallet. That's when I realized I'd forgotten my money.

The butcher had wrapped the bulging sandwich in white paper and was now cutting it diagonally. *What should I do?*

"Pickle?" the butcher asked

"Sure," I said meekly. *I can't borrow from Mary Jo. I did that last week when I ran short of change buying candy at Landis.*

"Here you go, honey." The butcher slid the sandwich over the tall glass countertop. Wiry grey hair sprouted clown-like at the rim of his little white cap. Did Jurgensen's take back sandwiches?

I hesitated before picking up the sandwich, still wondering what to do. I moved over to the small checkout counter at the front of the store. As usual, Helen was at the register. I spotted the familiar tablet for house charges right there on top of the counter. Did we still have a house charge? We were down to only two department store charges—Haggarty's in Beverly Hills, and Orbach's, a low-end clothing store two miles west of Fremont on Wilshire Boulevard in the Miracle Mile District. Mom hadn't mentioned losing Jurgensen's.

"This is a charge," I told Helen, masking confidence.

Helen tucked a clump of dyed brown hair behind her left ear. She hesitated, lips pursed. I'd seen the look. It was the same one that the woman at I. Magnin had given my mother a couple months ago when Mom tried to charge a nightgown. The saleswoman had sent the charge slip soaring in a canister through the long tube filled with air that connected to the credit office. It didn't take long for the black phone next to her on the counter to ring.

"It's credit, Mrs. Eaton," the saleswoman had said, handing the phone to my mother. "They want to speak with you."

Mary Jo was still waiting for her sandwich. I hoped that she wouldn't hear if Helen refused to let me use the account.

"We love your Mom," Helen said, looking around for the tall balding manager who always lingered around the front of the store. "So, just this time I'll let things slide for you." Then, leaning down close to me, she whispered. "The account is three months past due."

Instantly, I had a stomachache, the kind that's down deep in the gut. The way Helen looked at me, so sympathetically, made me want to cry. I swallowed hard, holding back. Helen was a kind lady. I knew she liked Mom. They always shared jokes, and often times the manager would listen in and laugh along with them. I was sure he would have let the sandwich slide "just this time," too.

"Thank you, Helen," I said as she placed the white paper wrapped sandwich in a small brown paper bag. Mary Jo had joined me at the counter and was signing the tab for her sandwich.

"Give my love to your mother, Heather. Tell her we miss seeing her."

Helen handed Mary Jo a yellow receipt to put in her pink plastic wallet.

On the way out of the store, I caught a glimpse of Balzar's, an extension of Jurgensen's that sold fine wines. I had spent many Friday afternoons in the cellar-like room with my mother as she meticulously chose wine for her parties. It was boring and I hated being trapped inside the dark, musty room, listening to Mom and the salesman discuss liquor, so I used to kill time there by counting wine bottles and playing with the collection of corks in the barrel by the door.

There were some advantages to our having money problems. No more Friday afternoons at Balzar's.

Still, I couldn't stop thinking about what Helen had said about our account on the ride home. Mary Jo, lagging behind again, called out for me to slow down as I shot across the intersection of Third Street at Rossmore without stopping. I knew I was rushing. It was a busy intersection and a driver laid on the horn as he slowed to avoid hitting me. I kept moving. I just wanted to get home and hide or something. I was sure Mary Jo had heard everything. Even though she probably suspected there were problems because of the way our house was starting to look, or that we never went anywhere on vacation. It was just so embarrassing.

The day before had been trash day and a number of the homes on Rossmore Avenue still had trash bins lining the curb. My stomach ached from the turmoil inside me. I no longer wanted the sandwich and stashed it in one of the metal cans along the route. I was unaware that Mary Jo had ridden up behind me just as I was closing the lid.

Cars rushed past us on the busy street. "Hold on," she called out over the noise of the cars. "Keep the lid up."

She tossed her sandwich in along with mine. "Let's go have lunch at my house," she said. Then, referring to their family cook, "Dolly's making tuna."

Chapter Six

Think. What would you do if you were dating him?
—Mom

Aunt Carolyn's home reflected her dislike of most things domestic. Her whole house was beige. The walls. The furniture. The carpets. The only color came from the oil painting of Don Quixote above the fireplace in the living room and my cousins Robert and Jonathan's plastic toys scattered around.

Mom had asked me to come with her to Carolyn's this evening after dinner, killing time until Dad came home.

The porch light in the small brick threshold wasn't on. "Maybe she's not home," I said to Mom.

"Oh, she's home," Mom answered. "She probably forgot to turn the light on."

My mother rang the doorbell several times. When there was no answer, Mom impatiently tapped the wooden front door with her car keys. I heard a click from inside as the porch light came on.

"Oh, good, he's not home, yet," Mom said, as soon as Carolyn opened the door.

"He's here," Carolyn corrected. "I'm just putting on his dinner."

"He's home and you're wearing *that*?"

Aunt Carolyn looked down at her worn Levis and rumpled shirt. Her shoulder-length blonde hair was pulled back in a pony-tail. She wore no make-up and was holding an empty Swanson's TV dinner box in her right hand.

"Yeah," she said, defensively. "This is what I'm wearing and, yes, Charlie's home."

"Christ, you're even wearing bedroom slippers!" Mom looked down at Carolyn's fluffy flat slippers. "You look like hell, Carolyn. Don't you even get dressed for him when he comes home?"

"Jesus, Marilyn," Carolyn snapped back. "Quit with the comments. I said you could come over. I don't need your crap."

I followed them into Carolyn's kitchen. As we passed the den, Charlie peered out from behind *The Herald Examiner*. "Hi there!" His voice was surprisingly cheery; not at all how Carolyn had described his outbursts to my mother.

"Heatherbean," he said, "Jonathan ate already. He's upstairs with his new train set." A glass of iced tea sat on the table next to his chair. I'd heard Mom tell Carolyn over one of their lunches that she was lucky because Charlie wasn't a boozer like Mom's Mr. Wonderful.

Aunt Carolyn tossed the empty Swanson box in the trash.

"Listen," Mom said in a whisper as we entered kitchen, "I don't want to bother you while he's here. I was going to complain about April and her new idiot boyfriend. You go on and eat your dinner."

"No. Don't leave," Carolyn said.

••

April had become bored of Bobby Sproul and her flock of admirers after she had been lured by the sound of rock music coming from Robert Goldstein's garage band around the corner. Watching the Devil's Disciples practice became my sister's new pastime. It didn't take long for her to fall for the lead guitarist, Ray Magee, seven years older with shiny black hair down to his shoulders.

Even though he came from a nice family who lived on Woodrow Wilson Drive in the Hollywood Hills, Mom wasn't wild about

Ray. It was the age difference and his annoying "yep" and "nope" response to everything. At sixteen, April was becoming more and more independent. She didn't care what Mom thought. Now, it was all about Ray Magee.

Had it not been for the sound of Ray's hot rod El Camino, my parents would never know when she came and went. April didn't stay out late, but she definitely was in charge whenever there was a confrontation with Mom. April was smart and she was strong. Dad had already checked out emotionally and with Mom relinquishing the reins, April had the freedom to make most of her own decisions.

"April was like this as a baby," Mom said to Connie. "Had tantrums all the time when she didn't get her way. I don't want to start a fight."

••

"Heather, you want to put Robert to bed?" Aunt Carolyn asked me. She looked over at Mom. Her skin was pale, making her old acne scars more prominent. She pulled the TV dinner out of the oven. "I just checked the timing on the box. It's ready and I'll give Charlie his dinner now. He won't mind. Trust me. He couldn't care less."

"That's what you feed him?" Mom was aghast. "Where's your dinner?"

"I'll eat later." She lifted the square aluminum tin filled with turkey slices, peas, and flat mashed potatoes. "He likes these." She looked down at the tray.

"I'll be right back," Carolyn said over her shoulder, as she carried Uncle Charlie's heated Swanson's dinner to the den.

I went over to Robert, who was poking around in a plastic laundry basket filled with toys. Dressed in cotton, snap-front pajamas, Robert's silky disheveled blonde hair gleamed under the bright kitchen lighting. The front of his pajamas was covered in food stains. Mom rolled her eyes toward the dull ceiling.

Heading home from Aunt Carolyn's, just one block down from where we used to live on Longwood, my mother sat poised at the wheel of her blue Mustang. She rarely drove the Mercury wagon, claiming that it just wasn't her style. I'd resigned myself to having a mother who would rather drive a sports car than be like a proper mom and drive a station wagon. Her long fingernails, now a frosted white, clicked on the walnut steering wheel to the beat of a pop music song on KHJ.

"Mom, what was Aunt Carolyn like when you were growing up?" I wanted to know because my aunt seemed so distant to me lately. She wasn't the Aunt Carolyn who'd been such a fun, involved aunt, thinking up local adventures for April and me, taking us to the LA Zoo or Griffith Park.

Mom lowered the music on the radio. "What?"

"It's weird, Mom. You and Carolyn are so different, but you guys seem so close. Was it always like that?"

"Well, for starters," she said. "Carolyn's five years younger. Poor thing, she was born cross-eyed. Had to have a doctor fix it."

"When we were kids," she continued, "we played 'Jungle' a lot in our backyard over on Las Palmas. You remember that house. I showed you, right?"

I nodded.

"I was always the princess," my mother said. "Poor Carolyn, she was always the monkey."

"Were you mean to her?"

"No, that was just the way things were."

"Really?" I said. "But, Carolyn's kinda pretty now."

"Oh, yeah, now she's fine, tall and all. Great figure. But as a kid, she was knock-kneed and not that cute."

We had stopped at the traffic light on Rossmore, ready to turn into the gate on Fremont. I wished we'd been farther from home. As we got there, our conversation would end and my mother's focus would be the telephone and her friends. It was what she did when Dad wasn't home.

And he wouldn't be home. He never was on Saturday. He was always "out playing golf," a game that, for him, lasted all day and into the night. That's why on Saturdays Mom dragged us on outings with Aunt Carolyn. Uncle Charlie was gone on Saturdays, too.

Uncle Charlie wasn't a golfer. His big interest was his new sailboat. He named it "The Sagita," after a mythological constellation of stars. He spent every moment he could in Marina Del Rey where it was docked. Aunt Carolyn hated The Sagita. She told Charlie that the minute she stepped foot on deck, she felt seasick.

"Who the hell cares?" Mom said on one of our outings over a plate of El Coyote's famous puffed-up chile rellenos. "Go out in the boat and fake it, or he'll find someone else to take sailing."

Jonathan and I never looked up from our cheese enchiladas. We were used to that kind of talk.

Now, the light on Rossmore turned green and Mom eased the Mustang forward. Soon, we'd be home and Mom had only started to tell me about Carolyn.

"A square peg in a round hole," Mom said, pressing on the gas pedal with her right foot. "Your Aunt Carolyn's always been a loner. The intellectual type. She loves to read books that make you think, like *The Invisible Man* and *Mila 18*. Heady stuff. She writes in her journal, ride horses, that kind of thing."

Passing by Hank, asleep at the wheel of his cruiser at the corner in front of the Cardinal's house, Mom added, "But, she's gotta hang on to her marriage. There's not a lot of time for that other stuff."

"Hopeless," my mother said, turning into the driveway. A couple more bricks framing our driveway's edge had broken loose, right next to the Birds of Paradise. I felt one under the right front wheel.

Mom's dangling, pink rhinestone keychain swung back and forth as we came to a stop under the porte-cochere. "I don't know what's gotten into her. I worry about her."

I sat in the passenger seat, listening, amazed that she wasn't dashing inside to the phone.

"She's walking like she's underwater." Mom stared straight ahead, not at me.

Behind us, Ray screeched to a halt at the curb out front. My mother didn't turn around to look, much less make the usual snide comment about him.

"I don't think Aunt Carolyn cares anymore, Heatherbean," Mom sighed, opening the car door. "About anything."

Chapter Seven

Men leave for one thing—another woman.

—Mom

It started with the roast beef. Mom had overcooked it.

"Inedible," Dad said to her after he took the first bite. "You really botched the dinner up." He shook his head in disgust and took a drink of his scotch.

"Here, have my piece," Mom offered her slice, which still had a hint of pink.

Dad refused.

"I'm sorry," she groveled. "I don't know what went wrong."

I didn't want to see the desperate look on my mother's face and concentrated on the fake centerpiece in the middle of the dining room table, a tiny plastic Christmas tree with miniature wooden soldiers and little glass ornaments glued to wire branches. One of the soldiers had come loose and his bayonet was pointing down. Across the table, April seemed oblivious as she continued to cut her meat, dipping the overdone beef into Mom's homemade concoction of horseradish and sour cream. I tried to eat, chewing my meat into mush, then swallowing hard. It gave me something to do.

The lighting was soft at these Sunday night dinners Mom orchestrated, barely enough to see the food. Mom claimed that she looked better by the candlelight than the glare of the overhead chandelier. She was thirty-nine.

The only other illumination came from small lights on the still life above the side buffet and on the etching of George Bernard Shaw that Mom had hung above Dad's chair at the head of the table. My father's face looked slightly twisted, his bushy black eyebrows squeezing together like a giant caterpillar resting above his eyes.

He attempted another bite. Almost to his mouth, he slammed his fork back down, landing hard on the porcelain plate. "Marilyn! Damn it! I can't eat this!"

"God, Dad," April snapped, scooping up a forkful of peas. "It's not *that* bad."

My mother sat motionless at the other end of the table. Usually, their fights took place down in the living room when Mom accused him of seeing another woman after we'd gone to bed, or behind the closed door of their bedroom when he told her to stop nagging. This time was different.

Dad pushed back his chair and headed for the living room. His purple cloth napkin (to match the upholstery in the chairs), fell from his lap and lay forgotten on the beige high-low carpet.

Mom followed him.

"Make me another drink," he said to her without looking back.

Focused completely on him, my mother followed his orders and turned to go through the swinging door in the dining room that lead to the bar area in the butler's pantry.

April looked at me across the table. "Why doesn't he get his own drink?"

I was worried. The yelling scared me. My mother's meek reaction to him scared me even more. It was one thing to hear it all—to hear her complaints to her friends, the restaging of every fight—but to see the action myself and the pain in my mother's face was too much to absorb. I looked back down at my plate. One of my favorite dinners was getting cold, going to waste. I guessed that it was alright because tomorrow, even though she was supposed to go out to dinner with Dad for their anniversary, Mom promised to make roast beef hash, my ultimate favorite, with big chunks of tonight's left-over meat, onion and potatoes all fried up in the big skillet with the copper bottom.

As soon as Mom passed though the swinging door to get his drink, Dad called out to April and me from the living room. "April, Heather, come here."

"Now what?" April sighed, rolling her eyes. We pushed back from the table and made our way into the living room, leaving the half-eaten dinner.

"Sit down," Dad said, leaning against the mantle. He'd lit a cigarette and was patting down the hair covering his bald spot on the back of his head.

Mom entered the living room and handed him a scotch on the rocks. April and I sat on the edge of the white sectional.

"I'm leaving," he announced. In front of the mantle, he looked taller than his 5-foot-9-inch frame, commanding and completely in control. I wondered at that moment if he had staged the whole evening.

"Don't be mad at me, Bob," my mother pleaded. "I swear. I'll cook it right next time. I swear. Give me another chance. *Please?*"

The light was brighter in the living room, every lamp on. My mother looked desperate. Her shiny blue eye shadow had formed creases in her eyelids. The moisture from her tears had caused her false eyelashes to lift and curl slightly at the ends.

She walked over to the side table and reached for the pack of Larks. She managed to strike the match on the side of the ribbed holder, but then her hands shook as she brought the match to the cigarette in her mouth.

"Dad, please don't go." I hoped he'd listen to me, his Heatherbean, his Smiley.

"I can't take it anymore, Heatherbean," he replied.

"Take what?" April asked, strong and self-assured.

My mother continued to cry, and sat down on the couch next to April. "Bob," she sniffed. "The girls. Please don't leave. Think of the girls. Heather's grades are bad."

I sat silent. Was this really happening?

Mom stubbed out the cigarette in the crystal ashtray and began nervously rubbing her manicured hands on the tops of her thighs.

"Let him leave, Mom," April said. Her words were brave but I saw the hurt in her watery eyes. "Can't you see that he wants out of here?"

"I love you girls," Dad said, taking a sip of the scotch. "I do. But, I can't live with your mother anymore." He was talking to us as if Mom weren't in the room.

"No," Mom cried. "Please. *Don't* go."

"Please, Dad," I said, moving over to my mother.

April stood up from the sofa. "Look, you guys figure this out. I'm going upstairs to call Ray."

"Marilyn, I just don't love you anymore." My father sounded exasperated.

"Yes, you do. I know you do." Mom was defiant through her tears.

Scotch in hand, Dad walked over to Mom.

"Marilyn." His voice was firm. My mother reached for his free hand and he quickly pulled it away. "I'm leaving you." He walked out of the room.

He was still holding his drink and was halfway up the stairs when Mom, following close behind, started in again. "How can you do this, Bob?"

He was losing control. "Jesus, Marilyn. Stop!"

It was surreal, like watching in slow motion as he pitched the heavy crystal glass against the wall. It exploded into pieces with the brown liquid dripping down the aged gold-toned wallpaper. The oil painting of a clown, Mom's favorite from her art class three years earlier, escaped the scotch by a hair.

I followed, climbing the stairs cautiously to avoid shards of glass, and went straight to the safe haven of my pink-walled bedroom. It was dark in there and I left the light off but kept the door slightly ajar so that I could see partway into my parent's room across the hall.

The next thing I heard was the click of the door latch to Dad's walk-in closet. From behind the crack in my door, suits flew from the closet, landing on top of their huge bed.

"Please. Don't leave me, Bob. Pleeeease." Mom wailed.

Next, my father pulled a suitcase out of the hall closet and dragged it back to their room. I heard the thump of shoes and the clink of belt buckles hitting the bottom of the suitcase followed by a loud thud from the stack of suits.

He pressed both latches on the suitcase to close it, and pulled it off the bed. I closed my door quickly and switched on the light in my room. I didn't know what to do with myself, so I sat on my twin bed and waited for what, I wasn't sure.

"Heather," Dad said, opening my door, suitcase in hand. "I love you, Smiley."

My lip had started to quiver and although I tried to hold back, I began to cry. "If you really love me, Dad, you won't leave Mom."

Dad hesitated a moment, his eyes looking side-to-side, his lips pursed.

Right behind him was my mother, her smoldering cigarette in one hand, a wadded wet Kleenex in the other.

"Bye, Smiley." He left my door open. Mom followed him like a lost puppy as he continued down the hallway to April's room.

"Go," April said. Tears dripped down her cheeks. "Just go, if that's what you want."

51

I followed April to the stair landing.

Down the stairs, his hand gripping the heavy glass front door knob, my father turned to my mother at the bottom of the stairs. It was right out of *Gone with the Wind*, but, instead of telling my mother "he didn't give a damn," he said: "Don't worry, Marilyn. I'll pay all the bills."

He walked out and shut the door behind him.

She turned to my sister and me, above her on the landing. "Don't worry," she said, through more tears. "Tomorrow's our eighteenth anniversary. He said he'd take me to dinner."

"You think he'll really do that still?" April said. "I mean, he's gone, Mom."

"I know, but he promised." She peeled off her false eyelashes and wiping more tears with the soggy tissue. "He'll do it, even if it's just out of guilt."

"He'll take her," I piped in, but I wasn't so sure.

••

"You mean today's your parents' anniversary?" Anne asked the next morning. I had arrived early at the Woodward's house to get a ride to school. I wanted to be around a normal family.

"Yeah, December eighteenth."

"And, he left your Mom?" We were in the Jack n' Jill bathroom between her parents' bedroom and hers. Anne spoke softly, squeezing the toothpaste onto her toothbrush. Just before putting the brush to her teeth, she asked, "Why did he leave, Heath?"

"Because Mom burned the roast beef."

Chapter Eight

She was all dressed up like Mrs. Astor's pet horse.
—Mom

My father kept his promise to take Mom out on their anniversary. I tried hard to wait up for her, but by 8:00 I was asleep. "No wonder," April had said as I nodded off at dinner in the Green Room. "Last night with Dad leaving and Mom crying...it was exhausting. You're just an eleven-year-old kid. You need to go to bed early."

I hated it when she bossed me around. But this time, April was right.

The sound of Dad's car pulling in the driveway woke me. The clock on the nightstand read 9:45—a bad sign. It was way too early for my parents to have had a good time.

I stumbled out of bed and ran over to the window and peeked under the heavy plastic shade. There they were, sitting in Dad's Lincoln. Opening my bedroom window just a crack, I could hear their muffled voices inside the car. The overhead light went on inside as Mom opened her door. Dad's face was fixed straight ahead, away from her. I ran down the hall to April's room. As usual, she was on the phone with her boyfriend. "Call Ray back. Mom's home early."

Although Ray usually came first in her life, this time April followed my lead.

Mom's key turned in the lock just as the two of us reached the bottom of the stairs.

"He's not coming back," Mom said when she saw us.

The headlights from Dad's car beamed through the open shutters and bobbed slightly as he backed down the driveway.

I froze. Mom had it wrong. He'd be back. He'd miss us too much.

I'd miss him too much. He never scolded me about my gaining weight. Only talked about my smile.

My mother looked horrible. Even with all the make-up and a new set of false eyelashes from the Larchmont Pharmacy, her eyes still looked swollen. Earlier in the day, she'd put cucumber slices on them for an hour to get rid of the puffiness from crying. It hadn't worked.

Mom slipped off her high heels. There was a small run in her stocking near her red-painted toenails.

"I don't know what I'm going to do without your father." The way she talked, it sounded like he'd died.

"He might come back," I said, hopefully.

Mom's hands shook as she picked up the shoes. "No, Heatherbean. He won't."

We turned to follow her. I tried to grasp what she was saying but my sister wanted the facts.

"So, what happened?" April asked. "Is it another woman?"

"He says it's not." Mom fingered a damp bubble on the wallpaper where his drink had splashed the night before.

"Then why'd he leave?" April asked.

"He said," Mom started to cry, "that he..." She choked. "That he...he meant it last night when he said he didn't love me anymore."

I swallowed hard. He didn't love her anymore... What about me?

••

54

When we reached our parents' bedroom, Mom went straight to her dressing room. April and I sat on the bed, watching as she dipped a hand in the jar of Abolene Cream next to the Kleenex. Scooping out a lump onto her cheeks, she spread it mixed with tears all over. After wiping the cream with tissue, she came back to the bedroom and asked April to unzip her cocktail dress. "Know what that bastard had the guts to order for dinner?"

"Chicken pot pie?" I asked, knowing that they had been at Chasen's and that he loved their chicken pot pie.

"Nope," she said, slipping her dress off. "He ordered goddamn roast beef!"

••

Dad came home six days later on Christmas Eve. It had been a weird six days since he'd left. Mom had stayed in bed all day and cried on the phone to her friends at night. April was with Ray. Lupe hung out in her room, and I was left alone. When I wasn't in school or asleep, I was around the block at Anne Woodward's house. The big evergreens out front blocked the sun and made the rooms dark inside. It wasn't scary, though. Anne's brothers and sisters came and went with their friends and Mrs. Woodward was always busy cooking or sewing or playing cards with friends. And there was Mr. Woodward, always so nice. Mom called him "John the good."

••

On their anniversary dinner, Dad had been wearing pricey grey flannel slacks and a brand new brown suede jacket. My mother had asked how he could afford such an expensive new outfit.

"If you have to know, it's Freddy's," he'd replied. "Borrowed it from his closet." He was living with Freddy now.

55

The next morning, I heard Mom on the phone with Aunt Carolyn. "Freddy's shorter and heavier than Bob," she said. "What he was wearing looked custom-made. I'll bet a woman paid for it."

It didn't make sense to me. There couldn't be another woman. He had come back to us for Christmas.

My father stayed over on Christmas Eve, but, slept downstairs on the couch in the Music Room, the same couch where Mom had spent so many nights talking with friends while waiting for him to come home.

On Christmas morning, he hauled in a heavy box from the trunk of his car. "Go ahead, Marilyn, open it."

Mom tore at the red wrapping paper. Inside was a color television set. "It's for all of you," he beamed.

"Another guilt gift," Mom muttered. "Only this one isn't just for me."

"Jesus, Marilyn," Dad said.

Mom pulled it together for Christmas night. Papa and Virginia arrived early, followed by Uncle Charlie and Aunt Carolyn with my little cousins, Jonathan and Robert.

I loved Papa. He was larger than life. He entered the house with a huge smile and did a little soft-shoe tap dance that he always did when he saw us.

Mom told me once that her real mother, Arvella, couldn't keep up with Papa and his political ambitions. "She put her head in the bottle; became a raging alcoholic. Eventually, it did her in."

Papa had met Virginia after Arvella died. He was giving a speech as the Governor of California on Veteran's Day. Virginia, a war widow, was there selling paper poppies in honor of America's war dead.

Mom said that Virginia was from "the weed patch," meaning the wrong side of the street. A lot of people though it was a big deal that he used to be Governor of California. I just thought it was neat that he cut the ribbon to open Disneyland and we got a special free pass now.

At Christmas dinner, Dad sat at his usual place at the head of the table, Mom sat at the opposite end, and the rest of us sat in between.

Mom and Dad didn't say a word. While Papa told stories and Virginia looked adoringly at him, Mom sipped her wine and Dad sipped his scotch. Carolyn and Charlie barely looked at each other, fawning all over Jonathan and Robert to distract themselves. The last time we'd had lunch with my cousins at El Coyote, Aunt Carolyn had just found out that Uncle Charlie was seeing another woman. Her name was Sherry, and her boat was docked at the Marina in the slip next to Charlie's boat, "The Sagita."

I thought about Mom's warning to Carolyn months ago. "If you don't go on that boat with him, somebody else will."

I'd hoped that my father's being home for Christmas was a sign that he was moving back, but as soon as everyone left after dinner, Dad reached into the pocket of so-called Freddy's pants and peeled off a couple hundred dollar bills from his money clip and handed them to Mom. "This is for next week," he said.

Next, he handed Lupe, who was clearing the table, two weeks' back pay and tucked an extra $20 in the pocket of her apron "for working Christmas night."

"I've gotta go, Marilyn." He grabbed his suede jacket from the hook on the antique umbrella stand in the hall and pulled out his car keys.

"Why are you leaving so fast?" she asked with the pleading sound to her voice again. I prayed she wouldn't cry.

He ignored her as he turned the doorknob. "I'll call the girls next week."

Then he was gone.

Ray came through the door minutes later. He greeted us with "Hey," and joined April in the Music Room to listen to records.

I helped Mom carry the empty glasses and dirty ashtrays from the living room into the kitchen. I felt sorry for her. Dad had been mean to leave.

Lupe was busy drying dinner dishes. *"Senor Eaton no vive mas en casa?"* Lupe asked, innocently. Lupe was lucky. Her room was in the back of the house, far away from all the drama.

"Si, Lupe," Mom said in her best high school Spanish. *"Mi esposa no vive mas en casa. Su matrimonio termino."*

I was starting to believe my mother. Dad wasn't coming back.

••

A month later, Lupe told April in broken English that our mother stayed in bed past noon while we were in school.

April, at sixteen, took charge. "Mom, you've got to get it together," she told her. "Does Papa know that you're sleeping 'till noon?" she asked. Papa called every day to ask how Mom was doing.

"Yes, he does," she said, lighting another cigarette. It was 3:30 in the afternoon. My mother never smoked until after five in the evening—another sign that things were bad.

"He told me to go see Dr. Ferguson, Carolyn's shrink, who'll help me through this."

"The same doctor that Aunt Carolyn goes to?" I asked.

"That's the one," Mom said, taking another long drag off her cigarette.

"Can I go with you?" I asked. Since Dad had left, I hadn't wanted to leave my mother's side.

••

Dr. Ferguson's office was on the corner of Normandie Avenue and Sunset Boulevard, not the nicest of neighborhoods, but Papa had assured Mom that he was "the best."

Inside, the clinic looked shabby. One wall of the main hallway was painted dull yellow. A colorful mural covered the opposite wall. It was a mixture of drawings—rainbows, cows stopped at a street sign, people wearing odd-shaped hats, a yellow bus with no windows, butterflies and a large fairy with wings and a halo.

I asked Mom what it all meant. "I haven't a clue," she replied. "I think that it was painted by a bunch of the nutty patients who come here."

We stopped at the door near the end of the hall. "Dr. James Ferguson" was on the name plate. Next to the door was a tiny red light and a switch. Mom flipped the switch, and we sat down on two cracked vinyl chairs next to the door. Soon, the red light turned off and Dr. Ferguson appeared at the door. He was tall, thin, and had light brown hair. His face was pock-marked near the jaw, and he smelled like cigarettes.

He took a leathery hand out of his tan sport coat and extended it to my mother. "You must be Marilyn," he said in a gravely voice.

My mother began sobbing on the spot.

He wrapped a long arm around her shoulders and guided her into his office. Then he came back outside the door and leaned down to meet my eyes.

"I'll be talking with your Mom for about an hour," he said. If you need us, just come inside the office. O.K.?"

I liked him. "O.K.," I said.

I took out the little diary I had gotten for Christmas. "My Diary—1968" was printed on the pink cover. A gift from Aunt Carolyn. "This is a place where you can write your secret thoughts and feelings," she told me.

I took out a pen from the pocket of my new blue and white gingham-lined straw basket, a Christmas gift from Papa and Virginia.

"My Mom is sad," I wrote. "She's so sad that she needs a special doctor."

Just then, a pair of pointy high-heeled shoes came into view. I looked up from my diary to find a strange looking older woman dressed in an old-fashioned jacket and skirt the same color as the shoes. She stared down at me. Her eyes looked wild, distant and scary. She said nothing, just stared.

I felt uneasy and looked back down at my diary. I pretended to write, hoping that the crazy lady would go away.

"Please leave me alone," I thought. My mind raced. Should I go get my mother? Dr. Ferguson said that it was all right. No, she needed Dr. Ferguson. Please, God, make this lady go away.

I checked the clock on the wall above the mural. Five minutes had passed and the strange woman hadn't budged an inch. Just when I had gathered enough courage to move away from her, the door across the hall marked "Dr. Joel Simon" opened.

A middle-aged man poked his head out. "Mrs. Tanner, you may come in now."

I looked down at my diary. As soon as the red shoes passed through the door, I began writing again.

"Is my mother crazy like this, too?"

Chapter Nine

A day late and a dollar short.

—Mom

Dad opened the menu as soon as we sat down for dinner.

"Aren't we going to get Shirley Temples first?" I asked.

It was the end of January, the first we'd seen him since Christmas night.

When he picked us up, Dad had stayed in the car and honked his horn with the motor running. April and I dashed outside while Mom stayed up in her room. I could feel her eyes on us from the bedroom window as we got in the car.

"Sure. Sure," he said, as a waiter placed a Scotch in front of him. They knew him well at Perino's.

"Shirley Temples for the girls, Adam," he said to the waiter. "And, we'll order as soon as you bring them."

"So soon?" April asked. "We haven't seen you since Christmas. Can't we wait a little with our drinks before we order, Dad?"

"Yeah," I piped in, sliding my pudgy hand under the folded cloth that covered the silver bread tray. The dark Parmesan cheese toast was warm.

"It's a school night," he said, pulling out a new gold lighter. "You both need to get home to do homework." He lit a cigarette and flipped the lighter shut. The familiarity of a simple sound of his lighting a cigarette, of everything about him, hurt.

"My homework's done," April said. "And Heather never does any."

"That's mean." I narrowed my eyes at April.

"Stop it, girls," Dad interrupted. "It's our first visit. Let's make it nice."

Dad barely touched his dinner, but managed to finish two scotches and part of a third. He only half-listened to what April and I said, and asked us several times to repeat things. He checked his watch twice, trying to be inconspicuous, slowly moving the white cuff of his monogrammed shirt back when he thought we weren't looking. The watch was new, one with a big round face and thin, black Roman numerals. It looked expensive and lay flat and shiny against the dark hairs of his wrist. I wondered how he had gotten it. According to Mom, he was broke.

On the short ride back home, April sat up front and talked to Dad about horses—her other big love besides Ray. I sat in the back watching the rain fall. I felt secure in the warm interior of the car. The smooth leather and familiar smell of the old Continental was comforting, reassuring. But, I worried. Should I tell Mom about the new watch?

Making circles with my finger on the moist window, I thought about Mom back at home, alone. It was all wrong. We weren't a family anymore. Dr. Ferguson was trying to help Mom feel better. She was going to him three mornings a week, but still cried a lot and talked on the phone for hours with Connie and Aunt Carolyn.

Drawing squiggly lines, I thought about Dad, deep in conversation with April up front. I had missed my father this past month. I had missed our Sunday night dinners, his sleeping on the itchy brown couch in the den after he and Mom had a fight. I had missed Mom getting dressed up for him and looking pretty. I had missed watching her comb her hair all high on her head. I had missed sitting with her as she put her on false eyelashes they went out at night. I had missed watching her coat her real lashes (when she didn't wear the fake ones) with the cake mascara that she spit in to make the brush glide smoothly.

I had missed the smell of scotch on Dad's breath and the scent of his aftershave. I had missed listening for his voice in the hallway late at night when he'd come home.

I thought about Anne and Mary Jo's dads. They were different. Their fathers came home at regular times. Took them to baseball games and helped them with their homework sometimes, even drove them to school. But, my father, even though he didn't do stuff like that, was still my father.

The way it was before Dad left felt normal to me, even though I knew that my parents weren't happy. At least my father lived with us.

Now, Mom was scared about having no money. "There's no back-up," she told us. "I have no real family money." She sighed, adding: "I've never had a real job. I don't even know what I'd do."

Everything depended on the weekly check from Dad. It came in the mail every Friday, and if it was late, Mom went crazy calling bars and restaurants and friends' houses until she found him. "Where's the check?" she'd screech when she finally got him on the phone.

The check was never more than a day late. Mom made it clear to us that the weekly check was only temporary until the settlement was done and the divorce was final.

Words like "settlement" and "divorce" scared me. Good things didn't come out of words like that.

••

Mom held nothing back from April and me. I knew who we owed, what we owed, and how much we owed.

"He's a bastard," Mom told us. "He got us into this financial mess."

I absorbed it all, escaping to Anne's house where the constant action among Anne's four siblings was fun and distracting.

Slowly drawing the squiggles again, my mind wandered back to that first weekend after Dad had left.

I'd been at Anne's big wooden breakfast-room table, eating my second helping of spaghetti. Mrs. Woodward made the best spaghetti. "Comfort food," Anne called it. I had been worried about the situation with my parents, but was swept away with the chatter around the table. John, Anne's older brother, regaled us with stories about Friday night's football game. He was a star player for Loyola High School and the big man on campus, or, so he told us.

Anne's parents were upstairs getting ready for a night out. Anne and I were in charge of babysitting Andrew and Gerry, her younger brother and sister. As soon as they were in bed, we'd be free to watch the big TV in the "Ballroom," their name for the large family room that had once been a ballroom when their house was built. We'd be free to dig into that big chocolate cake, freshly made, that sat under the clear cake plate in the pantry.

Finishing my second helping, I tried to hold on to the taste and the feeling of the warm, yummy spaghetti and easy chitchat. Tomorrow was Sunday. The Woodward's would go to Mass and I'd go home to Mom who was a mess. To Lupe, who barely spoke English and to April and Ray, who spent most Sunday afternoons kissing out front in his gold El Camino.

Anne and I never talked much about our families. She'd ask about my Mom, or how it was with my Dad, but she didn't pry. If I felt like talking, fine. If I didn't, that was okay, too.

We talked a lot about the boys we had crushes on, or what we were going to wear on free dress school days or to Cotillion each month.

Even though all the boys went for Anne, who was so beautiful with her long black hair and pale blue eyes, being around her helped me forget my life at home.

By the time Dad pulled in the driveway bringing me and April home, the damp car window next to me was covered with circles and squiggly lines, remnants of my faraway thoughts. Peering through my finger drawings, I saw a flash of light through an open shutter upstairs in Mom's dressing room.

She must have heard us.

She was upset enough these days. I wasn't going to tell her about the watch, I decided. What good would it do?

After saying goodbye and promising to see us soon, Dad quickly backed down the driveway the minute we got out of the car. Mom waited at the top of the stairs.

"So, how does he look?" she asked, followed by, "Is he still living at Freddy's?"

The questions didn't stop. "Did he mention another woman? Did he say anything about me?"

I felt bad for her and wanted to tell her something good. Something that she'd want to hear, that would make her feel good. But, there was nothing. He had never even mentioned her name.

Later, I had trouble falling asleep. The bedroom light was off, and I watched the fluorescent dial on my nightstand clock until the hands pointed past ten. It had been my first visit with my father, and he hadn't called me "Smiley" all night.

Chapter Ten

A dog that will take a bone will carry it.

—Mom

Four months after that first visit with Dad at Perino's, my parents jointly filed for divorce citing "irreconcilable differences," two big words that meant they didn't get along. There was no formal agreement suggested in the divorce settlement for child visitation. No set time or day, such as "every other weekend" or "every Wednesday night" which, Mom explained, were the normal times for divorced fathers to see their children.

"He goes by his own set of rules," Mom told us. "He has no morals and he'd screw a snake."

Not kind words to hear about one's father coming from one's own mother. But, I was beginning to believe her and not disregard her nasty comments about Dad like I had before. I tried to accept that my father, who I had once thought favored me, was drifting away.

Most of my our visits with him had been like the first one at Perino's. Always dinner, always rushed, and, always, according to Mom, "at a convenient time for him." Sometimes we saw him once a week. Then it might be two weeks before another phone call from him or an invitation to dinner. Not once since my father had left had he called me "Smiley." April said that it was because I didn't smile anymore. She was probably right.

My father never mentioned another woman but Mom said that all the signs were there after April told her about the new things that Dad had on every time we saw him. Since the watch, he'd worn another new suede jacket, new monogrammed shirts, and last time we had dinner with him, a shiny new gold ring was on his pinky finger.

"Forget hurting Mom's feelings," April said after I'd accused her of upsetting Mom with the details of dad's new wardrobe.

"Listen, kid, the bank called yesterday about our past-due mortgage payment," April explained. "Mom needs to know this."

Maybe April was right. But, I was too afraid to ask Dad how he paid for the clothes. His answer might be what Mom had suspected.

"Mom, why do you act so crazy when the weekly check from Dad was only two days late?" I asked.

"For Chris sakes, Heather, I'm hanging on to Lupe by a stem. Henry's only mowing the front now, and I'm about ready to clean the pool myself. Hell," she added, "I may have to, after the divorce, anyway. Then, again," she emphasized. "There may *be* no house or pool to clean when the divorce is final."

"O.K.! Forget it!" I shouted at her, then ran upstairs and went to the back of my closet. I crouched behind the clothes in the dark where I felt safe. I didn't want to hear her complain anymore. Away from her rage, in the darkness at the back of my closet, I needed to think of something good. Wherever Dad was getting this stuff, maybe, just maybe, there might be little left over for us.

I'd stopped crying myself to sleep about my parents' split months ago. It was spring now. He'd left in December. He wasn't coming back. Instead of crying, I ate. Food was comfort and I grew fatter by the minute. At eleven, I was already edging my way up to a size 16 Preteen.

Even my feet were getting bigger. I went from a size 7 Medium to an 8 Wide. We went shopping for shoes at The Larchmont Jr.

Bootery that year. Ed, the shoe man with the craggy skin and nervous tick, leaned over from his perch on the vinyl stool with the rubber runway, Ed's pack of Winston's teetered precariously from the pocket of his Hawaiian shirt. Pressing my foot hard into the measuring stick, he practically shouted. "Heather's hard to fit, you know." Cringing, I was sure everyone in the store had heard. Then, sitting up to face my mother, his right eye twitched wildly. "Her feet are *really* wide."

"I know that she wants the pink patent ones." Mom pointed to the sample shoe I held in my hand. "But, honestly, let's just get something cheap that fits."

I had my heart set on those pink shoes. I begged her. "Please let me try them."

Reluctantly, Ed returned from the stockroom and pulled the shiny shoes out of the tissue from inside the box. "These run narrow," he warned, struggling to guide them on my foot with his silver shoehorn.

Stuffed into the tight-fitting Mary-Janes, my feet throbbed. "They fit fine," I lied.

"You should walk around," Ed said, probing my toes through the shoes with his thumb, his eye twitching. "They feel awfully tight to me."

"No, no, they're not tight." I stood and walked around the store. The shoes were so pretty I masked the pain with a frozen smile, silently hoping they would stretch out.

Mom wanted to be done with it. "We'll take them then," she sighed.

••

My mother's eye wasn't on my overeating like it had been before Dad left. She hadn't checked under my bed for dried-up bowls of ice cream and hadn't searched my nightstand drawer for candy wrappers in weeks. It wasn't that she didn't care that I was getting fatter, she was worried about everything else. But, she still served Jell-O instead of pudding and steered me away from my favorite: Tiny Naylor's Drive-in on Sunset, where the cheeseburgers were wrapped in wax paper and smothered in Thousand Island dressing dripping down the sides. We still went to Mrs. Hannibal's Health Food Store on Larchmont. My mother thought that health food meant diet food. Healthy food had calories too, but my mother insisted that Mrs. Hannibal's egg salad sandwich made with "Hollywood" brand safflower mayonnaise was better for me. After eating lunch at the long counter, my big treat was to pick a health-food candy bar from the assortment on the shelf next to the vitamins. No matter how much my mother tried to get me to like the sesame seed candy and the carob bars, none of it held a candle to an Almond Joy or a Peppermint Patty.

Now that Mom wasn't checking on me so much, I felt a guilty about eating fattening food behind her back, like when her friend, Louise Flemmng took me out to dinner with her daughter. Eleven like me, everyone called her Little Louise. When we went to the Hamburger Hamlet on Sunset in West Hollywood, Little Louise's mother Louise let me eat everything. I had a cheeseburger with onion rings and a double chocolate malt topped with a mountain of whipped cream. I was so stuffed, I felt sick. Louise had to take me on a walk around the block to get some air before she took me back to their house in Bel Air to spend the night. Louise had been separated from her husband, Carl, for a whole year. I felt comfortable with them. Little Louise's Dad wasn't around either.

••

That Spring my mother's sessions with Dr. Ferguson three times a week seemed to be paying off. Each month, there'd been progress.

It had been scary to see my mother so weak and vulnerable right after Dad left. Being in what she called "analysis," seemed to help her.

The first month with Dr. Ferguson, she stopped sleeping late during the week and purposely scheduled her appointment with him for 10:00am so she'd have to be somewhere early.

By Valentine's Day, she'd stopped chain-smoking all day and was back to the first cigarette at five o'clock in the evening. By March, she started wearing lipstick again, but the rest of the make-up remained untouched on her dressing room table.

On Easter Sunday, Mom put false eyelashes on again.

"I'm back in business," she laughed when I told her how beautiful she looked.

On her own, Mom put Easter on that year like nothing had changed. The egg hunt was the same. Papa stole eggs out of our baskets for fun and did his little tap dance when he won the prize for "finding" the most eggs. The colored eggs Mom had hidden were still in the same places in the crook of the branches in the big sycamore tree out front, among the now-neglected roses and the Birds of Paradise, and on top of the first floor shutters. Uncle Charlie came, and, like always, took movies with his camera. Uncle Charlie and Aunt Carolyn had separated, too, not long after Mom and Dad, but he came to Easter with Aunt Carolyn anyway. Dad didn't. He was "with clients."

"On Easter?" I'd asked him on the phone earlier in the week.

He gave no answer. And I gave up.

••

Carolyn tried hard with Charlie that Easter. Dressed up in a lavender broadcloth shirt-maker dress, she served him ham and hot cross buns from the buffet, even placing his napkin on his lap for him, a big change from the time when we dropped in on her and she was dressed sloppy and was serving him a frozen dinner.

Aunt Carolyn wore lots of eyeliner and made sure that my cousins, Jonathan and Robert, were settled quietly at the dining room table. Her actions seemed fake and desperate. I wasn't sure that Charlie was buying it either, but he was all smiles.

"Of course, he's buying it," Mom had said later while I watched her take off her lashes. "He's got two women after him. It's a man's world," she told me, placing the lashes carefully in their molded plastic container. "And don't you forget it."

••

Twilight on that May evening seeped through a slit in the yellowing burlap shades covering the Music Room windows. April and I sat opposite Mom on the couch facing her. My mother's vodka and water was next to her on the end table, the glass all sweaty with a cocktail napkin underneath wrinkled and wet. Mom had wanted to prepare us. The divorce would be final in a few months.

"The divorce settlement isn't great," she told us. "This is it and I've got to get my act together, or I'll have to work at The May Company."

"You'd be a saleslady?" I couldn't picture my mother selling clothes at a department store.

"Your father doesn't have any money," she said. "He's let his law practice go and he got nothing from his father." She took a sip of her drink and continued. "He probably banked on his father leaving me lots of money, but all he got were few pairs of cufflinks. Everything went to the second wife. Hell, she deserved it more than Mr. Wonderful."

"God, Mom," April groaned. "You're so frigging dramatic."

"Listen," Mom snapped. "We may have to sell the house."

72

While April and Mom continued to discuss our bad money situation and take guesses at who might be the "other woman," I watched the beads of water dripping down my mother's glass. Between each sentence, Mom took a long drag off her cigarette, then put it back in the silver framed ashtray. It was easier to watch something than to try to make sense and accept what they were saying. Another woman? Part of me didn't want to know.

That night, I hated my mother for telling the truth. I hated my father for leaving. I hated my sister for being so know-it-all, and I hated myself for hating all of them.

••

A few days later, the powder-blue princess phone in April's room rang off the hook. She'd gotten her own phone line from Dad weeks ago for her birthday. Now, he only called us on April's line, which drove Mom crazy. I'd heard the subtle clicks on the house phone when she'd tried to eavesdrop on our calls on the main line. Dad had probably heard them too.

"Get it, Heather," Mom called out from her bedroom. "It's probably your father. April's out with Ray."

"Hi, Smiley," my father said. He sounded cheery. "How about dinner Thursday at The Bistro?"

"We've never been there," I said. "Is it fancy?"

"Very. So make sure you and April are dressed up. O.K?"

"I better ask Mom, though. She likes to know when we're going to see you."

I hadn't noticed my mother standing in the doorway of April's room. "Ask me what?"

Startled, I turned around to face her. "Dad wants to take April and me to dinner on Thursday. It's all right, right? We haven't seen Dad since before Easter."

Mom groaned, but nodded her head. She hated it when we saw him. "Your father's always fun and games for you," she told us. "Out there at the great restaurants, and I'm home with the tuna sandwich over the sink."

April shot back the last time she'd started in. "Mom, quit the guilt. He's our father, for God's sake."

That image of my mother and the sandwich was imprinted in my mind, though, and I worried about her while we were with Dad. It was hard to love both parents who didn't love each other.

"Mom says O.K." I said, moving closer to the window in April's room. I needed more space between my mother and the phone. The large window was open and the screen smelled like tin and dust. Below, our next-door neighbor was cutting roses in her pristine backyard.

"Great," Dad replied. "Oh, and Louise Fleming's coming with us."

I was confused. "You mean, Mom's friend, Louise? Little Louise's mother?"

Mom leapt from the doorway and grabbed the receiver away from me. "LOUISE!?" she shouted into the phone.

I stood stunned, still staring down our neighbor, who had moved on to another rose bush by the fence. No wonder Louise had let me eat so much at The Hamburger Hamlet that night. She wanted me to like her.

Chapter Eleven

Don't let the Peter Pan collar fool ya.
—Mom, on promiscuous women

"Shit!" Mom yelled after breaking a fingernail—painted mod frosty pink—when she slammed down the phone on Dad.

She nursed the jagged edge with her tongue. "That bastard isn't worth breaking a nail." Mom's pale blue eyes, top-heavy with fake lashes, shifted side to side, following each thought buzzing around in her head.

"So, I guess April and I won't be going to The Bistro with Dad and Louise, huh?"

She ignored my question and ordered me to get in the car. "I need to get out of here. I need to go talk to Richard and Connie."

"Are you mad?" I shifted uncomfortably in the front seat of the car. What a stupid question, I thought. Of course, Mom's mad. She had just found out Dad had been seeing her oldest friend, Louise.

"Yes." Mom's full lips tightened, the frosted pink lipstick moving into a thin line. "I mean no," she corrected herself. "Not at you."

"How could that bitch Louise do this to me?" she said, turning left outside the Fremont gates onto Wilshire Boulevard. I sat quietly bracing myself for the outburst of emotion that I knew was coming. Thankfully, the Rossi's only lived five minutes away.

She turned to me at the first stop light. "Well?"

I started to answer, "I dunno..."

"I mean, what the hell was that broad thinking?!"

"I dun…"

"My oldest friend! We've known each other since in high school. Jesus!" She gripped the wooden steering wheel tighter. "I was a bridesmaid in her wedding! She was a bridesmaid in *my* wedding! *She's* the irreconcilable difference!"

She shook her head in disgust. "I should have known. Your father always liked Louise. She's the feminine type. Delicate. And, she's got *a lot* of money!"

When the Rossi's' street came into view, Mom slowed the Mustang to a crawl so that she could finish her tirade. Connie was her best friend and her husband, Richard, had been her lawyer for the divorce, but I sensed that Mom wanted to get some of her anger out before we got there.

"Louise's really rich," she said, her eyes never leaving the road. "I think she's worth something like fourteen million."

I was confused. Louise had always been so nice to me with her sweet, breathy voice. How could she do this to Mom? To me? I'd always liked her. She let me eat whatever I wanted when I spent the night last February. Mom would have had a fit over my overeating, but Louise didn't. She just waited patiently with Little Louise until I felt better. That's the way she'd always been, easy and calm. She even stayed that way after she and her husband, Carl, separated. Little Louise had said that her mom never cried about the breakup the way my mom did after Dad left. Little Louise wasn't being mean. She just always said what was on her mind.

We'd never been good friends, more forced into friendship by our mothers. Little Louise acted like she was older than me. She could be too much, like when I was brushing my teeth in her bathroom after I'd spent the night a year ago, and she burst in with, "I have to change my pad and can't wait!"

She lifted her nightgown, pulled down her underwear, and sat down on the toilet. "Look," she had said, showing me her used

76

Kotex pad still attached to the little belt that held it in place, "look how much I bleed on my period. Have you started yet?"

Shocked that she would show me something so personal and so gross, I couldn't tell her that I hadn't. She'd think that I was a baby. "Yeah," I garbled with a mouth full of toothpaste.

••

"No wonder Big Louise never got upset after Carl left," Mom explained after I'd asked her why Big Louise was always so calm. "It was her idea to separate and she's the one with the money. Nothing changed for Louise. She kept her house and she doesn't have to wait for some lousy check every week. Louise's scene is not like mine, Heatherbean. She doesn't have to depend on anyone."

Now, Little Louise got to stay in her big house and have lots of money *and* my Dad.

We came to a stop at the curb in front of the cement walkway leading to the Rossi's' front door. Mom shut off the engine and turned to me. Her voice softened.

"How could I have competed with fourteen million dollars?"

••

Angela, the second youngest of the five Rossi children, answered the door.

"Hi Auntie Mare," she said, using the "Auntie" that our mothers insisted we call them. "Hi, Heath."

Her scrawny arms and spindly legs jutted out from a loose-fitting blue and white seersucker romper that was cinched in at her tiny waist with a rope tie. She hung on the big iron doorknob, sheepishly swinging a skinny right leg back and forth.

My mother and I followed Angela into the family room, an add-on to their moderately sized Mediterranean-style home. Now at 3,500 square feet, the house approached the mansion realm.

At the far corner of the large room, there was a bar for the grown-ups. "So, here's the heartbeat of the house," Mom had joked when she saw the new addition.

Connie bragged that it was built to duplicate the bar at Scandia, their favorite restaurant. But, Connie was wasting her time if she wanted to make Mom jealous with her new addition.

"Connie's got the world by the ass," she told me once. "Richard really digs her." Now, *that* made my mother jealous.

Perched on the barstool, Connie greeted us with an over-sized smile and raised a half-empty glass. "C'mon in."

My mother's best friend was blessed with high cheekbones, wide-set eyes, and sensual lips. She was the spitting image of Ava Gardener, and, like Ava, she wore her chestnut hair the same way in a French twist and accentuated her full lips like Ava did with a vibrant red lipstick.

Connie put the glass down on a cocktail napkin and reached for the pack of Pall Mall non-filters.

"Thank God it's cocktail hour," Mom said, taking the stool next to her and dropping her heavy wicker handbag with a thud on the glazed terra-cotta tile floor.

"What's wrong?" Richard asked, standing at attention behind the bar. "You seem beat, Mare."

Angela and I joined them, our legs dangling from the high leather bar stools. The brass pushpins that made the diamond pattern in the burgundy leather cut into my fleshy thighs. I pulled my skirt underneath me and looked down. There was a real brass foot rail.

Connie took a long sip of her drink. Her thick gold charm bracelet jingled as she emptied the glass. "What is it, Marilyn?" she asked with a slight slur and a fixed smile. The alcohol was taking effect.

Uncle Richard wiped the copper countertop with a small white rag, making it sparkle under the recessed light. Like a bartender, he placed a cocktail napkin in front of my mother. "The Rossi's'" was printed across it in bold script.

"First, the drink," Richard said. "What'll it be, Mare?" They'd been close friends for years. I was surprised that he didn't know what my mother drank.

"Vodka, short on the tonic," Mom said, pulling out a pack of Tareytons from her overstuffed handbag below.

She'd changed cigarette brands recently. "I'd rather fight than switch," the Tareyton ads touted in Mom's favorite magazine, *Photoplay*. Mom said that the ads were reason enough for her to change from Larks. "I'd rather fight to stay married than switch," she'd told me. "But, I didn't have a choice."

"You girls go play or watch TV," Connie said, placing an unlit cigarette in her mouth.

"That's right," Mom agreed, also putting a cigarette in her mouth.

"I know. I know," I sighed. "Kids and cocktails don't mix."

Richard leaned over with a thick match he'd just struck on the ridges of the ceramic match holder on the edge of the bar. Connie and my mother leaned in together to meet the match with the end of their cigarettes. As the match hit the tips, they took huge drags to make sure the cigarettes were lit, then leaned back and blew out the smoke in unison. Richard smiled, satisfied with his accomplishment, and blew out the match.

I followed Angela over to the game table at the other end of the dimly lit family room. I took a seat at the small game table while she scaled shelves in the nearby closet to pull out the Clue game from the top shelf. Like Mary Jo, Angela was agile. Thin people moved so easily.

"I'll be *Miss Scarlett*," she said, setting up the game board. "Why don't you be Colonel Mustard."

"Sure," I said, more interested in my mother at the other end of the room.

Angela handed me the dice. "You go first."

Positioning myself to face the bar, I rolled the dice as Richard reached for the vodka. He began pouring Mom's drink.

I moved my little yellow plastic figure six spaces toward the "Dining Room."

"Bob's been seeing Louise Fleming," Mom blurted out. I could hear the quiver in her voice.

I looked down at the dice for a moment, then back over at the bar. Richard and Connie stared at each other, saying nothing. The only sound was Angela loudly tapping "Miss Scarlett" her seven precious spaces closer to the *Hall*.

Mom watched Richard set her drink down on the napkin, meeting his eyes. "Do you know something, Richard?"

"Now, we can tell you," Connie sighed, stubbing her half-smoked cigarette out. "Richard and I saw them at Scandia a couple weeks ago." There was a pause "I knew you'd referred Louise to him as a client a while back. You said it would drum up business for his fading law practice."

Richard looked down, rubbing the already glistening bar top. "But, it didn't look like they were doing much business, Marilyn," he mumbled.

"You knew? Jesus. And, you didn't tell me?" Her quiver had turned to a tremble. Mom cleared her throat. "I mean, I knew that he had other women. I even heard him say a name once. Gwen. He slipped one night and called me by her name."

Mom cleared her throat a few more times and continued. She was trying to pull it together in front of Richard and Connie.

"Bob always had these so-called clients that he had to take to dinner," Mom said. "Clients with names I'd never heard before." Facing Connie, "You remember that crocheted knit dress that Bob gave me, right? I swear another woman, not some salesgirl, picked that dress out for me. Something about it just didn't feel right."

Angela handed me the dice.

I rolled quickly, landing two spaces closer to the Dining Room and prayed that Angela hadn't heard what was being said over at the bar.

"We didn't want to upset you, Marilyn," Connie said, softly. "You'd been through enough."

"Another woman, I get. But, my oldest friend? Jesus." Mom took a gulp of her drink and stared off into space. Every corner on her face had turned down, her eyes, her blonde brows, the corners of her mouth.

I started to stand up and go over to try and comfort her, but Angela pulled me back with a strong, reedy arm. "Let's keep playing."

Connie inched her barstool closer to my mother and put her hand on Mom's. "Marilyn, please know that we didn't want to hurt you by being the ones to tell you. I mean, we thought, hey, maybe this is just a passing thing, you know?"

My mother let out a moan. "I know why you didn't tell me. I understand," she said, reaching for another. "But, God, Connie, Louise is—was—my oldest friend."

I wanted to go outside in the car and be by myself. Lucky April, she was out with Ray.

Richard came out from behind the bar and sat down on the other side of Mom. "Now that it's out," he said, "you've got to face this, Marilyn."

"Mare" had become "Marilyn." The festive mood had turned somber.

I hesitated, holding the tiny pewter candlestick, hating Angela for making me concentrate on this stupid game.

"I'm mad. Hurt. Christ, I don't know what." Mom put a fresh unlit cigarette down on the bar.

"Listen, you think you're mad, Marilyn," Richard said. "That name you heard before, 'Gwen.' Well, according to the word on the street, she paid the last three payments on your house in Fremont thinking that Bob was going to marry her!"

Mom was defeated. Her eyelids grew heavy. "Jesus Christ, I knew that Gwen was the mistress's name."

"So, basically, Marilyn," Richard said, matter-of-factly, "the son-of-a-bitch dumped the wife *and* the mistress for the rich girlfriend."

The past-due mortgage... the Gwen lady had stopped paying it.

Angela startled me back into the game. "So, who do you think committed the murder?"

"I haven't a clue."

Chapter Twelve

She's as clever as a tree full of owls.

—Mom

Dad pulled up to the house and honked twice. April quickly hung up from Ray and hollered at Mom to help her find her other dressy sandal. Mom rushed in and found the stray shoe at the back of April's cluttered closet. I'd been ready in my empire waist party dress for an hour. It was a big night, dinner out with my father and Louise for the first time. Little Louise and her older brother, Teddy, would be joining us. Carl Jr. and Bonnie, Louise's older kids, were visiting their father. I hadn't talked to any of them since Dad started seeing Louise. I was nervous and also worried about my mother who would be at home alone.

April sat up front with Dad, as usual, but didn't say a word. So, I jabbered on about Anne and Mary Jo and how much I wanted to go to Gold Arrow Camp with Mary Jo this summer, hoping maybe, that my father might feel sorry about the divorce. Even though Mom said there was no money, he might pay for me to go. If he gave in, I would be gone for a whole month up in the mountains, away from everything except my close friend. I had to go.

But Dad was focused on April now, taking her silence to mean she was angry at him. "Does my seeing Louise upset you?" he asked her. "Is that why you're so quiet tonight?"

"No, Dad, it's because I'm mad at Ray," April answered. "If you want to be with Louise, that's your business."

"What's up with Ray?" Dad relaxed his shoulders. I could sense relief.

"I don't know. He gets so uptight. He thinks he owns me." She looked out the side window, again. "I hate that."

I wished that Dad had asked me if I were mad, because I was. Of all the women he could be dating, why Mom's old friend?

Our table at The Bistro was long enough to accommodate all of us. Louise was already seated in the center of the table when we arrived; Teddy next to her, and Little Louise across. Louise looked the same, all porcelain, powdery and soft with her coiffed light brown hair swept up on one side in a puffed wave. Mom said that Louise's hairdresser went to the house to comb it out almost every day.

Dad kissed Louise lightly on the cheek and motioned for us to sit, pulling out the chair next to her for me. She smelled of Joy perfume as she leaned over to give me a weak hug. April sat down across from us next to Dad's chair, and Louise greeted her with a warm hello, rounding her bow-shaped lips that were lined in a darker shade of pink.

Mostly, the talk was with Dad and Louise. I was nice to Little Louise from across the table. "Hi, Louise," I'd said weakly.

She was nice back. "Hi, Heath."

The whole thing felt awkward and I wondered how Little Louise felt about it all. Teddy was weird. Fat like me, he had always seemed miserable, but even more so tonight. Every time that I'd come over to play with Little Louise, he was alone in his bedroom with the red and green plaid carpet. The shutters were always closed, making the room feel dark and scary. When Little Louise and I went to look for him, he'd be in there watching television, sitting in one of his overstuffed chairs. Although Teddy was a couple years older than Little Louise and me, he didn't kick us out or anything and tried to be nice. He had all these theories about stuff and seemed really smart. But that night at dinner, he didn't say a word to April or me.

The way Dad looked at Louise: it was love, for sure. He'd never looked at my mother like that. Never focused all of his attention on Mom the way he did with Louise. He barely took his eyes off of her except to order from the menu. He even knew what cocktail she liked, and ordered it for her. Louise beamed at him while Teddy played with his napkin. I reached for the bread. Little Louise passed the butter to me. April rolled her eyes.

Mom's voice played in my head. "Is he in love with her, or the money?"

Louise adored my father. It was obvious because she tried so hard to be nice to April and me. She acted different from before, almost motherly. "What do you want to order, Heather? Do you like lobster, April? Do you girls want a special dessert? They'll make one for you here."

I ordered the Lobster Newburg, but only ate a few bites. The thick sauce with bits of lobster was way too rich, even for me. When I passed on the Crepe Suzette, Dad gave Louise a look that read, "Not like her to pass on dessert."

Little Louise and Teddy ate with gusto. They were used to seeing my father and Louise together. This was new to me and I'd had mixed-up butterflies in my stomach all night. April seemed fine, though. She practically licked her plate clean.

••

After dinner, I needed to use the restroom. As I started to rise from my chair, Louise put a pale, delicate hand over mine. "Wait," she said, in her breathy voice. "You might need some money for the bathroom attendant." She opened the satin evening bag on her lap and handed me a pale manicured fist full of twenty-dollar bills. The purse was below the table top. No one had seen. I didn't know how to react. Looking down, I saw the contents of her purse. It was stuffed with cash, wadded up like the paper the department stores use to keep the purse's shape while on display. When I hesitated, she whispered, "Take it."

Maybe this was what Mom meant when she said that Big Louise was extravagant. Or, maybe, this was Louise's way of giving me money.

I put the clump of bills in the little white purse I'd gotten to go with my Easter dress and headed for the restroom. The attendant was an older woman, dressed in a maid's uniform. She handed me a linen towel to dry my hands. By the door, was a plate with coins. I fished out a quarter from the side pocket of my purse and put it on the plate. "Thank you, sweetheart," the attendant said. She seemed so nice that I debated leaving her one of the twenties, but it was too weird for some eleven-year-old kid to leave a twenty-dollar bill for the attendant.

On the way home, April was fine, chattering away up front. The dinner must have put her in a better mood.

"You O.K. back there?" Dad asked

My mind was on the cash in my purse. "Fine, Dad."

••

Mom was upstairs when we got home.

"C'mon up!" she yelled from her bedroom when she heard us.

Taking the stairs two by two, I made my way to her room.

April stopped at her bedroom at the top of the stairs. "Start telling Mom about tonight, Heath. I've got to call Ray back. I'll be in there in a minute."

My mother sat upright on top of her bed, talking on the phone. The television was on but the sound was low. "Call you back, Carolyn. They're home." She put the powder-blue receiver back in its cradle. A TV tray was next to the bed with the crusty remnants of a burnt Stouffer's cheese soufflé still in the aluminum tray. She hadn't even bothered to put it on a plate.

Mom patted the bed, motioning for me to sit down. "Well? How'd she look?"

"Fine. The same." Then, I opened my white purse.

"Look, Mom. It's for you," I emptied the wad of bills onto the blue bedspread. "Louise gave me money for the bathroom lady, but I kept it."

"Jesus, I knew that Louise was a big spender," Mom's eyes widened over the stack of money, "but, all this for the bathroom attendant?"

"I haven't counted it, but it looks like a lot, Mom."

She hesitated a minute, then scooped up the money. Her latest orange nail polish looked harsh compared to the pale pink on Louise's nails as she smoothed out the wrinkled bills on the bed.

"Twenty, forty, sixty.... We deserve this, Heatherbean."

Chapter Thirteen

Proceed as the way opens.

—Mom

I knew it was coming. My mother had talked about it, but I wasn't ready and now, there it was: the For Sale sign perched in the center of the front lawn of our 4,500 square foot white colonial home.

The house still looked stately with balconies flanking both sides and pillars at the entrance despite the need for paint and a few dilapidated shutters. Our home in Fremont Place was like family behind the big cement gates at the entrance of Rossmore and Wilshire. The Woodward's. The Duque's... Where would we go?

"Oh, no!" I cried when Mom turned into the driveway and I first saw the sign.

She came to a stop under the porte-cochere. "They put the sign up today while you were in school." Turning to me, she added, "I was worried you'd be upset. That's why I picked you up from school."

I couldn't say a word. Instead, I opened the car door and ran over to where the offending sign was planted in the ground. Underneath the big bold letters was the realtor's name, Linda Calhoun. Not Mrs. Calhoun! Her daughter, Susan, was in my class at Cathedral Chapel.

Mom looked on from the front door as I grabbed the sides and tried to yank the sign up. It wouldn't budge. Then I worked it side-to-side, like an umbrella in sand, struggling to loosen the deeply rooted stake. The harder I tried to pull it up, the more frustrated I got. Finally, I plopped down on the grass, defeated. The sign was askew. I started to cry.

Mom called out from the front door. "Come 'ere, Heather! No need to get in a thing, honey. Not to worry," she emphasized, "At least, not yet!"

"Yet?" I picked myself up and headed inside, following my mother to the kitchen, making sure to slam every door in my path. The crying had stopped. Now, I was mad.

"I hate Dad for making us do this," I yelled. "And, why'd you ask Mrs. Calhoun to be the realtor?" I opened the refrigerator door, glanced inside for a second and slammed it shut. My mother must have sensed my need to let off steam. Twisting her hair, she just stood at the sink and listened. She didn't pick up the phone, like she usually did.

"She's Susan's mom! Now, everybody at school'll know that we have to sell our house!" I opened the refrigerator again, but my eyes were on Mom. "And, didn't Mrs. Calhoun just *start* selling houses?" I slammed the refrigerator door. The glass jars rattled inside.

"Susan said that her mom's working because they need money to buy a bigger house. So, what does Mrs. Calhoun know about real estate?"

My mother unwrapped a package of frozen hamburger that was thawing on the Formica counter. "First of all," Mom said, "Linda's my friend. She understands my scene." She poked the meat to see if it was thawed.

"Hold on a minute." She turned to call Lupe who was resting in her room. "*La carne esta lista, Lupe.*"

Turning back to me, Mom continued. "Secondly," she paused, "Linda's agreed to list the house at a ridiculously high price that nobody in their right mind would pay."

April padded down the back steps in bare feet. She was still wearing her navy blue Immaculate Heart uniform. Typically, April changed right after school, but nothing about today seemed normal.

"I heard the last part of your conversation." She reached for a glass in the cupboard. "You guys talking about the house?"

"I was explaining to Heather why Linda's pricing the house too high."

"It buys you time, right?"

"Exactly," Mom said. "I'm buying time to keep the house."

It was a ray of hope.

••

My mother had taken Uncle Richard's advice to face reality after she found out about Dad and Louise. "I'm dealing with the fact that your father's not coming back," she told me a few days later. "I've taken off the blinders."

"He has no money. Probably just what he's giving me every week," she went on. "His law practice is falling apart. Hell, he's never there." Mom's blunt words spilled out as she moved around her big bed, sloppily tucking in the sheets—so different from the way Lupe made the bed with tight corners that made the bed look like a wrapped package, tight and cozy, so that when I'd get under the sheets, I felt all secure.

Sitting in the blue chair by the bed, I studied Mom. It was Lupe's day off and my mother was lost without her help. If the housekeeping was left to Mom, it would be a disaster. Her idea of cleaning was to shove everything into the nearest drawer.

Mom tugged at the lopsided ends of the large wool blanket. "And, I don't want to make beds for the rest of my life," she said, pulling the worn blue quilted bedspread over the top. "I've got to hang on to this house," she added. "It's all I've got. It's time for me to get out there, Heather."

"What do you mean?" I gathered the small throw pillows that went on the bed in matching shades of blue.

"I've got to get out there and find a guy," Mom replied, "I'm not educated, and I have no trade. It's always been about the husband and I need to find someone to support us. Dr. Ferguson said to get my eyelashes on and hustle."

The pillows felt cheap and slippery.

"You mean, like get a man to come live here? Are you going to get married?"

"First, I'm just gonna look for a gentleman caller."

So, this was my ray of hope?

Chapter Fourteen

Put on the party hat and keep moving.

—Mom

"It's time for the drapes," Mom said, out of the blue. We were in the car on our way to Larchmont to get her hair done. With no phone around to distract her, it was a good time for us to talk.

"You know, Heath, drapes. Just like Scarlett O'Hara in *Gone With The Wind*."

I was confused.

She explained. "When Scarlett didn't have any money and was about to lose Tara, the family plantation, she pulled down the velvet drapes."

"Why?" I still didn't understand. Sometimes, my mother talked in circles.

"She had her Mammy turned them into a dress so she could catch a man. Which is what I need to do so that we don't have to move to a walk-up apartment somewhere on Wilshire's Miracle Mile."

Mom stuck her hand out the window to signal a left onto Larchmont from 3rd Street. "I have no Mammy, no tired drapes, and Papa doesn't have any real money to support us, so I did the next best thing," she continued.

"What?"

"I called Charlotte."

Charlotte wasn't Uncle Freddy's girlfriend anymore. The two of them had split up for good after Mom and Dad had separated. "They took sides," Mom told me. "Charlotte has really hung in there as my friend."

Whenever Charlotte came over, she was all talk about her modeling at Sak's Fifth Avenue in Beverly Hills or the latest fad in the fashion magazines. Charlotte knew and loved fashion. I never let on that I missed having Freddy around because Charlotte was so good to Mom. "She has lots of gentlemen callers," Mom told me, "and she's going to help me find a man."

"This is the first step," Mom said, as she maneuvered the car into the small angled space in front of the Larchmont Pharmacy. There was a hint of excitement in her voice. "Charlotte says that I need a set of hot rollers. She says I have to lose the dated hair-do."

I looked at Mom's hair. It was the usual. The style was supposed to look like the smooth, tight bubble on my Barbie doll, but, somehow, Mom's was messy. It always looked like she'd taken an egg-beater to it. Charlotte was right, Mom needed the rollers.

Clearly, Charlotte had an agenda for Mom. After the hair, it was time to go through Mom's closet. I watched from the vanity chair in Mom's dressing room as the two of them sifted through Mom's clothes.

"Nothing hip enough." Charlotte slid dresses along the closet's wooden pole at a steady clip. "Time to go shopping, Marilyn."

"With what?" Mom laughed, eyeing the heap of belts on the floor that Charlotte had placed in the "no" pile. "Blue chip stamps?"

"Nope. Giorgio's." Charlotte was now shuffling through the side drawers where my mother kept her underwear and bras.

"Are you kidding? Georgios on Rodeo Drive?"

Charlotte closed the top drawer and turned around, holding two worn-out bras in her hand. "That's the one."

"Giorgio's cost's a fortune! They serve *wine* to the customers. Connie said that they have a pool table to occupy the men while the women shop. Are you crazy? Jesus, you wanna tell me how I'm going to pay for expensive clothes?"

"Look," Charlotte replied. "I'm friends with the owner. I'll ask him to send the bill to Bob. He's still living with Freddy, right?"

Mom looked confused. "As far as I know."

"Your ex-husband likes to be the big man around town." Charlotte smoothed her thick blonde pageboy as she gazed into the mirrored closet door. "He'll pay."

••

At Georgios, Charlotte helped Mom pick three outfits for her "new job." A white leather mini-skirt with a silk, navy-and-white polka-dot blouse, a basic black cocktail dress with a slight plunge to the neckline, which, according to Charlotte was to "give just a hint," and a powder blue silk skirt suit. "In case you get lucky," Charlotte told her. "The suit will be a perfect second wedding dress."

I watched my mother carefully hang up her new clothes, silently hoping that I'd look as good as she did in a white mini-skirt someday. She tied the plastic store garment bags into a knot at the bottom and stuffed them into the small wastebasket in her room. "Just habit. I've always done this, you know. When you and April were babies I didn't want the plastic to smother you."

A week after my mother's shopping spree, Charlotte arranged Mom's first date.

••

"Give us the details," April pressed. "When are you going out?"

We were all in the kitchen, joined by Aunt Carolyn. Mom was by the stove preparing Carolyn's favorite, *coq aux vin*, to cheer her up. Since she and Uncle Charlie had separated, Charlie took my cousins, Jonathan and Robert, on a regular basis, accompanied by Sherry, the woman he'd met whose boat was in the slip next to his.

Aunt Carolyn gave up on the marriage when Charlie told her after Christmas that he was in love with Sherry and wanted a divorce. Carolyn went into what Mom called "deep depression," which Mom says is like being sadder than sad.

Whenever Charlie had the boys at his new place, Mom or Papa and Virginia, invited Carolyn over. They didn't want her to be alone. Although Carolyn was a loner, she seemed to enjoy coming over. Mom said it was good for her to be around other people.

As long as April was home, having Aunt Carolyn around was fine. She and Carolyn shared horse stories. But, if April was busy with Ray or friends, Aunt Carolyn would just follow Mom around with a pained look on her face. Mom worried about her, constantly calling her, making dates with her and my cousins, having them over to swim, encouraging her to write fictional stories, something that Aunt Carolyn used to do regularly.

This afternoon, Aunt Carolyn was particularly good, more talkative than normal, almost chatty. She even asked if I was writing in the diary she'd given me and seemed interested when I told her I was. "What're you writing about?" she asked.

"Friends mostly." I didn't want to tell her that I wrote mean things like "I hate April" when she made me mad or "Mom's mean today" when she scolded me for something. Those thoughts were my own.

Aunt Carolyn's "deep depression" frustrated me. Why couldn't she just put on her eyeliner again and pull it together like Mom had? Her moping around bugged me. When Mom was sad after Dad left, she got help, went to Dr. Ferguson. Aunt Carolyn was going to

Ferguson, too, but she wasn't getting better. Mom had enough to worry about with the bills and the house for sale. Worrying about Carolyn was just one more problem my mother didn't need.

"The date's tomorrow night and his name is Dennis Shelly," Mom said, adding pepper to the chicken. "He's a friend of Charlotte's. British. Divorced with one son, but the son lives with the mother. I'm wearing the new leather mini skirt. Brit's love anything mod."

"Sounds interesting," April said.

"Sounds frightening," Carolyn added.

"He's got something to do with the Queen's horses over there in England. That should impress you two," Mom said, looking over at April and Carolyn.

With that my sister started in about English saddles, and she and Carolyn were off in their own horse world again. I slid down from my perch on the metal kitchen stool and went over to Mom. I wasn't sure I liked this whole idea of my mother and another man.

Mom handed me a wooded spoon to stir the bubbling mushroom sauce surrounding the chicken while she turned down the gas flame. "So, you have to go out with him?" I asked.

"Well," Mom replied. "Now that I've got all the trappings, you know, the new clothes and all. I need to get my feet wet. And, I'm ready!"

••

The next day my mother took me with her to The Golden Comb, the "hair house" on Larchmont, to get ready for her date with Dennis. Normally, Mom went to John Viola's beauty shop in West Hollywood. It was right across the street from Red-i-Go Italian take-out where they made the best meatball sandwiches ever. Going there was a tradition for Mom and me. If I had a Friday off from school, her normal hair day, she'd bring me along and let me cross the street to Red-i-Go for the sandwiches. While Mom was under the dryer, John and I would huddle around her on the rolling stools and eat together. I loved it, and I loved John. If he was running ahead of schedule after Mom's appointment, he'd say, "Hop up in my chair, Heather, I'm going to make your hair look beautiful." He combed my dish-water blonde hair until it glistened. But Charlotte had insisted Mom change hairdressers. "John makes your hair look dated, Marilyn."

••

"Keep the curls loose," she told Bill, the new hairdresser. "And don't rat it up too much. I've got my first date tonight, and I don't want my hair to look over-done."

There would be no meatball sandwiches today, so I occupied myself on an extra stool near Mom, looking at pictures in movie magazines.

The large woman in the salon chair next to my mother was an old acquaintance. She uncrossed her thick veiny legs and leaned over to Mom's chair. Her jet-black hair was in big curlers with one small curler up front, setting a thick shock of grey at her forehead. "Marilyn, if this date tonight doesn't work out, I know a recent widower, and I can set you up."

Bill reached for a can of spray, and Mom placed her hands in front of her face. He began spraying her hair with the same wild arm movements he used to shape her hair, managing to get spray all over Mom's friend and me. Mom's voice was muffled behind her hands. "Really, Marge?"

"Yep, he lives over on Plymouth, right around the corner." Marge returned to an upright position in her chair, and her hairdresser began taking the curlers out.

My mother smiled at Bill's reflection in the mirror. She was pleased. Less teasing and a little more curl in the front, but I thought John did a better job.

"There's just one thing," Marge said, her hair half in curlers, the other side all springy. "He's got four kids."

"Four kids? That's a lot to take on, Marge. Let's see how this guy tonight turns out."

All the curlers were out now, and Marge fished in her purse and pulled out a small piece of paper and a pen, scribbled something, and handed it to Mom. "Here's my number. Call me if you change your mind."

Four kids? Stepbrothers and sisters? I closed the movie magazine.

••

Dennis was tall and lean with inky dark hair that shone under the porch light.

"Hello," he said, as I opened the front door wider.

"Hi," I replied, sheepishly. This was so weird. "Mom'll be right down," I added, knowing that she wanted to make what she called "an entrance."

"May I come in?" he said with an English lilt.

Behind me, Mom was halfway down the front stairs. In a sultry voice, she said: "Dennis, so nice to see you."

Dennis raised his eyebrows, his tight grin growing into a smile. "You look great, Marilyn."

"Bye Heatherbean," she said as they walked out the door. "Be good."

I watched them head to Dennis's fancy green Jaguar. He towered over my mother's five-foot-five frame. Dad was short. It all seemed so out of kilter.

Later that night, Mom said they'd had fun eating at The Egg and Eye, a restaurant near the art museum that serves only egg dishes.

"Eggs for dinner?" I asked, thinking it a strange place for a first date. But, Mom said that it was "in."

The second date was a day trip to the Bull Fights in Tijuana. My mother had convinced Aunt Carolyn to come along on a sort of blind date with a jockey friend of Dennis's. "Jockeys love tall women," she told Carolyn. "And, Dennis says that he's a great guy."

The jockey never called Carolyn back, but Dennis must have liked Mom because he took her out on two more dates. Afterwards, they came back to our house, and Mom put on records in the Music Room. They drank a lot of wine and the sound of the records on the Hi-Fi reverberated a continuous thump-thump from below that kept me up for hours. In the morning, Lupe quietly cleaned up the ashtrays and the stained wine glasses. It was a good thing that Molly was back in Ireland. She would not have approved.

"Tonight, Dennis is cooking lamb chops for me at his apartment," Mom announced after the fourth date. She'd been worried that she'd blown it with him. He'd taken her horseback riding, and she'd looked great in Carolyn's borrowed jodhpurs, but once she got on the horse, she was terrified and they had to settle on walking around the ring.

"He's a horseman," she'd said when she got home. "That didn't go over big." I figured that it must have been all right if he was cooking her dinner.

••

The following morning, I heard Mom talking to Carolyn on the phone in the next room. "So, then he said that we should see other people, not tie each other down."

Silence.

"I know. Can you believe that?! Right after I took the last bite of dinner and complimented the hell out of the food, he lays this on me."

Silence.

"No way, Carolyn. I've got to keep moving. So, know what I did?"

Silence.

"No, I *didn't* help with the dishes to make him happy." Mom laughed. "Dr. Ferguson is teaching me a few things." She paused for effect. "I left Dennis alone to do them by himself, and I went into the den with my purse. Ever since I saw Marge at the hair house, I've kept her number with me."

Silence.

"No, I picked up the phone, right then and there, and called her. 'Marge,' I said, 'I'm ready for the widower!'"

.

Chapter Fifteen

A plain-faced woman looks like a peeled grape.

—Mom

Mom worried about money more and more. The weekly checks from Dad weren't covering the basic upkeep of the house. Lupe, on her modest salary of $250 a month, did her best to clean, but no amount of elbow grease could bring back the dull hardwood floors that needed refinishing. The paint had started to peel on the front of the house, and Mom tried to "touch up" the areas she could reach. But, the cheap brush she used left hairs imbedded in the pillars out front.

With help from The Akron on Sunset Boulevard, Mom got good at concealing frays and stains on the sofas with cheap satin pillows She even tried *Elmer's Glue-All* to press down the linoleum flooring that had curled up on the back porch.

Although the "For Sale" sign still loomed on the front lawn, Mom had played it smart hiring her friend, Linda Calhoun as our realtor. True to her word, Linda priced the house way over what it was worth and we hadn't had a single showing in weeks. My father was so preoccupied with Louise he hadn't pressed about the sale; however, he wasn't offering any extra money for upkeep and repairs either. My mother still hadn't figured out a way to keep the house and warned us that the clock was ticking. "Thank God, Marge has arranged a date for me with the widower," she told us. "There's still hope."

"Ray joined the Air Force yesterday," April told her when Mom poked her head inside April's room to check on us. I was sitting on the purple throw rug between her twin beds. April was on the bed propped up on one elbow. I liked being below her on the floor, where I was looking through the new thick August issue of *Seventeen.*

I thought my sister sounded detached, as if she were reciting a grocery list. Then, I remembered her telling Dad that night we had gone to The Bistro that Ray was too possessive. Ray had accused April of flirting with other guys, and they'd fought about it.

"Ray figures it's better than going into the Army," my sister added, never looking up from *Gone With The Wind*, which she was reading for the third time.

"This is a big deal," my mother said. "He could be sent to Vietnam. Isn't that what all you kids are protesting? The Vietnam War?"

April didn't respond.

"When does he leave?" Mom asked. "Doesn't he have to go to Boot Camp?"

I stayed quiet, studying the latest teen fashions. I wondered if Mom, too, was happy that April and Ray wouldn't be able to see much of each other now.

April finally looked up from the book. "He takes off in three weeks." Her face was blank. No tears. Nothing. Did she really love the guy?

"Don't get too excited, Mom. We're not breaking up. We'll write each other letters and stuff."

"Oh, that'll last about a week." Mom leaned against the dresser. "Jesus, April, you're only sixteen. You need to go out with a lot of boys. Not tie yourself down to one. Trust me; sticking with Ray is a woeful waste."

April jerked up. *Gone With The Wind* fell to the floor, landing beside me with a loud thump. "You just don't want me to have a boyfriend. Do you?" she yelled.

"That's not true," Mom shot back. She reached up to twist her hair, something to do with feeling insecure, or so Dr. Ferguson had said.

"What about the boy that you and Ray fought about?" I blurted out before I could stop myself. "You know, the one who always calls you on the phone?"

"What boy?" Mom asked.

April looked down and gave me a mean stare. "Mind your own business and get outta here."

I stood, clutching *Seventeen.*

"Don't take this out on her," Mom barked, which really surprised me. If there was a fight, it was usually the two of them against me. Whenever I ate too much, they always seemed to gang up on me.

"Sit back down, Heather," Mom ordered in a low, controlled voice. She was trying to stay calm, twisting another strand of hair. "Break up with the poor bastard, April, but *don't* string him along and see other guys on the side." She looked right into my sister's eyes. "God, I hope that you're not like your father."

••

Dad's girlfriend Louise bought a vacation house in Newport Beach. "On Linda Isle," Dad boasted. "Right on the bay."

"Wait 'till you see it," he said to me over the phone. "It's fabulous. Louise sure has great taste. Everything is top drawer. You'll love it."

"Sounds neat, Dad." I wanted to be nice even though I could imagine my mother saying, "Of course, she's got great taste. All it takes is money."

"How about coming down with me this weekend?" he suggested. "Only Louise and Little Louise will be there."

"What about April?" I asked.

"I already asked her," he replied. "She wants to stay home and be with Ray before he goes to Boot Camp." He paused to take a long drag on a cigarette. He was smoking all the time now, probably because Louise smoked constantly. "Like a chimney," my mother used to say before Louise stole Dad away. Mom had harsher words for her now.

I could hear Dad exhale. "Bonnie and Carl, her two older children, will be with their dad," he told me. "And, I think Teddy is spending the weekend over at a friend's." He went on about the house and how great the Robinson's store was at the new Fashion Island. "It's dramatic," Dad said. "There are these bells on the face of the Robinson's store building. Modern and upscale." He said I'd have a good time at The Fun Zone across the bay on the Peninsula. "It'd be good for you to come down and spend time with Little Louise."

I didn't want to spend time with Little Louise. Ever since Dad started seeing her mother, I dreaded being near Little Louise. Things that never bothered me before about her were magnified now. I didn't like it when she acted older than me. I thought she was showing off when she smoked cigarettes in front of her mother, who allowed Little Louise at only twelve to smoke.

Even though Little Louise had always been nice, I never really liked her that much. Before, if I admired something of hers, such as a shirt or something, she gave it to me. It felt strange, but she would insist. The last time I was over before Dad started dating Louise, I innocently commented on how much I loved her porcelain collection of 18th-century French courtiers that lined a small curio cabinet in her bedroom. I told her that my favorite was the lady in a beautiful pink ball gown sitting on a fancy sofa. She looked so real, so elegant. When Little Louise told her mother that I liked it, Louise said, "Give it to her, honey."

Without a second thought, Little Louise opened the cabinet and handed it to me. I knew that it must be worth a lot of money and refused to take it. Once again, Little Louise insisted. I took it home and set it on my dresser in a special spot so that I could see it from my bed. "Typical," Mom had said when she saw it. "Louise's very generous."

I didn't understand how Little Louise could behave exactly the same with me after my dad started dating her mom. I could tell that she really liked Dad and didn't resent his being there, but I was confused. Didn't she care about how her father felt? She never even mentioned him. I put on a good act, never letting on how much I resented her mother for stealing my father away, and Dad for leaving Mom. I pretended to be like Little Louise, acting as if the whole situation was fine with me, too. I didn't have any other choice, though. It was either that, or not to see my father. And, how could I do that after he'd offered to pay for me to go to pricey Gold Arrow Camp, the camp I'd been begging to go to with my friend, Mary Jo. If he was going to pay for camp, I needed to do my part, too.

"Sure, Dad. Sounds fun." I lied.

••

When Dad honked the horn for me the following Friday afternoon, I said good-bye to my mother eating a tuna sandwich over the sink in the kitchen—a freeze frame that stayed with me all weekend.

It took only an hour to drive to Newport and the sea air smelled good when we arrived. We pulled up to the back of the house and

Dad unloaded my things from the trunk. "Where's your suitcase?" I asked him.

"Oh, I keep a few things down here so I don't have to pack every time I come."

I followed him around to the front of the house. Just beyond the small manicured front lawn was a cement sea wall separating the lawn from the bay. Large baskets of colorful flowers dangled from two tall white wooden posts that led down to a small private dock. "No boat, yet," Dad remarked. "We're looking, though."

I wondered why he said, "we." Wasn't Dad still living with Uncle Freddy?

Little Louise opened the huge sliding glass door that faced the bay front and greeted us. She was grinning from ear to ear. "Hi Bob! Hi Heather. C'mon in, you guys."

"Hey there, Fred," my father replied, tousling the hair on top of Little Louise's head.

"Fred?" I asked.

"It's my new nickname," Little Louise piped in. "Your dad gave it to me."

"You know," Dad interjected. "Like when I call you Smiley."

"That you, Bob?" Louise was half-way down the stairs. The white carpet was so plush, I hadn't heard her. One of her manicured hands was on the heavy nautical rope that served as a banister.

"Hi Heather, honey. Well, how do you like it?" she said, sweeping her hand across the room.

Dad had said that it was a casual place. "Not like Louise's home in Bel Air," he'd told me on the drive down. "More beachy."

"Beachy" was anything but casual with the thick white carpeting, matching white sofas and tall beamed ceilings. A collection of exotic seashells spilled out of a huge glass bowl on top of the bleached wood coffee table, and the glossy white bookshelves that framed the marble fireplace were filled with matching books in subdued shades of beige and pale green with no glossy jackets. My mother got rid of her book jackets too when she read her movie star biographies.

"Your house is beautiful," I replied. "Have you guys read all these books?" I asked, pointing over to the bookshelves and trying to prolong wherever I was supposed to go with Little Louise.

"Are you kidding?" Little Louise laughed. "They're fake. Hollow. Not a page in any of 'em. The real books are in the study upstairs."

Big Louise looked fragile to me with her see-through skin and slim body. She was wearing a pair of white slacks with a defined crease down the legs. Her pink blouse was silk and had big ruffles at the neckline. Louise never showed cleavage. "Now, you know our little secret about the books," she said coyly.

My father handed her a vodka tonic in a small cut-crystal glass. He'd already poured his scotch and when they clinked glasses, I saw their eyes meet.

"Can we go now?" Little Louise asked. Her skin had started to break out in pimples making her seem even less attractive. She turned back to me. "Mom wouldn't let me go on the ferry to the Fun Zone until you got here."

"Maybe I should unpack first?"

"Oh, don't worry about that, Heather," Louise coaxed. Her hair didn't look as poofy as usual. Her hairdresser must not have been able to make the drive down south for her daily comb-out. "It's good for you girls to go have fun. You can talk about what you're bringing to camp."

"Camp?" What was Louise talking about? "Not my precious Gold Arrow camp!"

"Yeah," Little Louise said. "I'm going, too."

Dad must have seen the panicked look on my face. "Louise and I thought that it would be a good way for the two of you to become close," he said. "You know, going away together and all."

I wanted to burst out and cry right there, but I managed to hold it together. I had a sick feeling in my stomach. So that's how Dad got the money to send me to camp! Louise paid. And the pay back was for little Louise to come along with me so we could become better friends.

Louise handed each of us a wad of cash from the endless supply that seemed to be in every one of her handbags. I could smell her Joy perfume mixed with my father's Cezanne aftershave as she extended her hand with the money.

As soon as we left the house, Little Louise pulled out a cigarette. "Your Dad hates it when I smoke."

I didn't know how to respond, so I turned to look out on the bay. Large yachts and some small sailboats were peacefully gliding past. How, I thought, was I going to stand going to camp with her?

Dad dropped me back at home on Sunday afternoon. Mom was at the market and April was somewhere with Ray. Lupe let me in, back from her day off.

I felt exhausted from the weekend and plopped my overnight case on my bed. My eye caught the French figurine on the dresser. I walked over to the dresser and set it carefully under my slips in the drawer below.

It was good to be home.

Chapter Sixteen

Need to know the program before the play.

—Mom

Upstairs, our house was sweltering in the August heat. All the windows, including the balcony doors, were wide open, but there was no breeze blowing through, only hot air. My mother was busy in her dressing room, trying on different outfits for her blind date that night with "the widower," Allan. My sister was sitting on the vanity stool close by, giving her input on each outfit.

"That's the one," April said, pointing to the short yellow dress my mother pulled out of the closet. The dressing room door connecting my room was open, and I watched my mother's reflection in the mirror as she slipped it over her head, smoothing the dress with her hands. It was from her second shopping trip to Georgio's with Charlotte. "Bob won't have gotten the bill yet," she'd counseled Mom. "You better get a couple more things before he cuts you off."

I was in my room getting ready for camp. I'd always wanted to go. I'd learn how to ride a horse and sail a boat on Shaver Lake. It's where the rich kids went. A whole month away from home in the High Sierras!

That afternoon, Dad would be picking me up. I would spend the night with Dad at Uncle Freddy's apartment in Beverly Hills before leaving for Gold Arrow the next morning. At the crack of dawn, Dad would get Little Louise, and then the three of us would drive together to Union Station, where Louise and I would board the train. This arrangement worked well for Mom. She hated mornings.

My new footlocker (a "must" according to the Gold Arrow packing list) was open and empty in the middle of my bedroom. Stacks of clothes stood in neat piles all around. Louise had taken Little Louise and me camp shopping at Robinson's the weekend I'd visited Newport. Everything was new and I labeled each piece of clothing with my name in a black marker after I'd seen the cloth strips with Mary Jo's name sewn in her clothes.

I was excited about going and hadn't thought about being away from home for a whole month until my mother gave me that last big hug before she left for her hair appointment at The Golden Comb. Dad would be coming soon to get me. It was my first time away from home for an extended period. This was our good-bye.

Mom tried to lighten the mood. "I'll write you all the time, even though, I can barely write my own name."

I tried to laugh a little; then, I loosened myself from her hug and looked up at her. "Will you come up for Parent's Weekend in two weeks?"

Apparently, she hadn't planned on it. My throat closed. I felt my chin quiver. "Dad and Louise aren't coming," I reassured her. "You won't run into them. I swear."

She took a deep breath, looked away and exhaled slowly, like she did when she smoked. "I'll try."

"You promise?"

"I promise," she replied, now looking me straight in the eye.

••

From the front seat of the car, I waved to April while Dad loaded my footlocker into the trunk. She was dolled up in white hip-hugger pants and a tight blue poor-boy short-sleeved top. Her blonde hair was tied back in a low ponytail by a thin blue ribbon that matched her ribbed shirt. My sister was a picture of summer beauty as she waved back to me.

April's boyfriend, Ray, had only been gone a week. Mike, the guy who'd been calling her, was on his way over.

Yesterday, she'd received a letter from Ray and he'd included a small snapshot of himself standing at attention wearing his baggy Air Force uniform. He looked scrawnier than ever, and seemed to be gripping his hat like he was hanging on to it for dear life.

April had cried when she read his letter, and later Mom told me that he'd written about how much he loved her, and how hard the training was. My sister stuck his picture in the frame of the big mirror over her dresser.

••

"Smiley!" Uncle Freddy said, jumping off the white leather couch where he'd been watching golf on television. He wrapped his arms around me in a big bear hug. The familiar scent of Brylcreem in his salt-and-pepper hair was comforting.

I wished that my visit with Freddy could have lasted longer. But he had to leave shortly for his job at The Star on the Roof. Grabbing the tuxedo jacket and music folder, he dashed out the door. No sooner had he left, than Louise and Little Louise appeared at the apartment unexpected. At least for me, it was unexpected.

They were dressed up. Louise wore a sleeveless tan cocktail dress with a boat-neck collar of brown feathers that accentuated her slim neck. Little Louise was in a red cotton shift that hung straight and did nothing for her athletic figure. Her hair had been cut short, and the curls around her face helped to soften her plain features.

"We've got a surprise!" Dad said, smiling as we walked through the small entryway. "We're going out to dinner to celebrate. The four of us."

"Celebrate what?" I asked.

My father put a hand around Louise's tiny waist. Her arms and neck looked so pale next to the dark hair on Dad's arms. For a moment, my mind wandered to the vision of my mother sitting by the pool this past week trying to get a tan for her date with Allan.

Dad straightened his shoulders. "Louise and I are getting married."

"So soon?" The words popped out of my mouth before I could catch them. My body felt numb and I sat down to get my bearings. My parents had only been separated ten months and not even divorced yet.

An awkward silence filled Freddy's apartment. Dad and Louise exchanged glances. Little Louise and I just stood there and I focused on Louise's lips again. The shape fascinated me, the way she outlined them with a darker pink liner. Were they really bow-shaped? I'd never seen her without her lipstick.

"Isn't that wild?!" Little Louise finally said, knocking us out of our silence. She came over and a took a seat next to me, acting like she already knew. She leaned back in the chair with a wide grin. "You and I are going to be related." She *did* know! Little Louise was actually excited about this.

I looked away from her to my father.

"Wow, Dad." I looked at him, shocked and trying to recover. "When?" My voice sounded meek.

"No date yet," Dad beamed, oblivious to my distress. "But, soon, we think."

"But, not 'till we get back from camp, right?" Little Louise asked.

Dad and Louise looked each other as if there was no one else in the room. "We'll wait. Don't worry."

••

I could feel my heart beating in my chest. My own father could care less about how this was affecting me. That it was just fine that he was marrying Mom's friend. That it was ok that Big Louise's kid knew first. Before me!

My mind raced. I had to tell Mom. But, how? I'd be leaving before she even got up tomorrow morning. What would she say? How would she feel? How did I feel? What would April say? Would she even care?

"Carl and Bonnie aren't that happy about it," Little Louise said of her two older siblings. I always liked her honesty. "They're on my dad's side," she added. "But, Teddy and I think it's cool. We like Bob. I mean, your dad."

Louise dismissed her daughter's comment in a whispery voice. "They'll come around, Little Louise. You'll see."

"We're going to call April tomorrow to tell her." Dad's voice was calm, almost subdued.

"Have you told Mom?" I knew he hadn't. No way my mother would keep something like this quiet. My mother kept nothing quiet.

"I'll talk to her when I call April," he mumbled. My father, too, wanted to brush off any unpleasant thoughts.

Then his tone brightened. "Show her the ring, honey." Dad was smiling again. Mom always said that he liked shiny things.

Louise extended her left hand. The ring sparkled. Set in platinum, it reached all the way to her knuckle in a spray of diamonds and sapphires. It looked more like a Christmas ornament than an engagement ring. I stared hard, trying to photograph it in my memory. Mom would want a complete description.

115

Dad clapped his hands together. "Off to celebrate at the Bistro!"

"Yeah," Little Louise chimed in, hopping up. "Our last good meal before camp food, huh Heath?"

"You know," I reached down to feel my stomach against my striped-cotton tent dress. "I'm not feeling so great. My stomach or something." It was a ploy. I had to get away from them. I needed time to absorb this.

"Really?" Big Louise's voice was so soft I could barely hear her.

Dad looked puzzled, and upset. He frowned and his dark eyebrows did that caterpillar thing. This was not going according to his plan.

Big Louise saved me. "Bob, maybe Heather wants to sleep in her own bed the last night before she leaves. You don't want her getting sick just before she goes to camp."

I nodded, crouching over, my hand still on my stomach for effect.

Dad moved over to the phone on the fiberglass mushroom-shaped end table. I stood up, still holding my stomach. He took his time picking up the receiver, giving me an opportunity to change my mind. "Guess I'll call Marilyn."

He held the phone to his ear for a few minutes as we stood motionless. "No answer," he hung up the receiver hard.

I knew there'd be no answer. I was buying time. Mom was out with the widower. I had to think fast.

"Now what?" Dad reached for a cigarette from the open pack next to the phone.

"What about the Duque's?" I offered, knowing that Mary Jo would have to be at the train early for camp, too. "I know their phone number by heart and I can stay there until Mom gets home. They can take me to the train with Mary Jo in the morning." I winced a little for effect while rubbing my round tummy.

Louise and Dad shrugged. Little Louise looked disappointed. I felt bad for her right then. Deep down, I knew this whole thing with our parents wasn't her fault. "I'm sorry," I turned to her. "I just don't feel so great, you know?"

"Yeah," Little Louise replied, her wide grin, now a frown. She wasn't convinced.

••

The minute I arrived at the Duque's I felt relieved. Mom was still out, and Mrs. Duque insisted that we head to bed straight away. "We have to leave at four-thirty tomorrow morning, sharp." Then, turning off the light in Mary Jo's bedroom, she added, "Don't worry, Heather, I'll let your Mom know what happened later after we get back from the train."

In the dark, Mary Jo whispered from the other twin bed. "Sorry about your dad marrying Louise."

"Me, too," I whispered back. I hugged my knees to my chest, closed my eyes, and said a hushed Hail Mary. Lupe prayed every night at the little altar in her room. She said that the Virgin Mary listens to our prayers.

Chapter Seventeen

Avoid her like the plague.

—Mom

I waited, hidden on the platform after I saw Little Louise board the train. It would be a long ride up to Fresno, followed by another hour and a half bus ride to Huntington Lake in the High Sierra's where the camp was located. Mary Jo had already boarded and promised to save me a seat far from Louise.

From the platform, I watched through the windows of the train as Little Louise passed by the empty seat next to Mary Jo and into the next car. Only then did I move forward and give my name to the lady with the clipboard. Then, I boarded the train.

••

The first two weeks of camp were filled with challenges. The biggest was when I arrived and discovered that I wasn't in Mary Jo's cabin, as I'd requested. My cabin counselor told me that Louise had made a request to put Little Louise and me in the same one, different from Mary Jo's.

"Please," I begged her on our group walk to dinner that first night after asking her to hang back with me so I could talk. "Don't make me stay in this cabin. It'll ruin everything."

She wouldn't give in. "Those are the orders."

I sighed and shuffled the loose dirt below my feet, turning my white Ked's a dirty brown. This was going to be a long month.

After dinner, while the rest of my cabin was at the campfire, I wrote Mom a letter. I told her about Dad getting engaged to Louise and I drew a detailed diagram to the best of my memory of Louise's ring with arrows pointing to indicate which stones were diamonds and which were sapphires. My cabin counselor came in and took a seat next to me on my bunk. The letter lay open beside me.

"Everyone is at the campfire," she said, giving a side-glance at my letter. "You sure you don't want to join your cabin?"

"I'm sure," I said, tears welling up.

"Why are you crying?" she asked.

I looked across to Little Louise's bunk. She'd brought her own fluffy pillow from home.

"My dog died," I lied.

The next day I was moved to Mary Jo's cabin.

••

My first activity was horseback riding. My horse, a chestnut beauty named "Princess," broke free from the long line of fellow campers on slow-moving mounts and burst into a canter. I pulled on the reins with one hand, gripping the pommel of the western saddle with the other. I couldn't stop her, or even slow her down. What would Aunt Carolyn or April do? They would know how to stop this horse! Princess was heading toward a clump of trees in the distance. Terrified, I screamed at the top of my lungs. "Princeeeesss!!!"

The riding instructor was quick to respond and came to my rescue. She commanded Princess to a quick halt at the base of a huge hanging branch. My knees shook as I dismounted. It took a few steps for me to feel my legs again. The counselor patted me on the back. "You did great. You held on and didn't give up."

120

"I didn't know what else to do."

Next, I was nervous but excited to water ski on Shaver Lake. The other three campers in the speedboat, all skinny, seemed to get up effortlessly on not only two skis, but then on one! I watched in awe and envy as they zipped in and out of the water's wake. When they were done skiing, they pulled themselves easily out of the deep lake water and back into the boat with one swift movement, their lithe bodies gifted with agility.

Then, it was my turn. After the first attempt to get up on the skis I was mildly discouraged. The second time, I was despondent. The others in the boat encouraged me. "Try one more time, Heather!"

With the third attempt, the counselor sped up the engine, the boat moved forward and I fell flat. "That's it," I yelled back at them. I finally gave up. The young male water-skiing counselor tried to help me back in the boat, but my weight held me down. I couldn't lift my leg up over the side. I was too fat.

He held onto my fleshy forearms with his lips pursed in a forced smile, his jaw clenched behind a closely cropped beard. He looked disgusted with me. That's when I took matters into my own hands. "Hey, I got an idea," I said, dropping back and holding onto the side of the boat, "I'll drag the boat to shore and then, get in. See, watch." I pulled it slowly toward the shore nearby.

The three other campers in the boat laughed. "Heather, you are so funny."

"Okay," the counselor said, joining in the laughter. He leaned back on the stern of the boat, arms crossed behind his head. "Let's see how you do it."

Once I hit solid ground, I climbed in. "There! See? I did it!"

My fellow campers applauded me, including the counselor, but I knew that his look of disgust would be etched in my mind forever.

••

Parent's Weekend fell on the second weekend at camp. I'd eaten lunch with Mary Jo and her parents earlier and had managed to stay away from Little Louise (like I had all through those first two weeks) who was also alone. Thankfully, she'd made new friends and was hanging around with one of them and their parents. Most of the parents had left and the staff was setting up a BBQ dinner for the stragglers. I'd been looking over my shoulder all day. Would Mom really come to see me? She said she'd try... I felt that familiar pit in my stomach as the afternoon came to a close. My mother wasn't coming.

••

"Who's that man with your mom?" Mary Jo saw them first. They were standing on the hill at the entrance to the camp, mingling with some of the parents.

I strained my eyes to get a better look. "I don't know. I've never seen him before." I took off towards them, lumbering up the steep hill. By the time I reached my mother, I was out of breath, blubbering with pent-up emotion. "Mom! Mom! You came!" I'd missed her so much.

Mom opened her arms wide to hug me, but her smile was fixed and frozen. The strange man next to Mom greeted me with a smile.

"Heather's so sensitive," she said to him, excusing my outburst. Her body was rigid and her smile tight and static. She'd scanned my body with disapproving eyes. My weight embarrassed her.

"That's a good thing," he replied.

"Really?" I replied wiping my tears with the back of my hand.

"Yes," he said. "It shows you have compassion."

I liked him right away for saying that. I looked up at him. He had a solid build, neither fat nor thin. Taller than my father, he had sharp facial features with high cheekbones and a strong jaw line. His thick auburn hair was parted on the side and his brown almond-shaped eyes were intense and tilted slightly upward when he smiled.

He shook my hand firmly. "I'm Allan Stubbs."

So, this was the widower.

"Sorry we didn't come earlier, but we got lost."

"You can say that again." Mom fluttered her false eyelashes at him. "Wasn't Allan wonderful to drive me here so that I could see you?"

My mother was really pouring it on. And, I could tell by his expression that Allan adored the attention.

"Instead of Gold Arrow, this place should be called 'Lost Arrow,'" he laughed. "I thought I knew my way around the Sierras, but this place was hard to find."

I reached for Mom's hand which was more relaxed now, as we headed to the area set up for the families. "Thank you so much for getting here and not giving up, Mr. Stubbs."

He looked down at me. "No big deal. And, hey, call me Allan."

"Allan's a mountain man," Mom said coyly, as we walked toward the BBQ picnic. Later, when he was off getting a second helping from the buffet, Mom confessed that she had fallen hard for Allan on that first date.

"I walked into Marge's living room, and there he was," she told me. "It was like a bell rang off—chong! I was attracted to him right away. He was wearing white buck lace-up shoes and a brown-and-white seersucker jacket." She scooped up some cole slaw with her plastic spoon and continued. "His hair matched his eyes and the first thing he said was that he liked my dress. 'Yellow,' he told me 'is my favorite color.'"

"Mom, he must like you to drive you all the way up here to see me." I picked up my corn bread and started to butter it.

"Hope so. Do you like him?"

"Yeah, he's nice." I *did* like him. It felt good not to have to lie to her.

"I haven't met his kids yet, though," she said, taking a small bite of her chicken.

Allan returned to the picnic table carrying a plate of spare ribs and corn.

"I'm from Kansas City," he said, sitting down next to Mom and me. "And, I haven't had ribs this good since I left there."

Mom leaned over to me and whispered. "Mid-westerners. Glued-together people, those Mid-westerners."

I asked about his kids and Allan told me that he had three boys and one girl, ranging in ages from thirteen to twenty-one. "You'll meet them when you come home," he said, picking up a sparerib. "You guys will all get along fine, I'm sure."

••

Despite the rough beginning, I loved my month at Gold Arrow Camp. After the first week, I immersed myself in camp life and began to let go of the distraction of home. I managed to get up on two water skis—even if it was only for a second to look down at the water's wake and realize that I, "Hot Dog Heather," had pulled myself up. And, more important, I'd been able to climb back in the boat with a different counselor who'd helped me push myself up and in. I got a badge for being the funniest in my cabin and one for bravery, too. That was for getting on another horse two days after Princess had run away with me.

I had fun with Mary Jo and met new friends. Little Louise steered clear of me until the last week when her cabin and mine had at Archery at the same time.

I even cheered her on when she struck two bulls eyes in a row. "So, you still like me, huh?" she said, typically candid.

"Sure," I replied. "It was just the cabin thing. Too much togetherness, you know?"

"Yeah," Little Louise said. "It's all too much for both of us. I still like you, though."

"It's not *you*," I replied. "It's the whole thing."

Little Louise nodded. "I know."

But, did she? My father would be living with her. Not with me.

••

Sitting on the logs by the campfire that final night, I clutched my new badges and ribbons from the closing awards ceremony. In the morning, I would be headed home.

For what, I wasn't sure.

Chapter Eighteen

Fall 1968

The Ontra Cafeteria is God's waiting room.
Everyone in there is old and on the launching pad.
—Mom

A month after I got back from Gold Arrow Camp, Mom, April and I were on our way with Papa to have dinner at the Ontra Cafeteria on Wilshire's Miracle Mile. It was Papa's favorite restaurant and after my father left, Papa treated us to dinner there a lot. I wondered, though, if it was because he felt guilty. After all, Papa was the one who had introduced Dad to Mom in the first place.

Virginia never came with us. She was into health food (despite her love of cheap Chablis) and couldn't bring herself to eat "all that cardboard food sitting under heat lamps."

Mom didn't mind that Virginia never joined us. She'd never been wild about her. "She sold him a poppy and her world opened up," Mom said. "I don't trust her. She's always trying to push her brother and his family on us."

It wasn't as if Mom missed her own mother, Arvella, who had been an alcoholic and passed out most afternoons of her childhood on the living room sofa. Arvella passed away when my mother was just twenty-five of heart failure, but my mother had gotten used to life without a mother. And Virginia was no substitute.

Papa, a Mormon born in Provo, Utah and grandson of mining magnate Jesse Knight, was a man who believed that every man should earn his own way. As a boy, Papa and his mother and sister, Dolly, migrated to Los Angeles after his father left the family for another woman. As a teenager, he helped support the family by getting a job at a gas station with a clear view of the downtown courthouse. It was then, while pumping gas that he decided to go to law school. "I'm going to be a judge someday." And he did exactly what he said he'd do.

Usually, my mother was relaxed on these nights at the Ontra. Tonight, though, she seemed anxious, and had nearly run two red lights when we picked Papa up on the way to dinner.

"What's the deal?" Papa reprimanded. "Wanna kill us all?"

April and I, in the back seat, just rolled our eyes. We were used to Mom's driving.

"So, how's the widower?" he'd asked Mom while reaching for the rarely used seat belt.

"Allan," Mom corrected. "Fine. Why do you ask?"

I leaned forward resting my chin on the back of Papa's seat. "He comes over a lot to take Mom out. I like him. He's nice."

"April?" Papa asked, turning to giver her a side-glance from the front seat.

She didn't look up from inspecting the split ends of her hair in the light from the street lamps outside. "He's okay."

In line at the Ontra, I glided my tray slowly along the warm metal bars. I wanted it all: the turkey stuffing, the meatloaf, the creamy macaroni and cheese. My mother slid her tray close behind mine, monitoring my choices.

Stationed behind the stainless counter of hot food stood an old Chinese woman wearing a cloth apron and a hairnet. She held the carving knife close to the turkey under the heat lamp and nodded to me. "Slice turkey breast?"

Expertly, she shaved off a thick slice. Then, reached for the ladle in the stainless steel pot in the warming tray. Steam spewed from the sides. "Gravy?" she asked, her accent thick.

"No thank you," I replied, feeling my mother's eyes.

I probably could have gotten away with adding gravy if I hadn't had that check-up at the doctor's right before camp. At eleven, I measured 4-foot-7 and weighed 135 pounds. After that, Mom was really focused on my weight.

I inched my blue tray past the orange cubed Jell-O to the pies. I wanted a real dessert.

Boldly, I reached for a slice of lemon meringue pie. The plate was almost in my grasp, the overhead lamp illuminating my pudgy fingers.

"You don't need that!" Mom snapped. "You look like you've gained more weight since the doctor's appointment."

I looked down and away from Mom's glare. "All right, Mom, I won't get it." My voice was low so that no one would look. I pulled my hand back from under the glass and wanted to disappear. Why did my mother always scold me in front of other people? She never cared who heard what.

Thankfully, no one was behind us in line. Mom left her tray and stepped back to the beginning of the salad section. She grabbed a tiny bowl of cottage cheese topped with a maraschino cherry—a cherry, the only appealing thing about it—and plopped it on my tray. "Here," she said, "much better."

Mom sat across the table from April, Papa, and me. I began to slice the turkey meat. My sister, the know-it-all, was next to me babbling away to Papa and Mom about her high school friends.

According to Mom, when Papa was Governor, he'd paced and paced the night before a convicted killer was set to be put to death in the gas chamber. One word from him and the inmate would get a reprieve and be sent back to the cell. "It was so hard on him," Mom had said.

After such big responsibilities as Governor, how could he be interested in April's silly high school stuff? This man who'd had the weight of the state of California on his mind. Now, he was reduced to worrying about his daughters and listening to my sister in the faded appeal of the Ontra Cafeteria.

I caught Mom's eye. I could tell that she wasn't listening to a word April was saying despite shifting her eyes back and forth between April and Papa. Her mind was somewhere else. Why was she more on edge that usual? She hadn't taken a bite of her stew.

Instead, she'd pulled out her little spiral notebook, her "tablet," where she kept her daily list. From across the table I could see *Call Connie* had been crossed off.

The next line read: *Tell Papa and the girls.*

Giving up on the bland turkey, I turned to the cherry on the cottage cheese. Tell us what?

April was going on about how the nuns at her school were so "progressive." Her food, like Mom's, hadn't been touched. How could they let the food just sit there? For me, eating always came first.

Papa patiently listened, nodding as he picked up the catsup bottle and turned it upside down to pat the end. The catsup gushed out, slopping all over his meatloaf. Then, he took his spoon, poured catsup onto it, and ate it.

Even though Papa had been Governor, he didn't act like a big shot around us. He was a moderate Republican, Mom told us. "Not the high-brow kind," she said, "who thinks that they are holier than thou or a shyster like Tricky Dick Nixon." Papa's big thing as Governor was his sympathy for organized labor and those people on what he called a "fixed income."

Which is probably why he was drawn to places like the Ontra Cafeteria that was filled with retired old people. Papa was casual. He liked wearing beige cotton belted jumpsuits and black high-top Converse sneakers. Rarely did he look like the pictures of him that lined the wall in the den, the ones where he was a Judge of the Superior Court of Los Angeles, or when he pursued the Republican nomination for the U.S. Senate (and lost), and when he was elected the 35th Lieutenant Governor of California. My favorite was the picture of Papa all dapper in a suit, seated at his big desk in his office in Sacramento as the 36th Governor of California after Earl Warren resigned to be Chief Justice of the United States.

Mom put the tablet back in her purse and picked up her fork, taking a stab at a piece of meat in her stew. She brought it to her mouth and blew on it to cool it. "I can't eat," she said, putting the fork down. "I need to make an announcement."

April stopped the chatter. We all looked at my mother.

Mom's expression went from anxious to nervous to complete satisfaction in a matter of seconds. She was beaming. "Allan asked me to marry him!"

Silverware clinked and the muted tones of the other diners chatting floated by, amplified by the silence that had descended. It took a minute for the news to sink in.

My mind raced. Without Mom remarrying, there wasn't much help for us. It wasn't like Papa was going to bail us out. Even though he'd been Governor, he'd not been good with his own money; he'd lost much of it in the stock market.

I clasped my hands in my lap and silently thanked God.

April's eyes bulged. "What? God, Mom! Did you say yes? Jesus, we haven't even met his kids yet!"

"April!" Papa said sternly. "That's uncalled-for."

Mom went for her purse. "Where the hell are my cigarettes?"

Allan, I thought, ticking away at his statistics. He has four kids. Four. Hmmm. Ok, stepsiblings would be all right if it meant we wouldn't have to move to a walk-up apartment as Mom had been threatening. This might be okay.

Papa reached across the table and put his hand on her wrist to calm her. "Forget the cigarettes. April will be fine," he said, looking Mom in the eye. "Pay attention to me, Marilyn." He was speaking slowly now, measuring each word. "I'm happy for you, but I'm not going to give you my blessing until I check Allan out. I need to visit his company. Make sure that Western Concrete is above board. That this guy has some money to support you."

I thought back to the deal that he struck with Cal Eaton for Dad to marry Mom and how that hadn't exactly worked out well for us.

"I like the guy," he went on. "I'm just being cautious."

April stayed quiet. I tore at the paper napkin on my lap, shredding it into little pieces. I was sure that Allan would be rich enough to take care of us.

"I'm crazy about him, Papa!" Mom sounded like a lovesick teenager.

Papa let go of Mom's hand, picked up his spoon again, and reached for the catsup. "That's all fine and good, Marilyn, but you don't want to make another mistake, do you?"

She looked down at her hands.

I knew it wasn't going to be a mistake. Allan loved Mom! He'd driven her all the way to Gold Arrow Camp to visit me. Me! And I wasn't even his kid.

Maybe Allan wouldn't be the same as a real dad, but the thought of him as a stepfather made me feel happy and safe. And, the big thing was now, Mom wouldn't have to get a job at The May Company.

I felt relief, an emotion I barely recognized.

"So when do we have to meet his kids?" April sighed.

Chapter Nineteen

You can stand anything as long as it's temporary.

—Mom

Two days after our dinner at the Ontra Cafeteria, we had a surprise visitor at the door. It was a school day and April had already left for Immaculate Heart, catching an early ride with Anne's older sister, Mary. Wrenching to fasten the button on the snug waistband of my school uniform, I moved over to the window. My eyes went past the nearly leafless sycamore on our lawn to the black-and-white police car parked at the curb in front. The door was marked with a badge-like gold star, beside it: *Sheriff*.

I ran into Mom's room. "Mom! Get up! The cops are out front!"

Her room was so dark that I had to open the shutters to see. Thin slices of sunlight fell on her form underneath the blue covers. She didn't move. The sound of her voice came muffled under the blanket. "Go away. It's too early."

"Mom, please get up," I begged, wondering why the sheriff would come to our door. What did we do? I swallowed a few times to calm myself. "Please, Mom. There's a sheriff at the front door."

A few tufts of her frosted hair stuck out from the edge of a blanket, partially wrapped around her head. "What now?" she muttered. "You know I hate the morning."

Mom roused herself, flipping back the blanket. Sitting up, she pushed aside her black satin eye mask and squinted to adjust to the light, then stumbled over to the bedroom window to look out. "Jesus, what now?"

There was a loud knock, followed by more rings of the doorbell. Mom struggled to pull up the double-hung window. Moe, our slipshod painter, had painted the windows shut and none of them had opened right since. She wrenched it open. "Who is it?" she barked.

"The sheriff. I need you to answer the door, Ma'am."

Mom had her raspy morning voice. "Why?"

"You're in default on your car loan, Ma'am. We have orders to repossess the Mercury station wagon."

I spotted Mrs. Kuhns, our eccentric neighbor across the street, bending down to pick up the morning paper on her front lawn. Her aging brown dachshund, Peeser, had crossed the street and was yipping at the sheriff who'd stepped back from the door to address my mother in the window. What was going on at our house didn't interest Mrs. Kuhns. She was too busy staring down at the front page of her newspaper. Without looking our way, she whistled for the dog and made her way back to her front door with the yappy old dachshund in tow.

I followed my mother as she grabbed her blue robe and purse. She rummaged through the purse, the whole way down the front stairway. I sensed her panic at not being able to find them the car keys. Before she reached the door, she found them in the side pocket and pulled them out, along with bits of loose tobacco from a stray cigarette clinging to the leather tab on her key ring. She asked me to open the door as she tugged to get the car keys off the key ring.

The sheriff was tall. The top of his hat almost touched the porch light. He had a broad brown mustache and green eyes.

"Morning," he said. No smile, he was all business.

My mother gave no greeting either, except "Just a minute." She barely looked at him and went back to tugging at the keys on the ring. "I have to get these off, but I don't want to break a nail."

I turned to see Lupe coming up the hallway from behind Mom. Once she saw who was at the door, though, she crossed herself and darted back into the kitchen.

Just then, the key ring snapped open and the entire set of keys flew loose, landing all over the entry hall carpet. The sheriff smiled with one eye cocked, amused as he stood silent, watching us on hands and knees, Mom's sleep mask still perched on the top of her head, groping along the carpeted foyer to find the right keys. Eventually, Mom stood to thrust the car keys into the sheriff's hands. "Here." Then, she pointed to the Mercury in the driveway. "Car's right there. Never could trust that bastard ex-husband of mine."

The sheriff tossed the keys over to a tow truck driver who'd come up behind him on the front brick steps. Then he turned back to Mom and me. "Thank's ma'am. Sorry 'bout this. Just doing my job."

The truck driver backed the wagon down the driveway to hitch it to the truck. The sheriff didn't move, as if he wanted to say something else. Instead, he tipped his hat slightly, accompanied by squeaking noises from his leather belt. "Have a good day, Ma' am." Looking at me, "You too, young lady."

Mom and I stepped out to the front steps and watched him with his neat square-shaped creases in the back of his tan uniform shirt go down the walkway. Once he got into his patrol car, the tow truck pulled away with the Mercury hitched to the back.

I looked up at Mom, "We'll be O.K., right?"

"All I can say is thank god the Mustang's paid off." She waited a beat. "Don't be late for the school bus. I'm going back to bed."

After Mom went back upstairs, I went into the kitchen, feeling unsure of everything. The sight of Lupe putting away the dishes from last night comforted me. The dishwasher had needed repair and she was doing them by hand now. She smiled. *"Buenos dias dulzura,"* she said, never mentioning the sheriff.

••

The For Sale sign loomed large on the front lawn and day by day, the debts mounted. Paint continued to peel on the house exterior where Mom couldn't reach with her paintbrush. The pool man only came once a month now and a faint green film appeared on the aqua tile. Henry the gardener, reduced to taking care of the front lawn only, hadn't been paid in two months. How long could Mom keep paying Lupe's weekly salary? And how long could our realtor, Mrs. Calhoun, stall the sale of the house by keeping the price too high? Dad had been pressuring Mrs. Calhoun to lower the price, but she'd stayed true to my mother, making empty promises to Dad, assuring him that she would find just the right buyer who would pay that overly optimistic price. "It's just a matter of time, Bob," she lied.

The bill collector calls multiplied. We owed everybody.

My mother had gotten good at fending off the collectors who called all the time. She'd pretend that she was the Mexican housekeeper who didn't speak English and couldn't understand the bill collector on the other end of the line. Or, she'd whistle into the receiver then hang up, hoping that the collection person would think that the line had gone dead. If a call caught her off guard, she had a tactic for that, too. She'd promise to pay five dollars on the past due bill. She'd "throw them a bone" and promise to pay more money next month. So much for my father's parting words: "Don't worry I'll pay all the bills."

The way she treated the bill collectors didn't bother me, but what Mom did to the thirteen-year-old paperboy who delivered *The Herald Examiner* made me feel bad. For months, he'd been coming to the door, his collection booklet in hand, waiting for someone to answer. I'd cringe when Mom would holler for us not to answer the door. I was sure that he'd heard her, but he'd still ring a few more times, then give up. I felt sorry for him as I watched him peddle away on his bike, a pencil behind his ear and the little booklet of pay stubs flapping in his back pocket.

I'd asked my mother why making up all these methods to dodge the bill collectors didn't seem bother her.

She looked me in the eye. "Survival."

••

Meanwhile, Mom suspected that Louise had foot the bill for my parents "proxy" divorce in Mexico. Mom really hadn't cared who paid because she and my father were in a rush to marry other people. It was simple. When Dad married Louise, he'd have money and could pay off all the creditors. When Mom married Allan, she could stop sweating it out every Friday, waiting for Dad's check.

Richard Rossi, my parents' old friend, acted as the attorney for both of them. There was lots of talk about Homesteads, Equity, Protection from Creditors, things like that. Unfamiliar terms and words to me but Mom seemed fine with it all because her name was now alone on the deed to the house. Allan agreed that once they were married, he'd pay the back taxes and take over the mortgage, even the delinquent payments. Dad didn't care. He was with Louise on St. Pierre Road in Bel Air now, living the life of a wealthy man. The Fremont house and all the problems that went with it, gone.

Down went the For Sale sign while I was at school.

Up went my spirits when I came home to find the front lawn without it. We didn't have to move! 127 Fremont had been the one constant in my life, this colonial. It didn't matter what it took to remain there, that the structure was beginning to fall apart, and that we had a whole new family moving in with us.

Except, I still had a problem. I hadn't told anyone at school about the divorce except Anne Woodward and Mary Jo Duque. None of my friends at Cathedral Chapel had divorced parents. "Because it's against their religion," Mom told me. "Catholics aren't supposed to get divorced. We're Episcopal. Our rules are different."

"Episcopal people are allowed to get divorced?"

"Look," Mom said, "Don't be afraid to tell your friends at school. Tell them the truth. Tell them that your mother hung in there for twenty years. Tell them that it was your father who left."

"It's not a big deal," Anne said on the way to school the morning after I knew the divorce was final. "And, nobody needs to know that you guys had money problems," she said. "You don't need to say all that."

"I'm sure people already know anyway," I sighed, looking out the back window of Mrs. Woodward's Country Squire station wagon.

Anne began listing our friends. "Look, Laurie already knows. Louise is her aunt, or, used to be until Louise divorced her uncle. Maybe Moira doesn't know but Susan's mom was selling your house, so she knows, and don't worry about Margaret. She's so Catholic; she'd never have a bad thought no matter what went on in your family."

"Don't forget about Kathy," I said. "She'll make this hard. She's such a nosey gossip, always talking about people behind their backs. Actually, she probably knows. Her mother's a big gossip, too. Can you believe that her dad owns a religious store? I mean, wouldn't you think that some of that holiness would rub off on her?"

Anne laughed. "Kathy *is* a gossip."

I was quiet the rest of the ride to school, thinking about Laurie. She'd told me long ago that she didn't like her cousin, Little Louise. She knew that I knew Little Louise and that our mothers were friends. "She's weird, Heather," Laurie had said. "She has everything and thinks that she's a big shot."

I'd been careful not to say too much to Laurie. That was before Dad started seeing Louise and Little Louise was only a minor annoyance, someone Mom made me be nice to because she and Louise were old friends. Actually, I'd envied Little Louise and her plush pink and red bedroom with all the fancy porcelain figurines in that curio cabinet near her bed. Everything in her house was rich. The carpets. Thick drapes. Overstuffed furniture. My friends all had nice houses, but nothing like Little Louise's house in Bel Air. Sonny and Cher's house was just down the road. "A movie star house." That's what Mom called Louise's house.

Little Louise had everything. Including my father.

My mood lightened a little when I saw the Helms Bakery truck parked in front of school. It usually came on Wednesdays, but this was Friday. A cherry-filled glazed donut would make me feel better.

On Fridays, school mass was on the schedule which would be the perfect place to break the news to my school friends.

Cathedral Chapel Church was on La Brea Boulevard between Olympic Boulevard and 9th Street, walking distance for the entire class from Cathedral Chapel School on Cochran Avenue and 8th.

The La Brea Car Wash across the street from church was busy that morning. The clanking noise of the automatic brushes seemed louder than usual. That, combined with four lanes of traffic zooming by on La Brea, made the church seem even more serene when I stepped inside. As we marched through the entrance, I dipped my finger in the bowl of holy water. It felt cool on my forehead as I made the sign of the cross. *Dear God, please help me. Please help my mom. And, thank you for giving her Allan.*

I slipped into the pew behind my friends so that I would be at the end of the row for an easy exit in case I needed to cry or something. Anne gave me the opening and whispered softly down the row. "Heather has something to tell us."

It shocked me when Moira, the quietest of the crew, ordered me to stand up. She took her hand and swiped it across my behind.

"I don't feel any Kotex belt, so it can't be that you've started."

Anne read the desperate look on my face. My eyes started to sting, so I lifted my head to keep the tears from falling and focused on one of the pictures in the Stations of the Cross on the wall. It was Jesus in the final stages of carrying the cross to the mount.

Anne covered for me. "Heather's parents are divorced now."

Moira looked genuinely surprised and strangely disappointed. She, it seemed, had wanted to be the one who discovered my secret.

I changed my focus to the front of the church and zeroed in on the thick gold filigree that framed Jesus on the cross. Laurie leaned over Moira and Susan between us.

"Pssst, Heather."

Father Mayer and two altar boys positioned themselves at the altar. The church was quiet.

Margaret, next to her, piped in with a whisper. "Laurie, you shouldn't talk in church."

Laurie ignored her.

"Heather," she whispered again.

We all stood. Mass was about to begin.

I dreaded what Laurie would say. Would she not like me now? Tell everyone not to be my friend? Say that my father's a bad guy? I turned to look at her. Laurie's face was tan. Her face was always tan.

"Guess that we're kind of related now that your dad's with my ex-aunt."

I smiled and whispered back. "Guess so."

Kathy, on the other side of Laurie, didn't dare say a word, deferring to Laurie, the most popular, who'd saved me.

If Laurie thought it was no big deal that my parents were divorced, then it would be O.K. with everyone. I should have known that Laurie would get it. Laurie was the only adopted kid in our class. She would understand about feeling different. I debated telling her about Mom dating Allan, but decided against it. The news of the divorce was enough for one day.

Chapter Twenty

The devil lurks behind the cross.

—Mom

It was a Sunday morning and the clock on my nightstand read 10:20 am. My room was cold, so I stayed in bed, hanging out under the covers and writing in my diary. I had been listening to the steady drone of my mother's voice on the telephone in her bedroom across the hall for almost an hour. She was talking with Connie.

From what I could make out, she was nervous about the dinner tonight with the Stubbs. It would be the first time the two families would meet. Eventually, her drone stopped. Mom must have gotten off the phone.

"April! Heather!" she barked, as if there was a big emergency. But with mom, the smallest thing could be an emergency, so I didn't rush.

I arrived in her room first and perched myself on the corner of her bed, tucking my feet under my long flannel Lanz nightgown. April, who'd slept late, wasn't far behind, shuffling through the door in fuzzy yellow slippers.

Mom was in her morning position, sitting up in the bed, coffee cup in hand, phone next to her on the blanket, daily tablet by her side. The scenario never changed.

"Why'd you get us out of bed?" April dumped herself into the little blue chair near the bathroom door. "It's too early to deal with anything."

Mom ignored her and took another slurp of lukewarm instant coffee. "Connie and I were talking. I've decided to cook the dinner tonight."

April rubbed her eyes under thick coke-bottle glasses. "Why?"

"Aren't we going to a restaurant?" I asked.

"I thought the plan was to stop by Allan's first and go from there?" April said. She looked so different without her lenses. If only those boys could see her now.

Mom adjusted herself against the pillows. "Allan keeps a stocked refrigerator, so I'm going to surprise them all and wing it with what he's got on hand."

April groaned and tightened the loose sash on her bathrobe. "Oh, Jesus, all that effort for *them*?"

Mom ignored her bitchiness. "I think it'll be much more spontaneous and relaxed than Allan taking us all to Mario's. And, I'll bet Allan's kids will appreciate a good home-made dinner in their own house." She took another gulp of coffee, swallowing hard. Her voice turned slightly nervous. "Let's face it, you two. I'll be *on* tonight and I need to impress them with my cooking."

April and I had no real clue what to expect. None of our friends knew the Stubbs. All we knew was what little Mom had told us.

The older ones, Sarah, 19, and John, 21, had been away at college. Mom hadn't met them. But, she'd met Jim, 16, and Bill, 13, when she and Allan had made a quick stop by Allan's house two weeks ago. As they drove up, the two boys were tossing a football on their front lawn. She described the boys to us when she got home.

"Jim's blonde," Mom said. "Kind of nondescript. He hung back on the lawn, clutching the football. Bill's the opposite. Dark hair. Fur on a bear, very out-going. Came right up to the car. Allan called Jim over to meet me and the kid seemed like he wasn't tracking. The whites of his eyes were red and he could barely look at me. I think he's shy."

"Or, stoned." April said.

"You mean on grass?"

"Blank look. Bloodshot eyes. Not-tracking. Mom, he sounds like a pot-head to me."

"But, Allan says that Jim is the smartest of his kids. Genius time."

"Smart people get stoned, Mom."

"I hope you're wrong," she told my sister.

I understood why Jim maybe smoked pot. It had only been three years since their mom died.

Marty Jo had only been 41 but she'd been sick for years. I wasn't really sure what the sickness was, but Mom had said that she was in bed a lot. So her being in bed that evening when it happened hadn't been unusual. Allan had been downstairs reading when he heard the loud thump.

He'd run upstairs and saw smoke coming out from under the doorway of their bedroom. He burst through the door and saw Marty Jo's bed was on fire—with *her* in it.

On the carpet next to the bed, Allan saw a smoldering cigarette with the heavy ashtray beside it that must have made the thump. He rushed to smother the flames with a blanket and hollered for Jim and Bill to help. They got the fire out fast and called for an ambulance.

Marty Jo ended up in the hospital with third-degree burns. She died three months later. I'd noticed the burn scars on the back of Allan's hands. Mom said they were from trying to put the fire out that night.

The burning bed, the loud screams, the ambulance... I couldn't imagine how scary that must have been. I'd probably smoke pot, too, if I'd had to witness that. And, what did they do with the burned-up mattress? Did they try to set it out for the trash men? Wouldn't it be creepy to see the burned-up mattress out beside the trashcans? The burned-up mattress where your mother lay burning? How do people get rid of something like that?

I didn't dare ask.

When we pulled up in front of Allan's house, it was obvious, even in the dusky autumn light, that the years of having a sick wife, four kids, and a company to run had been way too much. My mother had warned us that the house was a little run-down. "Keeping his home up," she told us, "had been last on his list."

The house was hard to miss on the corner of Plymouth and First Street. It looked less like a house and more like a big stucco box the color of vanilla ice cream. It loomed large, an eyesore among all the other well-kept homes in the Windsor Square neighborhood.

There was no distinct architectural style and no one had made an attempt at a garden, unless you counted the rim of low-lying shrubbery that bordered the house. The windows were small and thinly framed with brown trim. Clay tiles were missing from the roof. The lawn, wrapping around the property, had only erratic clusters of faded grass. A garden hose stretched halfway across it in a hopeless attempt. Silently I thanked God they'd decided we'd live in our house after they got married.

April pointed to a huge crack in one of the second-story windows as we started up the cement walkway. "Look! This place is a dump compared to our house. No wonder Allan wants to move to Fremont."

"Be pleasant, April." Mom buttoned her blue blouse to cover her cleavage. "Please, for me, will you? I'm trying to survive here."

The front door opened before we reached the worn rubber doormat that still had traces of an embossed "Welcome." Sarah, Allan's only daughter and a student at the University of San Diego, stood tall in the doorway. Her lips were bare and she wore no eye make-up. "You must be Marilyn and the girls." She forced a grin with big square teeth.

146

Sarah was pear-shaped with fair skin sprinkled with different-sized moles. Her brown eyes were set close with a large nose in-between. Her eyes matched her shoulder-length brown hair that had an unattractive wave to it. She wore grey tweed pants and a violet button-down sweater set.

The porch light bounced off a strand of pearls at her throat. She resembled Allan. "Allan in drag," Mom would later tell Connie, "which is fine for a man, but not so hot for a woman."

I was comforted by Sarah's conservative style of dress. Mom wasn't, but she tried discreetly to button her own blouse another notch higher.

Allan came up behind Sarah, wiping his hands with a dishrag. "Sarah, don't just let them stand there. C'mon in ladies!"

I'd never seen Dad pick up a dishtowel. As far as I knew, men didn't get involved in domestic stuff. Other than BBQ'ing for a dinner party (while drinking Scotch and most of the time burning the steak), my father had never done a thing around the house.

Sarah and Allan stepped aside for us to come in. "Bill and Jim were just helping me tidy up the kitchen," Allan said, then looked back and forth between Mom and Sarah. "Hey, you two haven't formally met."

Mom smiled, straightened her shoulders and walked inside. She smoothed her slim-fitting black wool skirt and extended a hand to Sarah. "Nice to meet you, honey. Your father's told me so much about you. He says that you're a great help to him."

Sarah fingered her mother's pearls, still holding that forced grin. It took a long minute for she respond. Finally, she reached for Mom's hand. Her blunt colorless fingernails clashed with Mom's nails, all long and polished bright coral. "Guess that's why daddy calls me 'Sarah Doll.'"

I could tell that it was instant hate.

147

We walked deeper into the house and everything looked bare in the dimly lit foyer except for a large sepia portrait of Jesus Christ on the wall above the stairway—the religious kind of picture, with His hands clasped in prayer, an exposed heart, and wearing the crown of thorns—on the wall above the stairway! Was this one of those Catholic houses, I thought, with all the religious symbols? Where would Mom put this picture when they moved in? It would look odd between the painted clown and the photograph of Abraham Lincoln in our stairway wall.

The hardwood floor in the hallway had no rug and squeaked slightly as we made our way to the kitchen. Mom bent down to whisper in my ear. "My god, this place looks like something out of a Tennessee Williams play."

April dug her hands into the slit pockets of her tight grey hip-hugger pants and followed behind Mom and Allan. Sarah hung back with me. "Daddy says that you're sweet."

"Thanks," I replied, tugging at my black cotton dress that had glued itself to my dark tights. Mom says that black makes you look thinner. "And your belt's cute," Sarah added. "Looks nice with that outfit."

I wasn't used to flattery. At the last minute, I'd grabbed the yellow belt to show off my waist—the only small part of my body. She'd noticed my effort to look nice and her attention felt good.

In the kitchen, one lone over-sized bulb hung from an exposed wire over the sink. That was the only lighting.

Allan introduced us to the boys and explained that John, who was on the crew team at St. Mary's College up north, wasn't able to get away from team practice. Meanwhile, Mom wasn't wasting any time and was already digging around in the freezer.

"Isn't it great that Marilyn wanted to cook for us tonight?" Allan beamed.

No one seemed that impressed. Only Jim responded and mumbled. "Yeah."

Do potheads mumble? Or, was he just trying to hide that chipped front tooth. It was the first thing I noticed about him. That and his slimy yellow teeth. He was weird and I had no idea how he would fit in our lives.

Bill moved over to Mom, who was holding a package of veal, and led her to the cupboard where the pans were. His face was handsome in a chiseled way and he had huge brown eyes. I couldn't believe that this cute guy, a year older than me and a freshman at Daniel Murphy High School, would soon be my stepbrother.

"Thank you, Bill," she eyed him warmly.

"Your wish is my command," he laughed.

Jim rolled his eyes. "Oh God, Bill, you're such a suck-up."

Bill looked back at Jim with a devious grin: "Better to be a 'suck-up' than a 'f-up.'"

"Boys!" shouted Sarah.

"You're not our mother," Jim shot back.

"Now, kids," Allan, sighed. "No need for histrionics."

"What are histrionics?" I whispered to Mom, but she was preoccupied at the stove.

She'd tied a white flour-sack dishcloth around her wool skirt, and I could see a small line of sweat above her lip as she stirred the packet of noodles into the boiling water. "Where are the frozen peas?" she asked, the lilt to her voice sounding phony to me.

Allan rushed to the freezer past Sarah and April, leaning side-by-side against the kitchen island. Both had their arms folded across their chests.

Sarah, having finally let go of the pearls around her neck, was telling April about her alma mater. "Marlborough is the top school for girls," she bragged.

"I actually disagree," April, replied. "Marlborough has a repu-tation as a 'snob school.'"

Sarah instinctively reached for the pearls again. "And, your Immaculate Heart is known for being a hippie school."

"I'd rather be a hippie than a snob," April shot back.

"To each his own," Sarah said, lifting her large nose slightly and dropping the pearls.

Mom was oblivious at the stove but Allan was aware. "Hey, girls," he said. "No school talk now. Help the boys set the table."

Bill and Jim brought out the placemats while Sarah got out the silverware, handing it to April and me ("as if we were servants," April told me later). The dining room was another bare room except for a rectangular wooden table surrounded by eight wood chairs. We began laying the table. After the rest had gone back to the kitchen, I turned to April. "This house is so dark and bare. It's weird."

"Forget the weird house," she whispered. "Sarah's a bitch. I want to strangle her with those damn pearls."

"I kinda like her," I replied.

"Don't let her flattery fool you," April whispered back. "I don't trust her. And, Jim! So weird."

"Bill's good, though."

"He's the only normal one," she said.

Allan helped Mom put the veal slices and noodles on a big plat-ter that had to be dusted off first. The peas stayed in the large pot. We dished up our plates buffet-style from the kitchen because there wasn't a sideboard in the dining room and took seats at the table. I was buttering my peas and hadn't realized that Sarah had seated herself at the head of the table across from Allan. Mom was the last to come into the dining room. She hesitated in the doorway, her eyes wide, pressing her false eyelashes flat against her eyelids. Clearly, she'd been thrown by Sarah's bold move.

Allan stood up and pulled out the empty chair to his right. "Here, Marilyn, take a seat next to me."

April nudged me from under the table and whispered. "Shouldn't Mom be sitting at the head?"

"I think so," I whispered back.

Jim, seated across from us, saw our exchange and leered at his sister. No love lost between those two, I thought.

Bill reached for his glass of milk.

"Hold on, everybody," Allan ordered.

Mom, now seated next to him, took that as a signal and held up her glass of wine. April and I followed her by picking up our milk glasses, expecting a toast to their upcoming marriage, or maybe to all of us being together for the first time.

"We need to say grace first," he said.

Awkwardly, we all put down our drinks. Crossing himself, Allan began, "Bless us O Lord for these thy gifts..."

Chapter Twenty-One

He'd sell his own mother for a buck.
—Mom, about Dad

Papa checked out Allan's company, Western Concrete Structures. It was solvent. In fact, it was thriving after a big pre-stressed concrete job on the Gateway Arch in St. Louis. Papa also learned that WCS was doing the post-tension concrete on the Foothill Freeway, a huge job near the San Gabriel Mountains. With proof that Allan was financially secure, Papa gave his blessing for Mom to marry.

The first week of November, Allan put his family's house on Plymouth up for sale. Linda Calhoun got the listing, this time to sell for real.

I had no idea how his kids felt moving into our house. I was just glad that we weren't moving into theirs. I kept thinking about that burning bed. Our house had more bedrooms anyway, plus the pool house, which, according to Mom, Jim had already staked out as his after they'd come by with Allan to see their new home.

"Big mistake," Connie warned after Mom told her. "That kid needs to be watched." Connie would know. She had five kids of her own.

The rest of the bedrooms were yet to be determined. It was no surprise when April put up a big fuss about sharing her room. "No way in hell, Mom," she'd shouted. "So don't get any ideas."

"Then, Sarah can stay in my room," I announced to my relieved mother.

Later, I wrote up a list and showed it to Mom. Seated on the Music Room couch, she was just lighting a cigarette and about to take her five o'clock Bufferin. She put the pill down beside the ashtray along with the partially lit cigarette and read the list to herself. *Empty drawers on right side of bureau. Clean out middle bathroom drawer. Move some hanging clothes in closet to the upstairs hall closet.*

"You saved my ass," she said, reaching out to give me a hug. "April will make a big scene if she has to share with Sarah and I don't want to upset Allan." She paused. "Do you really like Sarah? You're fine with this set-up?"

"Yeah, I like her." It was the truth.

••

The Stubbs would move into Fremont after the wedding, maybe as early as the next month. "Probably around Christmas," Allan said, but I hadn't heard any real date for the wedding yet.

Mom and Allan were planning a honeymoon in Puerto Vallarta right after the wedding. That's when Allan came up with the idea that his kids should move in while the newlyweds were away so that all of us could "get to know each other sooner." He tried to assure Mom. "Since Marty Jo died, they've learned how to fend for themselves while I'm at work. And, now Lupe will be on hand to oversee things. They'll work it out."

Lupe barely spoke English, but Mom insisted that it would be fine.

"No, it won't, Mom," April warned. "It'll be a train wreck."

Though my mother was concerned about leaving us all together without them around, she was torn between pleasing Allan and my sister. It reminded me of how she used to act with Dad, kind of afraid, always going along with whatever he said.

Mom also followed Allan's suggestion that April and Jim could be in charge of the household while they were gone because Sarah and John would be back at school, leaving April and Jim as the oldest.

In that respect, April had gotten her way. She always did.

But, I was mad. "Mom, *that's* a train wreck. April's gonna be mean and Jim doesn't even really know us."

"You'll be fine," she said, dismissing the obvious. "I'm more worried about Lupe. Cleaning up after four more kids might be a bit too much."

"No one ever listens to me!" I shot back, running up to my room. At the landing, I shouted down at her. "What about what *I* think!"

"Oh, Christ..." Mom sighed.

••

Our house wouldn't be the same when Mom married Allan. In Dad's closet, where custom suits used to hang next to monogrammed shirts, the empty rods would be filled with Allan's off-the-rack Phelps's Wilger suits and short-sleeved Brooks Brothers button-down Oxford shirts. In the driveway, Dad's black Continental would be replaced with Allan's blue Pontiac GTO. There was nothing fancy about Allan. Somehow, that reassured me. Dad had wanted a fancier life. Allan would not.

There would also be two teenage stepbrothers living in our house. Bill would turn the Hong Kong Room into his new bedroom while Jim would take over the pool house. A stepsister, Sarah, would be sharing my bedroom, and John, the oldest stepbrother, would bunk with Bill in the other twin bed when he was in town. John wouldn't need a real room because he was going into the Navy when he graduated college in June.

There'd be six kids in the house instead of two. A dog named Ed who looked like a wolf would also join us. And, Jim's ugly Galaxy would be parked out front.

I consoled myself that it was a small price to pay for no more calls from bill collectors and no sheriff coming to the door.

••

Meanwhile, Dad had moved in with Louise back in August while I was away at camp. Since they were engaged, I suppose it was all right, but it still seemed wrong to me. They weren't even married yet. I'd learned at Catholic School that "living in sin" was wrong. Committing adultery was wrong, too. Perhaps, Mom was right when she said Dad had the morals of an alley cat.

He hadn't taken April and me out for dinner even once that fall. He hadn't come by to visit at all, and rarely called. It was my fault. At summer camp, if I hadn't changed cabins to get away from Little Louise, Dad wouldn't be mad at me. He said I upset Louise by trying to get away from Little Louise. I'd tried to explain that Little Louise was okay with it in the end, but he wouldn't listen. "It wasn't smart of you to upset Louise," he'd said. I was too afraid to say what I was thinking on the other end of the phone line. What about me? Didn't it matter that I was upset?

Now, when he had something big to tell April and me, like his getting married to Louise, he told us over the phone. When he told us that he'd married her, I pretended that it was good. I congratulated him. But, when I hung up, I ate a whole box of Van de Kamp's molasses cookies. I don't even like molasses cookies.

My diary became my new best friend. It was a safe place to let my secret feelings out. Not everything, though. Someone might go through my drawer and find it.

> *November 1ˢᵗ—Dad called. He eloped with Louise in Mexico. They're married now. I don't feel so bad because Louise's kids were excluded from the ceremony, too. Little Louise and I are stepsisters—ugh!*

Mom said that the real reason they eloped was that Dad had to "nail it down quick" to get Louise's money before she could meet someone else. I sort of believed her. Still, it felt strange that he didn't tell us in person. I wondered when they told Louise's kids. Did Dad love them more than us now? Would he still see me on my birthday?

> *November 7ᵗʰ—Mom isn't upset about Dad marrying Louise. She says that she's got someone new, too. She means Allan. April said later that she's relieved that Mom has Allan. Because if she didn't, April thinks that Mom would probably be on Dexamils and Milltowns for sure. Or worse, she might act like Aunt Carolyn.*

••

> *November 22—Today's my birthday. I'm 12 now. I'm having a sleep-over with my school friends. No one seemed to care that my parents are divorced because they are all coming to the party. Everyone's bringing sleeping bags and we're going to sleep on the floor in my room.*

Dad mailed me a check. It was for $100. He wrote it on one of his work checks with "Robert A. Eaton, Attorney-at-Law" printed above his old office address on Wilshire. It was a long blue check and folded in half to fit a small plain envelope with no return address. He must have used up all the letter-size envelopes. I showed the check to Mom. She said to cash it quick. But, I'm not going to.

Sitting on my bed, I held the check in my hand and studied Dad's signature with the big "R," the big "A," and the big "E." The familiar handwriting seemed foreign to me now.

I folded it, put it back in the envelope, and stuck it in back of the top drawer of my nightstand along with all the old candy wrappers. If I cashed it, what little I had left of him would be gone.

Chapter Twenty-Two

Leading her up an alley.
—Mom

Allan and his four children spent Thanksgiving with their mother's family, at their uncle's home in Brentwood on the west side of town. Like us, this was their last dinner as an original family unit before what Papa called "the merger."

Our Thanksgiving had been low-key. Usually it was at our house, but this year, Virginia offered to host. We were just a small group, Papa and Virginia, Aunt Carolyn, Mom, April and me.

My cousin Jonathan and his little brother, Robert, were now living fulltime with Sherry and Uncle Charlie because Aunt Carolyn's depression had gotten worse. Aunt Carolyn barely left her little house on Lillian Way. Papa, Virginia, and Mom constantly checked on her to make sure that she was all right. Most of the time, she wasn't. She didn't want to shower and stayed in her faded-blue cotton bathrobe all day.

It was so frustrating. Why couldn't Aunt Carolyn get it together? Why couldn't Dr. Ferguson fix her?

On Thanksgiving, there wasn't much talk about Mom and Allan's wedding. April told me earlier that Mom asked Virginia and Papa not to talk about it in front of Carolyn. My mother knew that it would be hard enough on Carolyn to be without her kids on

Thanksgiving, much less having to sit through wedding talk during a Thanksgiving dinner that Aunt Carolyn didn't have much to be thankful about.

I missed my cousin Jonathan. We liked the same things—Disneyland, the same TV shows, the same pink Hostess Snowballs.

Lots of times after a family get-together, he'd get to spend the night and we'd stay up late and watch TV in the den after everyone had gone to sleep. Our common bond stopped, though, when it came to the way our parents disciplined us. Jonathan was spoiled rotten.

As much as I missed Jonathan, I didn't miss his regular fit, the one he had every Thanksgiving and Christmas when he wouldn't eat the turkey and begged for a peanut-butter sandwich. Last year, when Uncle Charlie wouldn't swap his turkey for a sandwich, Jonathan slunk from the table, taking one of Mom's good cloth napkins with him. He headed straight for the fireplace and threw the napkin in the fire. Instead of scolding him, Carolyn and Charlie gave in and made him a peanut-butter sandwich. My mother kept her cool, but the angry look on her face said it all.

"Monster," she said under her breath. Turning to Papa on her left, she whispered. "It's all I can do not to mash that kid."

••

The day after Thanksgiving, we went to the Stubbs' house for dinner. It was the first time we would all be together other than that original dinner a little over a month ago. John, the oldest, greeted us warmly at the door. Tall with thick sand-colored hair, John was handsome with a groomed mustache. We followed behind him as he led us through the entry hall and into the kitchen. The house seemed even more empty and cold. Boxes were stacked along the walls in the hallway as if they were moving to Fremont next week.

A dull outline marked the place on the stairway wall where the portrait of Jesus used to be. I wondered if we would have to hang it at our house. Would it replace Mom's clown painting? I hated that clown with the dark eye makeup and the ugly, bulbous nose. Clowns gave me the creeps, but the picture of Jesus was even scarier with the blood drops trickling down from the crown of thorns on His forehead.

I hoped that we wouldn't have one of those Catholic houses with all the religious symbols everywhere. Why did those houses always seem so dark? I prayed to God and everything, but I didn't want His picture in my front hall.

••

Allan was all smiles at the kitchen stove, frying his specialty, hamburgers.

"So, Virginia was able to get Ellen for next Saturday?" he asked Mom. I knew he was referring to the woman who'd been the cook at the Governor's Mansion when Papa had been in office, but I couldn't figure out why.

"Yep," Mom replied, untwisting the tie on a large bag of hamburger buns. "She's all set."

From across the room, I shot my mother a confused look. My mind was racing. *Boxes stacked in the hall...pictures taken down from the wall...* Maybe this wedding was going to happen sooner than I realized.

"What's next Saturday?" I asked.

Allan flipped a perfectly rounded patty in the sizzling cast-iron pan. His back was to us. "Marilyn? Did we forget to tell Heather?"

April, who was leaning up against the kitchen counter studying the split ends of her hair, answered without looking up. "I assumed you knew, Heath. The wedding's next weekend at Papa and Virginia's house."

I looked over at Bill. He nodded and shoved his hands into the

161

side pockets of his tan cords.

"*I* got the information," Jim piped in, looking over at John who replied: "All accounted for over here," John said, military fashion.

Sarah was upstairs, but I figured that she knew too.

"Shi-it," Mom said, dragging out the swear word.

All three boys looked wide-eyed at each other. They'd never heard Mom cuss. Wait until they moved in, I thought.

"I can't believe that we forgot to tell you," Mom said, stacking the buns on a platter. "Yes, it's next Saturday, Heather. It was the only day we could get Papa's old friend, Judge Gidelson, to do the ceremony."

And here I thought that keeping that wedding talk on Thanksgiving on hold not to upset Aunt Carolyn was for some Saturday in the somewhat distant future, not a next-week future.

My mother left the buns and came over to me. She started combing my bangs away from my face with her fingers, her long nails scraping lightly against my forehead. She looked down at me, "Jesus, how could I have forgotten to tell you, Heatherbean?"

I was numb.

Allan came to her defense. "It's easy, Marilyn," he said, now sliding the burgers into the buns. "We have six kids between us now. One's bound to fall between the cracks."

"Yeah," I said, shrugging my shoulders. "No big deal. Really."

Mom held my bangs back and leaned into my face. "You sure?"

I pushed her hands away and combed my bangs back to normal with my own fingers. "Uh-huh."

••

Back at home in my bedroom later that night, I heard the familiar beat of Mom's favorite, "A Taste of Honey" by Herb Alpert and The Tijuana Brass, coming from below in the Music Room. She and Allan were having "nightcaps," a grown-up word for late-night cocktails, which tonight seemed to go on forever.

I gave up trying to sleep and switched on the bedside lamp. The clock read 10:20. I pulled out my diary from the nightstand, then changed my mind. Diaries were for secrets. What I wanted to write was no secret.

Knowing where I could find a piece of cardboard, I headed into Mom's dressing room. There, in the bottom drawer of her built-in dresser, I found my father's shirts that had come back from the laundry after he'd left for good. I pulled the cardboard out from inside the folds of one of the shirts. Back in my room, I grabbed a Marks-a-Lot from my desk and went straight into my closet, shutting the door.

I pulled the link chain to click on the light and sat down on the cold hardwood floor, the hems of my dresses grazing my forehead.

Marker to cardboard, I wrote in big bold strokes.

I HATE YOU, MOM! HOW COULD YOU FORGET TO TELL ME THAT THE WEDDING WAS NEXT WEEK! DON'T I MATTER? I HATE YOU, YOU BITCH!!!!!

I reached up for the chain and clicked the light off. I sat back down on the floor in a heap, like a heavy block of cement. Downstairs, my mother had turned up the volume on the record player. That's when I started to cry. Ugly crying. Loud crying, with moans and sobs ripping through my body. I was safe. No one would be able to hear me above the Tijuana Brass.

Chapter Twenty-Three

Out of the nowhere and into the now.
—Mom

On the morning of my mother's second wedding, a muted sun was coming through pale sheers that were pulled across the large double-hung windows in Papa and Virginia's living room.

"Happy is the bride the sun shines on," Papa said as soon as we came through the door. Papa looked commanding in his dark navy suit, starched white shirt, and blue-and-white striped tie. No jumpsuit today.

"Hope so," Mom replied, stepping into the entry hall. "I'm higher than a B-19 right now," she told Papa. Breathless, she added, "So excited. Jesus. I had April drive me here, I was so nervous."

Mom turned to April who was lugging the over-stuffed suitcase that Mom packed to take on her honeymoon. "Put that there next to the umbrella stand. Remind me, girls to put that suitcase in Allan's car."

April rolled her eyes and I gave her a knowing smile. Although, Mom's excitement was infectious to me, my sister had her reservations about what was to become our new family life.

Papa explained that Aunt Carolyn had arrived early and that Virginia was in the kitchen dealing with last minute details. Mom wasn't listening. Her mind was elsewhere.

"God, Papa, remember the rain on Bob's and my wedding day?"

I hadn't thought about Dad all morning, too caught up with Mom getting ready for the wedding. Was he relieved? Mom said he would be. "No more alimony checks to me."

"Should'a known," Papa laughed.

Mom took a deep breath, trying to relax. "Should' a known."

Papa and Virginia's two-story colonial on Arden Boulevard was bursting with cut flowers in small arrangements on every available surface. Virginia had really thrown her back into preparing for the wedding, given the short time she had to plan.

A small group of adult guests mingled in the foyer, oblivious to the four Stubbs children who were milling aimlessly around them. My sister and I sat together on the large sofa in the living room, away from the fray. None of us children seemed to know what to do with ourselves while we waited for the ceremony to begin.

Virginia, her rounded figure stuffed into a tight-fitting pink brocade suit, was a welcome distraction as she bustled about, lighting votive candles and adjusting cut roses in blue Wedgewood vases. In front of the fireplace in the living room, Judge Gidelson was consulting with Mom and Allan. Papa, who'd stayed by the front door to greet the guests, ushered in the last to arrive, Marty Jo's parents, Kay and John Roney, whom I'd met only once at their richly decorated duplex on Orange Drive.

Mom and Allan took their place in front of the small wooden pedestal that Virginia had rented for the occasion. My mother was dressed in the powder blue suit that Charlotte had claimed would be "the perfect outfit" for a second wedding.

Charlotte stepped closer to Mom as her maid of honor. Mr. Webb, Allan's close friend and best man, moved next to Allan.

Why had Mom chosen Charlotte and not Connie? Or, shouldn't Mom have picked Aunt Carolyn? I knew so little about how this wedding was planned.

Behind the pedestal, Judge Gidelson straightened his shoulders and buttoned his suit jacket over his rotund belly. Smoothing his white hair behind over-sized ears, he leaned forward telling my mother and Allan to come closer to the Holy Bible on the little pedestal.

My eyes caught the back of Allan's left hand as he gently ushered Mom, the muted scars on his knuckles from Marty Jo's burning bed.

The judge cleared his throat and announced that the ceremony was about to begin. Everyone, except the Roneys who stood in the back of the room, gathered around the wedding party in horseshoe fashion. The Stubbs on one side. April, Aunt Carolyn, and me, on the other. Virginia, Papa, Mrs. Webb (the best man's wife), and Connie and Richard Rossi rounded out the middle.

Aunt Carolyn smelled of mom's Ma Griffe perfume. I looked up at her profile, the chiseled nose, the sharp chin. Her shoulder-length hair was freshly colored and styled in a flip. I hadn't seen it combed and without dark roots for months. She'd lost a lot of weight and the skirt of her powder blue checked suit hung loosely around her hips. Mom had insisted that Aunt Carolyn wear make-up but the bright orange lipstick and dark eyeliner looked freakish against her sallow skin.

Mom had been so relieved when she'd seen Aunt Carolyn's beige Dodge Dart parked out front at Papa's when we arrived earlier. That meant not only was Aunt Carolyn there, she'd actually gotten in her car and driven herself, which would have been the first time she'd done that in weeks.

When the Stubbs family had arrived, Jim had been eager to take photos with his new camera and offered to take a picture of Aunt Carolyn and my mother. Mom posed, all wide-eyed and grinning with her arm around Aunt Carolyn who seemed to be wearing a forced smile. As Jim clicked away, I could tell that poor Aunt

Carolyn was trying desperately to hold it together. I felt sorry for her. She was trying hard to be happy for her older sister. April must have felt sorry for her, too, as she inched closer to Aunt Carolyn and gave her boney hand a squeeze.

In the large gilded mirror above the mantle, I saw Kay and John Roney's reflection at the back of the room. Kay stood stiffly in a plain black dress with a gold circle pin near her shoulder and a purple scarf tied loosely around her neck. There was no expression on her face. I couldn't tell if she was happy or sad. How must she feel? Was she thinking about her daughter, Marty Jo?

Her husband, John, looked distinguished in a dark blue suit with his thick white hair so neatly groomed that you could see the marks of his comb. He had taken off his heavy tortoise-shell framed glasses and was wiping them with his handkerchief in a slow methodical circular motion, taking his time, it seemed, to put them back on.

The Judge opened to a page in the Bible and began to read. The words rambled and I found it hard to concentrate. Fortunately, it wasn't long before Mom and Allan exchanged vows.

Judge Gidelson turned to my mother. "Do you Marilyn take thee Allan…"

The white orchids in Mom's small bouquet shook slightly. "I do."

"Allan, do you take thee, Marilyn…"

His response was strong and firm. "I do!"

Judge Gidleson pronounced them "Man and wife."

I checked the mirror again. The Roneys, stone-faced, looked away as my mother and Allan kissed. Charlotte, whose tailored green dress was the color of lime sherbet, turned around and winked at my sister and me. Sarah held a blank stare and a plastered smile. Jim and Bill snapped pictures with their cameras and John, like I had done, checked out the Roneys in the mirror. I'd heard that John had been the closest to his mother. Why couldn't I stop noticing the sad people here?

Virginia, always dramatic, turned to the Rossi's with tears streaming down her powdery pink face. "Weddings make me cry," she sniffed.

••

There was the pop of champagne. "Time to celebrate!" Papa called out.

The adults congregated around Mom and Allan, so April and I made our way across the entry hall to the dining room. The big rectangle table was laden with breakfast-type foods on silver platters adorned with paper doilies. Ellen, the cook, stood by, smiling as we filled our plates.

Sarah was the first to follow us into the dining room. Her short sleeved navy dress stopped right at the knee, revealing what Mom called "piano legs," legs with no definition. Through her pale nylons, I noticed that her moles weren't limited to her face and arms.

"Well, hey there," she grinned with those big teeth. "We're stepsisters now."

"We sure are," my sister replied, dryly. Sweetening her tone, April added, "So, when are you moving in *exactly*?"

I looked down and picked up a deviled egg from one of the platters. Those two together made me nervous. I was sure there would be a fight soon and I hoped that I wouldn't be around to witness it.

"Not 'till Christmas break. Didn't daddy tell you? I have to go back down to school in San Diego right after this."

April reached for a miniature crepe. "Mom did say something about that, but I wasn't sure. You know, 'cause Jim and Bill are moving in this afternoon and all."

Sarah picked up a plate from the stack and eyed the goodies on the table. Without looking up, she said: "John's going back up to school in Hayward today, too. You knew that, right?"

April's voice became abrasive. "Of course I knew that. Jim and I are in charge of the move-in."

"Hmmmm," Sarah said. "Maybe I'll come back up to LA to make sure the move is going fine."

"No need to, Sarah," April said, giving her a tight smile. "We'll do just fine without you."

I jammed the deviled egg in my mouth.

Just then, Allan came into the dining room holding a half-empty glass of champagne. "There you girls are!"

Still holding the empty plate, Sarah looked up and gave Allan a hug. "Congratulations, Daddy."

"Thank you, Sarah Doll," he beamed.

"I'm famished," Sarah said, surveying the table again. She reached for a roll. "You'll excuse me while I fill my plate."

Allan stood with April and me. He smelled of shaving soap as he put his arms around us and promised to do his best to be a good stepfather. He meant it, and right then I felt bathed in security. Over the shoulder of Allan's brown suit, I spotted John Stubbs in the hallway talking to the Roneys. In the living room, Jim and Bill were snapping pictures of Papa, Mom, and Charlotte smiling next to Judge Gidelson; Aunt Carolyn was standing off to the right with a blank stare on her face.

••

Right after they cut the two-tiered white cake, it was time for my mother and Allan to leave for their honeymoon. Allan had been worried about getting to the airport on time for their flight to Puerto Vallarta.

Everyone gathered out front and threw rice at the newlyweds as they darted down the walkway to Allan's blue Pontiac GTO. Allan started the engine and Mom rolled the window down. Jim and Bill took a few last pictures of them in the car as Virginia ran up to Mom's window to say one last good-bye. Among the photos developed later would appear an unflattering snapshot of the brocade fabric of Virginia's skirt straining across her ample rear as she bent down to the car window.

As they pulled away from the curb, Mom blew a kiss to April and me standing on the sloped front lawn with Sarah and John.

We all watched as Allan made a U-Turn in front of the house on Arden then a left on 6th Street just a few yards south. My mother never looked back, and, in a flash, the blue GTO was out of sight.

Chapter Twenty-Four

Walking into the buzz saw.
—Mom

As soon as the GTO turned the corner, everyone left. April and I hung around Papa and Virginia's for a little while. Aunt Carolyn stayed too, but not for long. She said that her head hurt and that she needed to get home. Papa suggested that she go upstairs and rest, but she refused. He looked worried when he walked her out to her tan Dodge Dart. I hated that car. Virginia had one too. Same beige color. Same smell inside, like stale vinyl.

April and I finished helping Papa and Virginia move chairs back into the proper places in the living room, then headed home. April drove me in Mom's car, which she bragged she'd be driving the whole week that Mom was gone. My sister hated the used Ford Comet that Dad had given her on her 16th birthday. Mom had told her to shut up and deal, that she was lucky to get anything from her "bastard father."

The Comet, April nicknamed "the vomit," had no power steering and in order to make a big turn, she had to crank the steering wheel hard. It was funny to watch. My sister, 5-foot-2, blonde and pretty, turning red in the face using real muscle just to make a lousy left turn.

When we got home, April went up to her room and immediately picked up the phone. She was still in her room later that afternoon when Bill and Jim drove up in Jim's grey Ford Galaxy 500. I'd been waiting by the dining room window for over an hour for them to come. Jim's monstrous car was old like April's and the color of a battleship. It was packed solid, including the trunk, which was overfilled with boxes and tied with a rope to keep it closed. Watching them turn in the driveway reminded me of the opening credits on *The Beverly Hillbillies* where the Clampetts drive to their new home in a rickety truck overfilled with their junk.

The car windows were down with the radio blasting loud rock music as the Galaxy came up the driveway. I quickened my pace, following the music from inside, through the pantry, through the kitchen and out to the laundry porch to the window in back next to the back door where I could spy on them.

The Galaxy jerked to a stop inches in front of the garage door. Jim and Bill hopped out at the same time and started to unload. First out was a turntable that Jim lifted, his grey pocket t-shirt loose and wrinkled against his fleshy body and marked with a line of sweat down the back as he carried it, cords dangling, it to his new room in the pool house. Bill followed, carrying two huge speakers and more dangling cords. His compact body showing no signs of strain.

No one had been inside the pool house for so long that when Jim pried the door open it made a cracking sound, as if it had been painted shut which it probably had been knowing Moe. It was dark inside and had been that way since Dad left a year ago. Mom had pulled the shades down, closed the door, and had never gone back inside.

Jim left the door open and Bill followed him in. There was a burst of light when Jim pulled on the cord of the plastic rolling shades on the two windows that faced the fig tree. Through the open door, I could see Bill open the tiny bathroom door. Up went the shade covering the little window above the toilet. More light. These guys were brave, I thought. There must have been a million spiders in there after being dark for so long.

"Get me a broom!" Jim hollered to Bill who had gone back outside and was unloading a big taped box marked JIM—CLOTHES.

I ducked out of sight and darted into the kitchen, pretending to be looking for something in the cupboard just as Bill burst through the backdoor. I'd die if he caught me spying.

"You guys got a broom?"

Bill's face was flushed and sweaty and he smelled like cardboard and dust. My heart skipped a beat—those brown eyes, and that thick dark hair that swooped over his forehead. Wow, this was my new stepbrother. He looked cool.

I called out for Lupe. Instead, it was April who answered from the top of the back stairway. She must have heard me through her closed bedroom door. "Why do you need Lupe?"

I yelled back so that she could hear me from the kitchen. "Jim needs a broom."

I heard the quick tap-tap of her bare feet on the metal edging of the linoleum stairs. She landed hard on the floor from the last step and stood motionless. Still wearing the dress from the wedding, she put her hands on her hips. I held back from laughing. Who did she think she was? God's gift to being a bossy big sister?

Staring straight at Bill, she said: "No way in hell is Jim going to make Lupe clean his goddamn room!"

"Why're you yelling at him?" I asked, annoyed. "It was me who called Lupe to get it."

"Oh," she paused, hands still glued to her hips. I could tell that she was searching for something else to say to show that she was in charge. "Well, just so you both know," she said, looking back and forth between Bill and me. "Lupe's not anyone's personal maid. Got it?"

Bill rolled his eyes. "Oh, man."

April stomped straight to the window in the laundry room and eyed the scene outside. Jim had been busy. Most of the car was unpacked and the driveway was littered with boxes.

April turned way from the window to face Bill. Finally taking her hands off of her hips. She pointed to the laundry room closet. "Broom's in there."

He opened the closet, grabbed the broom and was out the backdoor, fast. April and I stood together watching out the window as Bill handed the broom to Jim. Bill lifted a box marked BILL'S STUFF, and headed to the backdoor. We stayed at the window watching. Somehow, it didn't seem as sinister if my sister and I were both watching.

Bill breezed by us at the window, carrying his box. In through the back door, past us at the window when he realized that he didn't know where to go with his stuff.

"Hey," he said, stopping at the bottom of the back stairs. "Where the hell is the Hong Kong Room? Shit, *what* is the Hong Kong Room? Dad says that's my new room now."

I answered. "It's called the Hong Kong Room because all the stuff in there is kinda Oriental, or something, I don't know. Mom names rooms."

"It's at the top of the stairs, go right," April said, "Not left on the hallway toward Heather and Mom's room. Not straight into my room, either. Make a sharp right, and turn down that little hall with the balcony on one side. The Hong Kong Room's right there at the end of that hall, opposite the door to my bedroom."

"Thanks," he said, starting up the stairs. As an afterthought, he called back from halfway up. "New name for the room, you guys. It's now *Bill's Room*."

"They don't seem to understand that they are moving into *our* house," April uttered to me through clenched teeth.

Standing on tiptoes to see more of what Jim was moving in to the pool house. I was so close to the window my breath made a round spot of moisture on the glass pane. "Mom says that now that Allan's paying the bills, it's their house, too."

"Over my dead body."

April turned to go back to her room and I followed behind her up the stairs to see what Bill was unpacking. I stood at the threshold of his room, waiting to be invited in. He ignored me putting out the grey suit he'd worn to the wedding, now rumpled from the top of the box marked BILL'S STUFF. That was followed by a string of pocket t-shirts and thin-whaled corduroy jeans.

"Hey," he called out to me, finally. "There's no dresser in here. Where do I put my stuff?"

"I think in the shelves in those little side closets," I said, wary of stepping into his new domain.

"Great. No dresser in a room named Hong Kong," he sighed, resigned.

••

All my friends were surprised that Mom had gotten married so fast and asked how things were going at home with the new stepbrothers. The only thing that I could come up with to say was that it was never dull. Our once boring house after Dad left had become lively again, in a whole different way. This time there were no fancy parties with caterers or late night cocktails in the Music Room or drunken people, half-naked by the pool with the pool light on after a wild dinner party. And no more late-night arguments between Mom and Dad when he came in late with lipstick on his collar.

Lively now, as in never knowing what will happen next.

Jim slept in the first morning and didn't emerge from the pool house until noon when he used the powder room off the Green Room and left the toilet seat up. Bill got up late, too, and was in the kitchen eating dry cereal right out of the box. His brown hair was uncombed and he was wearing only cords and no shirt. Was this how boys lived?

Lupe had taken to hiding out in her room. She came out only to cook dinner and clean a little. I don't think that she was praying at her altar much, because the little TV in her room was constantly on, tuned to the Spanish station with the volume high.

Jim with his greasy blonde hair and slimy teeth stayed in his room most the time, too, and when he came out, he grunted, if he said any words at all. April basically ignored him except at dinner in the breakfast room (which we had to explain, was called the Green Room, because of the green carpet). On the second night after they moved in, Jim tried to light a cigarette after he finished his dinner. April reached across the table and snatched the matches out of his hand. "Don't smoke in the house."

He slammed his hand hard on the table, and dishes and flatware bounced from the force. "Mind your own business, bitch!"

In the background, the volume on Lupe's TV went up another notch while Bill and I sat silent as stones at the table between the two of them, waiting for a reaction from April.

"Fuck off!" she replied.

Then, Jim leaned across the table and snatched the matches right back out of her hands. He struck the match and lit his cigarette, exhaling a tunnel of smoke back across the table into my sister's face.

April stood up, narrowing her eyes at Jim. "Creep." She tossed her napkin on her plate and stormed out of the room.

Jim, satisfied, stubbed the cigarette out on the edge of his plate, finished his milk in one gulp, made a gross burp, and left the table.

"He's a lot of fun, huh?" Bill said to me, picking his fork back up and digging into his Swanson's Turkey pot pie on what would be our second of five more nights of boxed dinners stacked in the freezer.

On the third morning after they moved in, Jim discovered that Bill had finished the box of Cap'n Crunch cereal and had put the empty box back in the cupboard.

Jim motioned with the empty cereal box over to Bill who was standing by the refrigerator. Then, turned it upside down, releasing a rain of sugary dregs onto the kitchen floor. "You eat all this, you jerk?"

"Ya, so?"

"Stupid shit. Why'd you put the box back? I wanted it for breakfast and now it's empty!"

Bill shrugged. "Sorry."

"I get first on all the cereal. Got it?"

"Yeah, yeah..." Bill replied, opening up the refrigerator and taking a gulp of milk straight from the carton.

None of what Jim did bothered Bill. I wished that I could be that easygoing. When April was mean to me, I got mad. And, when I fought with her, I lost. My sister was smart and always had an answer that made whatever I had said sound dumb.

It wasn't just April and Jim who were at odds. Thomasina, our cat named after the Disney movie of the same name, took to hiding out under my bed. Ed, the Stubbs' dog, made a game out of barking and trying to get at her by trying to squeeze his muscular shepherd-mix torso between the bed frame and the floor. Apparently, I hadn't seen Ed, who had been cowering on the floorboard of the Galaxy on the move-in. Finally, Jim had dragged him out at which time we spotted Thomasina by the pool and the chasing began.

Nighttime was a truce. Ed slept in Bill's room and Thomasina, in mine. We shut our bedroom doors to keep any mishap between the two animals.

By the time Mom and Allan returned home from the honeymoon a week after the move-in, Jim had begun "painting" his room in the pool house.

And Bill had turned the old Hong Kong Room into his own except he kept the Indian-print bedspreads from Akron. He moved the big brass coffee table with all the Chinese etchings into the den right next to his room. He rigged up a stereo in one of his closets and had big white headphones so that he could turn his music up loud and no one would hear.

"You like Jethro Tull?" Bill had asked me over our fourth night of TV dinners.

"Who?" I dipped into the sectioned apple crisp dessert first.

"I'll let you listen to them on my earphones," he offered. "But, not in my room."

"Then, how will I listen with them?"

"I've got a long cord that'll stretch into the den next to my room. I don't want some younger stepsister hanging around in my room."

Later that night, I sat in Allan's big leather chair in what used to be my father's den. "In Search of the Last Chord" by The Moody Blues was blasting through Bill's earphones wrapped around my head. Gazing over rooftops, I spotted the big lighted Christmas tree on top of the Farmers Insurance Building on Rimpau and Wilshire and I wondered. Shouldn't I miss my Dad more?

Chapter Twenty-Five

The Golden Rule: He who has the gold rules.
—Mom

I didn't have a crush on Bill anymore. One week of living with him fixed that. He smelled like sweat when he got home after school. He burped a lot, especially when he drank Dr. Pepper and, like Jim, he never put the toilet seat down. Boys were gross.

As a stepbrother though, he was pretty good. He played albums for me I'd never listened to before, and I liked his music. Before, the only music around the house had been Mom's Herb Alpert and Burt Bacharach records or April's Leslie Gore and The Turtles. Bill introduced me to Jethro Tull. I was crazy about that band and could listen to Living in the Past *all* day long.

Maybe it's the music that brought us together, but Bill was becoming kind of a friend. He made April and me laugh with his imitations, like the one he did of Jim's goofball best friend, Tom Carter, a guy with thick curly bangs. Bill would stand in front of us and shove his brown bangs away from his eyes with his thumb. Using a dumb-sounding voice, he'd pretend he was Tom talking to Jim: "Hey, man, got any cigs?"

"More!" we'd say, laughing.

Next he'd be Jim, using the same motions Jim used to brush his greasy bangs away from his pimpled forehead. "Yeah, man, gotta pack of 'boros in my room."

Bill said that Jim was genius smart. "The guy may be lazy, but he get's all A's."

For a "genius," Jim hardly talked and spent hours out in his room in the old pool house with the shades drawn, the door shut, and the black light on. Finally, he let April, Bill, and me in to see it. Shutting the doors and pulling the shades for maximum effect, he proudly switched on the black light.

It all came to life like some sort of amusement ride in the dark. Everything he'd painted fluorescent glowed like neon. A *Peace* sign lit up bright orange. *End The War* scrawled in purple and green marijuana leaves of varying sizes painted green all over the walls. "Oh my god, Dad's going to be pissed off at all of this," Bill muttered under his breath.

"Has my Mom seen this?" I asked him, knowing Mom called his room a cave.

"Nope."

"Just wait," April said, shaking her head, fluorescent yellow bouncing off of her white t-shirt.

"How do you turn the black light on and off?" Bill asked.

Jim moved to the door. He pointed at the light switch. "Here."

April laughed, fingering *turn on* painted chartreuse above the switch. "This is hilarious."

Jim reached for the doorknob. "Out! All of you!"

"C'mon," April said. "You've got to admit..."

He cut her off: "Out!"

"Ok. Ok," April said. Bill and I followed behind. Once Jim slammed the door, the three of us burst into laughter.

The heavy bass of his music reverberated clear to the main house and he played the same song over and over again. "*In-a-gadda-da-vida-honey. Don't you know that I'm lov'in you. In-a-gadda-da-vida, baby. Don't you know that I'll always be true...*"

One afternoon, April went into the kitchen and found Lupe cleaning up a mess Jim had made when he'd accidentally spilled a bowl of cereal. A puddle of milk had started to drip down the sides of the counter and Lupe was madly trying to catch the drips with a dishcloth while Jim just stood at the counter staring at her.

Sensing a fight, I stepped away from the refrigerator closer to the back stairway for an easy exit just in case.

"Hey," April barked. "Lupe's not here to clean up your mess. You do it!"

Jim poured more Froot Loops into his empty bowl and reached for the carton of milk. He didn't look up. "Yeah, who made you the boss?"

April's voice went from sharp to shrill. "You're a goddamn pig! And, you eat cereal all day like a kid."

Jim brushed his stringy bangs away with his thumb so that she'd see his sneer, giving her the full effect on his pale, ashen face.

She shook her head at him. "You're so righteous, Jim."

"You calling *me* righteous?" He picked up the cereal and took a spoonful. With a mouth full of food, he said: "Look in the mirror, bitch."

Lupe finished wiping up the last of the mess and was at the sink focused on rinsing the milk out of the dishcloth.

"Look, Buster, this is *my* house! You're just living in it."

Jim looked up from his bowl. He'd turned red with rage. "Oh, really? Who do you think is paying the mortgage?"

That's when things really exploded. Bill came rushing down the back stairs. April was so frustrated with Jim, she'd grabbed the handles of the side-by-side refrigerator and was repeatedly opening and closing the doors, every bottle and jar inside rattling wildly. "I can't stand you," she kept saying.

Just back from her honeymoon, Mom was on the phone in the Music Room like she always was when we came home from school.

She rushed into the kitchen. "Jesus Christ! What the hell is going on in here?"

Jim was the first to answer. "April's being a bitch."

April pressed her hands to her hips and narrowed her eyes at Jim. "And, you are disgusting."

Jim turned to Bill and me. "You two mind your own business and get outta here."

My sister took a hand off of her hip and pointed at Jim. "No. *You* get out of here!"

Lupe, who'd wrung the dishcloth to the size of a Tootsie Pop quickly turned off the faucet and hurried back to the refuge of her room.

"Quit jinging!" Mom hollered. "Can't you see that we're all trying to get along here? I don't need the two of you fighting."

She turned to Jim. "You, back to your room." Then she turned to April. "And, you go upstairs and cool off in *your* room. Call Mike or something, but keep out of my hair, goddamn it, both of you!"

The three of them stomped out of the kitchen and Bill, his brown eyes wide, looked over at me. "What does jinging mean?"

"It's Mom's word for being hyper."

The kitchen became eerily quiet. Bill shrugged. "Your mom sure has some wild sayings." He reached over to the package of Van de Kamp's chocolate cookies sitting on top of the breadbox, grabbing two at once. I looked over the things in the fridge to check for damage. Miraculously, nothing was broken.

Bill took a bite of one, sizing up the other cookie with his eyes. He swallowed and sighed. "Ah, another day in paradise."

••

It had only been a few weeks since the wedding but I was getting used to having a stepfather who was up and dressed for work at the crack of dawn—more normal than a father who was out all night with "clients" who left lipstick on the collar of his white shirts. Mom, of course, slept in.

Allan had a daily routine and he stuck to it. On weekday mornings, he finished breakfast by seven. By the time I passed through the Green Room around seven-fifteen, he'd be smoking his third Winston absorbed in *The Los Angeles Times* alongside a breakfast plate scraped clean of the heavily peppered fried eggs that he cooked himself.

He had a system for reading the newspaper, folding each page he was reading in half. Finishing one side first, then flipping the folded paper over to the other side. He claimed this was the only efficient way to read a newspaper.

At arm's length, on the small wooden ledge that jutted out from the wood-paneled wall, he'd have a deck of playing cards ready. After the newspaper, he liked to get in a game of solitaire before he left for work. If I heard the slow, methodical, flap, flap as he placed one card on top of another to make a match, I knew I was running late.

On school mornings, April was up and out before seven in her Mercury Comet. She was already angling to buy a better car by working part-time job in the deli at Von's market on Crenshaw. She was saving for an MGB sports car.

"You'd better sell a whole lot of day-old macaroni salad to pay for a cool car like that," Bill joked to her.

April loved Bill's humor. "Either that or chicken that we roast when the due date is up!" she replied.

Even with a job and a boyfriend, she managed to maintain good grades. It was strange, though: I never saw her do any homework. I guess it was because she was such a fast reader. Maybe that's how she did it. Mom believed she could get into a good college. But, there was no talk about her going to college.

Bill and Jim were supposed to leave by seven each morning,

too, but they always ran behind. The scene was as routine as Allan and his fried eggs. At exactly ten after seven, Jim yelled for Bill from the back porch door. "Bill! Hurry up!" Followed by the sound of Bill's feet pounding down the back stairs.

Next, the back door slammed as he ran to Jim's car that had crept up the driveway. Jim gunned the engine as he waited. Finally came the screech of the Galaxy as he peeled away followed by the harrumph as the car lurched over the first speed bump in front the Gentiles house at 122.

Nobody in the entire household made time to eat breakfast. Except Allan. Lupe, like Mom, didn't come out until the coast was clear.

••

Mom wasn't all relaxed and calm as I had hoped she'd be after the honeymoon. Rather, she had a new kind of edginess. Not the kind that she'd had before when she was separated from Dad and scared about money, always worried about hanging on to the house. This new edginess was all about keeping Allan happy while handling four new step-kids and a dog that kept chasing our cat. My mother got edgy about everything.

"You just *had* to have tennis shoes for gym," she said, jerking the car to a stop in front of the Larchmont Bootery. "Jesus Christ, I have enough to do without this!"

Or, not being able to find her Bufferin bottle to take her daily tablet at five o'clock. I could hear "Where the hell is the Bufferin?" from two rooms away.

Big or small, most things put my mother on edge. She blamed her jangled nerves from taking Dexamils and Miltowns, which her doctor had prescribed back when she was married to Dad, in order to be "up" for him, along with pills to get "back down," so that she could sleep.

It was a relatively quiet Tuesday night when the doorbell rang. Opening the door to a man in uniform. Now, *that* made her edgy. A man in uniform at the front door was never good news.

••

Hank puffed out his scrawny chest and made an attempt to suck in the small pooch that hung over his leather belt with the holster on the side. For years, all the kids in the neighborhood wondered if the gun was even loaded.

"Ma'am," Hank said, taking off his hat and pressing it against his chest. "I just saw Mr. Stubbs come through the gate. I'd like a word with him, please."

Mom started to close the door, blocking any view from inside the house with her body. "Not now. He just got home and…"

"Marilyn?" Allan called out from behind. "Who is it?"

"Later!" she said in a harsh whisper to Hank as she tried to slam the door.

Hank stuck his thick boot in the door jam. "Mr. Stubbs?"

Allan joined my mother at the door. "What's up?"

Mom looked at Allan, her eyes darting about the room as if searching fro a way out of this. She spoke fast trying to fend him off. "It's-no-big-thing. I-can–handle-it."

"Marilyn, I need to know what's going on." He gestured to Hank with his right hand, "C'mon in."

Hank stepped into the hallway and I crept back up the stairs and hid near the landing so they wouldn't see me.

"Sir, your son, the one with the grey car. He drives too fast in the street here, sir." Still holding the hat in one hand, he placed the other one on the edge of his belt near the holster. "Sir, Mr. Stubbs, sir, he flies over the speed bumps and exceeds the Fremont Place Speed Limit every day."

Allan nodded. "Thank you, Hank. I appreciate your coming

187

here to tell me this. I'll handle it from here, now."

••

"But, Dad," Jim argued later when Allan confronted him. "That old geezer's asleep in that fake cop car every time I pass by. How would he know if I was going too fast?"

Allan was firm: "James Montgomery Stubbs. Slow down. And, you're grounded for a week."

The next night at dinner, April did something neither Jim nor I expected. She stuck up for Jim. "Maybe it's the loud engine that makes Hank think that Jim's speeding. I mean maybe Hank's wrong," April told Allan.

"Nice try," Allan replied. "There are rules around here and Jim broke the rules. He went over the speed limit. Speed limit's ten miles an hour in Fremont. Jim goes too fast."

"But, a whole week? How do you know Hank's right?" April pressed on.

"Another neighbor stopped me on my way out of the gate a few days ago and complained about Jim's speeding. Hank just confirmed what I'd already heard."

April narrowed her eyes. "Which neighbor?"

Allan ignored the question. "Jim's grounded for a week, April. That's my final word. When someone breaks the rules around here, there are consequences."

My sister shivered as if she were trying to ward off a cold. Not only had there never been a routine around our house, there had never been any rules. April blanched.

I, meanwhile, silently rejoiced. I loved rules. They made my life feel safe and more normal. The Duque's had rules. The Woodward's had rules. I'd never had rules. No bedtime. No set time for homework. Curfew was supposedly whenever the streetlights came on yet no one ever checked to see if I'd come home. The only rule our family had had when Mom was married to Dad was simple: cock-tails and kids don't mix.

••

On my way out the door to catch a ride with the Woodward's on school mornings, I made a point to duck into the Green Room to say goodbye to Allan.

Without looking up from the newspaper, his words were the same every time: "Good-bye, now. Study hard."

The morning after Jim was grounded, I said my usual good-bye but Allan didn't respond right away. I waited in the doorway. He methodically turned the page of the newspaper, folded the next page, and looked up at me. The lines on his forehead creased like an accordion. He took a long drag from the cigarette that had been dangling from his mouth. The ashes lit up fiery red. He gestured to the book basket in my hand. Little gusts of leftover smoke escaped his mouth with each word. "I see that you bring books home, Heather, but I never see you do any homework."

He tapped a long ash from the cigarette on the edge of the small cut-glass ashtray on the table "School's important and you need to understand your arithmetic."

I switched the book basket to the opposite hand. "We call it math in seventh grade."

He smiled. "I call it arithmetic."

"Okay" I shrugged, thinking that arithmetic sounded babyish.

"Do the nuns give you much homework?"

I was getting nervous. Was he mad at me? He didn't sound mad. "Yeah," I replied weakly.

"Bill's gets a lot of school work over at St. Brendan. He'll be going to Daniel Murphy next year. No problem getting him in with his grades. But, I just haven't seen you or April doing schoolwork. Next year, you'll be in the eighth grade and it'll be your turn to take the test to get into high school."

All this talk about school was making me uncomfortable. I hated school. Other than art and English, I struggled in my classes. I'd heard that there was no way to cheat on the high school entrance test and worried that I wouldn't get in anywhere.

I looked down at my book basket. Part of the powder blue gingham lining had started to rip away from the straw edge. "Sometimes I do my homework," I lied, thinking about one of Mom's sayings: "First, you tell the truth. If that doesn't work, lie."

Dare I tell Allan that I cheated to get through school? That I relied on smart people, like Margaret and Eric, sometimes, Brice, to copy from on tests? Or, that I copied Anne's homework every morning on the way to school?

He folded over another half-page of the paper without reading it. "I want to start seeing you doing some real homework around here. I'll check it and if you need help, I'll help you. Okay?"

I swallowed hard. "Okay."

"Your mother says that your grades aren't good, but I think that you're smart. You just don't seem to try."

I nodded, clenching my jaw to fight tears. I didn't know why I was ready to cry. Allan didn't seem mad. Still, I felt awkward, like I was on stage. The laser focus of his attention on me and my homework was completely foreign. I was used to fading into the background. That's how I got through everything. I didn't know how to respond to this awareness of me.

Allan checked the sturdy navigational wristwatch he wore with the face on the inside of his wrist. "Now, run along to the Woodwards' or you'll be late." He reached for the deck of cards on the ledge.

"Bye," I said meekly and dashed out the door. Funny, I wondered as I made my way over to the Woodwards' How did Allan know that I wasn't taking the bus?

Chapter Twenty-Six

She's about as exciting as a toothache.

—Mom

Three weeks after the wedding. Sarah and John came back from college for the Christmas break. It would be the first time that they slept in their new home. John stayed in Bill's new room (the old Hong Kong Room) and Sarah slept in the other bed in my room, the room that we would now share.

"It's great," Sarah said, looking around as she entered our room ,newly decorated with her bedroom furniture from the old house on Plymouth.

"So, you like how it looks?"

She seemed pleased. "Of course."

Her eyes went from me to the Degas' ballerina prints that hung above our beds, copies that my mother had put in thick gold frames back when we were rich. "I'm glad to see that you kept those ballerina pictures. You need to have something of your own in here." She turned to her suitcase and lifted out a stack of sweaters. "Hey, whatever did happen with your old furniture?"

"The wicker stuff? Mom gave it to The Salvation Army. She says they do good things."

"Not the church?" she asked.

191

"No, we just started going to Mass with Allan and Mom on Sundays because Allan says it's what we do now as a family. But, Mom says that the devil lurks behind the cross."

"The devil lurks... what?"

I realized too late that I'd opened my big mouth. "Oh," I tried to recover, "she thinks that, you know, not all the people that go to church are good." I was getting myself deeper. I paused to think up something. "Like bad guys, crooks, those guys that wear crosses but, like kill people and stuff."

"Hmmmm," she said.

••

The next morning, I noticed Sarah slip out of our bedroom. Allan had already left for work and Sarah and I were the only ones up because of the Christmas vacation. She couldn't have been planning to go far because she was still in her nightgown, but curiosity got the best of me and I made my way over to the door to our room to see where she was headed.

From there, I saw her creep into Mom and Allan's room across the hall. Their door was open and I heard Mom half-asleep ask what Sarah was doing going through her wallet.

"I'm going to Bullock's Wilshire today and I need the charge," Sarah answered in a loud whisper. Why she was whispering, I wasn't sure. She'd already woken Mom.

Mom must have been fully awake now. "Sarah, no one said that you could go through my purse," She said.

Sarah's voice got lower. "My mother always let me."

Wide awake now, Mom yelled: "God damn it, keep away from my purse!"

Sarah said nothing. I heard Mom's purse snap shut.

I stepped away from the door and headed back to the bathroom not wanting Sarah to know that I'd been eavesdropping.

Sarah came into the bathroom. Her face was flushed, making her moles look a little less brown against the redness of her skin. Was she embarrassed or mad? "Are you going to be long?" She demanded.

"I just have to finish with my teeth," I pulled out the toothbrush and fumbling for the paste. Her angry tone rattled me.

"O.K., but hurry up. I need to get in there."

This was not the Sarah who had been so nice to me.

Later that day, I was just coming home from Anne's when I saw Sarah dart out of the house to meet Allan who'd just pulled up the driveway from work. She was at his car door before he even got out. "Daddy, I need to talk to you."

She stepped away as Allan opened the door and pulled out his briefcase along with a stack of rolled-up blue prints. His tie was slightly askew. He looked tired.

"Marilyn's so mean to me," Sarah said, breathless, as if she were trying to get it all out before he got into the house.

"Now, Sarah, we all need to get along."

"Oh, Daddy," she said, reaching for the big rolls of paper, "let me help you and carry those blueprints."

He handed them over as he walked from the porte cochere toward the front door.

"She doesn't let me do anything. I needed to go shopping and she refused to..." Sarah stopped abruptly when she noticed me.

Allan looked down to separate the house key from the rest on his key ring. "Sarah Doll, we'll take this up later."

That's when Mom opened the front door. "Heading him off at the pass, eh?" she said. Sarah looked puzzled. She didn't understand my mother's sayings, but I did. Mom was onto her.

••

193

The next few days were better. John went to Western Concrete with Allan to help out and Mom decided that it was better to get rid of Sarah than have her around so she offered Sarah the use of her car. "The lesser of two evils," she'd told Connie.

Turns out, those few days without Sarah around were the calm before the storm. On day four, April caught Sarah red-handed going through Mom's jewelry box in the dressing room.

"What are you doing?"

Sifting through a heap of bracelets, she replied: "Just looking for something to go with one of my dresses."

"Sarah, that's my mom's jewelry."

"Oh, she won't mind."

"Actually, yes, Sarah, she will mind. And, you know what? I'm going to tell her."

"Go right ahead," Sarah said, trying on Mom's pearl and sapphire ring.

••

A few nights later, everyone was home and we had the first "family" dinner in the dining room. Mom had made one of the Stubbs' favorites—creamed chipped beef over English muffins.

Bill, next to me, was inhaling it as if someone was about to take his plate away. Jim, glassy-eyed and stoned ("He had the munchies," April said later), was seated by Mom at the head of the table and eating as if he hadn't been fed in weeks. John, across from me, was eating fast, too. Sarah, next to Allan at the opposite head, was already halfway through her second chipped-beef-covered muffin. My mother was on her second glass of white wine from the carafe that she had strategically placed nearby. She seemed to be "drinking her dinner," as she called it.

The table was silent except for a loud symphony of the flatware scraping the dinner plates.

"So, the Navy after graduation in June?" Allan asked John. Allan had been in the Navy himself and had wanted to fly for them, but he'd never had that opportunity.

"Baby Jesus," Sarah said, addressing John with the nickname their family had given him because they thought he could do no wrong. "You sure that you want to enlist? They'll send you to Vietnam, you know."

"I want to fly off of an aircraft carrier," he said, placing his fork at a perfect angle on his clean plate. "It's been my dream, and if I have to do time in Vietnam to do it, I will."

Allan beamed, though John showed no emotion. It was as if he were reading straight from a script. But, that's the way he always talked.

Vietnam was scary. Every night on TV we watched American men fighting in the swamp. Some nights, they showed coffins of young dead soldiers that were covered in flags being carried inside the huge airplanes to come home to be buried. I wasn't sure who was fighting whom. Was it us against the Viet Cong? And, who were the Viet Cong anyway? Why were we fighting there? Hippies protested the war and there were a lot of peace riots, too, but I really had no understanding of what the war was all about to be against it or for it.

What I did understand was that John must be awfully brave to be willing to go there and fight in the swamp and risk coming home dead in a flag-covered coffin inside a big hollow airplane filled with other dead soldiers in flag-covered coffins.

April stopped poking the peas. "I'm against the Vietnam war," she announced.

Mom ignored April's comment and tried to turn the conversation. "How patriotic, John, to want to serve your country."

The corners of his mouth attempted a smile. "Thank you, Marilyn.

Allan took a sip of his gin. "That's right, John. You're a real man, not one of those idiot draft dodgers running off to Canada."

"They're not all idiots, Dad," Jim said. "They don't believe in the war. That doesn't make them an idiot."

I thought about the peace signs all over Jim's wall. Hadn't Allan noticed?

"The hell it doesn't," Allan replied.

"Some people don't feel like fighting for something that they don't believe in, Dad," Jim said.

"You younger kids and your peace-love-groovy thoughts," Allan said, looking back and forth between April and Jim. "It's a privilege to serve in the Armed Forces."

April started to protest, "But, Allan..." only to be cut off by the sound of a loud clunk against the table.

Mom's gold stop watch on the long chain around Sarah's neck had hit the edge of the wooden table when she'd reached for the pepper mill that John had been handing off to her. It was Mom's grandfather's stopwatch—the one that Mom made into a necklace.

"What was that?" Bill asked.

"Marilyn's necklace," Sarah answered, grinding the pepper over the small bit of chipped beef left on her plate.

My mother must not have seen it on her earlier and looked amazed and mad at the same time. She stared at Sarah with heavy-lidded eyes. "Would you mind giving that back, please?"

"This oughta be good," Bill said under his breath, the rest of us shifting our eyes back and forth between Mom and Sarah while Allan continued to eat.

"Yeah, sure," Sarah said, lifting the necklace up over her head. She held it in her hand and stared back at Mom and slid it down the center of the wooden table. Our eyes followed it as it came to a halt at the edge of Mom's straw placemat. "I didn't really like it anyway," Sarah said, picking up the pepper mill again.

"Oh man," Bill said.

The stopwatch necklace lay there at the edge of Mom's placemat, the chain, crumpled and covering the face of the watch. My mother looked down at it in what looked like disbelief.

Mom looked back up across the table to her new husband, Allan. "Allan!?"

Allan finished his last bite of chipped beef. He took a sip of his gin, shaking the glass of ice as he set it back down on the table. He looked up at the ceiling, still not saying a word. I braced for an explosion.

None came.

Instead, Allan turned back to John. "Enlisting in the Navy," he nodded. "Good decision, John."

Sarah chimed in: "I agree, Daddy, I think..."

April interrupted her. "Wait a minute, Sarah. Who cares what you think? You stole Mom's stopwatch!"

"Not cool, Sarah," Jim said, shaking his head.

John ignored both remarks. "I think it's a good decision, too, Dad."

I turned to Mom. Wasn't it her turn to chime in here? Aren't you going to yell at Sarah? Or, tell John that enlisting may mean he comes home in a body bag?

Instead, Mom's face went blank in a stunned stare. She picked up her wine glass, downed what was left, and reached for the carafe.

Chapter Twenty-Seven

Facing Mecca.

—Mom

I'd been checking myself out in the three-way mirrors in Mom's dressing room, trying to memorize the best angle in my brand new velvet Christmas dress. I was settling on my sideways view when I heard a car horn honking outside. Instantly, I shut the mirror doors. Disguising my weight was hopeless anyway.

The honk didn't sound like Dad's car, but the timing was right. It was Christmas Eve and my father was set to arrive at five-thirty to pick April and me up.

The Stubbs family had gone along with our plans for a low-key Christmas Eve. Tomorrow, Christmas night would be the time for us to celebrate together. This way, they could spend Christmas Eve with their mother's parents, and their aunts and uncles at the Roneys, and, April and I could spend Christmas Eve with Dad and Louise's in the posh section of Bel Air.

I looked at the clock on Mom's dressing table. 5:30 pm on the nose. I grabbed Mom's brush next to the clock and quickly ran it through my long hair, my one attribute that always looked good. I dashed down the front stairs past my mother's gallery along the stairway wall: the portrait of Lincoln, the still life of fruit, the clown Mom painted in oils (with tiny stains marking the night that Dad

199

threw his scotch against the wall), and the newest addition, Allan's Jesus on the cross. I didn't know what happened to the sepia portrait of Jesus with the crown of thorns I'd seen at the house on Plymouth, and I wasn't about to ask.

"Dad's here!" I called out to April, excited but hesitant. It would be the first time in six months my father married Louise that we'd be together. What would he be like? What would it be like spending Christmas Eve with Dad, Louise, and her kids? At the end of camp, Little Louise and I had made up after the cabin change, but who knew if she was still harboring a grudge?

April was at the front door with our gift for Dad in hand, a big bottle of Jean Nate Cologne for Men. He'd told her that that was his new favorite. April and I had agreed to give nothing to Louise. "She's got the moon," Mom had said. "You don't owe that bitch a thing."

We called a hurried goodbye to Mom and Allan who were having cocktails in the living room.

"Wait!" Allan called back. "Girls, come here a moment."

"Dad's waiting," April, said.

"He can wait a minute," I heard my mother say.

April and I stepped into the living room and we stood silent while Allan stubbed out his Winston in the dented silver-rimmed crystal ashtray.

My eyes went from the ashtray to the Christmas tree. He and the boys had brought it home from a lot on Wilshire. It was tall, reaching almost to the ceiling and so full that no trunk showed. Allan boasted it was "the best on the lot." Bill and Jim had dragged it through the front door to the living room, leaving a long trail of pine needles on the beige carpet.

We'd decorated it two nights ago when everyone was around— everyone except Sarah and John who weren't home from school yet. Allan had insisted that we do it together. "We're a family, now," he said.

In the past, Mom had decorated the tree herself. It had never been a big deal.

All our ornaments were cheap colored glass bulbs from Landis Department Store. Mom bought them in molded plastic packages of six. Nothing unique. As I unwrapped wads of toilet paper, I made a silent vow that I would have better ornaments on my tree when I grew up. Santa Clause on a sleigh, reindeer, candy canes, stuff like that. Maybe I'd even get one of those pretty white-flocked trees like the ones in the Crocker Bank on Larchmont. I'd dress it up with lots of tinsel, too. Mom never allowed tinsel. She said it looked cheap.

My mother had been nervous about having enough time to shop for Christmas this year. Allan had put her on a so-called "budget" which, Connie reminded her, was better than shopping on credit like she'd done for the last few years.

Still, for Mom, Christmas was a chore and it always had been. For her, the "goddamn holidays" were a "drag," rather than a time for festive decorations and fun.

Christmas was even more work this year with the Stubbs around. I could tell that she was tired which made her even more high strung. Lately, she'd been snapping at all of us. Well, everyone except Allan.

Bill and Jim seemed to take it all in stride, though. April said that it was probably because they were used to getting yelled at by someone. Allan didn't yell, so I figured it was Sarah or John because their mother probably had been too sick to yell.

Now, Allan lit another cigarette and rested it on the edge of the ashtray. "Girls, your mother here is worried that you might be swayed by all the gifts that your father's probably going to give you for Christmas," he said.

"Swayed?" I asked.

"Won over," Allan answered.

"Oh god, Mom," April sighed, shifting her white wool coat to the hand that held Dad's Christmas gift. "You've got to be kidding."

"Well," Mom said, taking a sip of white wine, "You never know."

"Sheesh, Mom, don't worry," I said, grabbing April's arm. "Dad's been waiting out in his car. We gotta go!"

A vision of our tree caught the corner of my eye as we darted out the door; the boring colored balls, big colored lights clumped in sections. I couldn't help but think that the "best on the lot" had lost its luster.

Dad sat waiting in the driveway with the motor running. I hurried into the car, not noticing it, but once I slipped into the back seat, I recognized the new-car scent mixed with rich leather. I hooked my hands over the smooth leather of the front seat to see the dashboard. "Wow, Dad, you got a new car!"

April, up front next to Dad, had already started fooling with the radio dial. "Sit back down, Heath," she scolded. "Dad's trying to back out the driveway."

I ignored her. "What happened to your old car?" I asked.

"Oh, I got rid of it a few months ago," he said, checking the rear-view mirror.

I settled back into my seat. It had been longer than that since I had last seen him.

We passed under a street lamp and I saw that there was a wooden tray fixed to the back of the front seat. This car was a lot fancier than the Lincoln. At the next stoplight, I noticed that his new car had a hood ornament—RR. "Dad, what's RR stand for?"

"Rolls Royce, Heatherbean."

April let go of the dial, satisfied that she'd found KHJ. "Nice goin' Dad."

"Wow," was all I could think to say as I sunk back into my seat.

Bel Air is a twenty-minute drive from Hancock Park, but that night the roads were empty and we got to the black iron gates leading to Louise's in no time. The ride had been smooth in Dad's new car. It was as if we'd been riding on air as he steered the car through the curves on Sunset.

He pulled into the circular driveway under an umbrella of tiny white lights that had been strung on every manicured tree in Louise's (now Dad's, too) front yard. The house was lit up like a winter wonderland. "Dad, how does Louise do this?" I asked, awed by the magical beauty, thinking about how Mom complains when she hauls out the step stool to hang one measly strand of colored lights over the front door.

Dad ignored my question. He turned off the engine, but before he opened the car door, he said, "Girls, I want you to be friendly to Louise's children." He turned back to look at me.

"Yeah, sure," we answered in unison. He sounded like he meant business.

"And, be very nice to Big Louise," he ordered, his voice firm. "She's gone to a lot of trouble to make this Christmas pleasant for all of us. Understand me?"

We complied, nodding yes. We stepped out of the car and followed Dad dressed in a dark suit, his polished shoes catching the lights from the trees above.

The front door had a huge decorated wreath. It made me think of Mom again. Just like tinsel, she hated wreaths. Not because they looked cheap, but because they reminded her of death.

Dad unlocked the door. Inside, the entry was softly lit. Fresh garland and ribbon was curled around the banister of the front stairway, and I could hear Christmas music coming from the living room. I'd never been to Louise's at holiday time and the house looked like a scene right out of a Christmas movie set with Dad and Louise cast as glamorous central characters.

Louise was seated on the sofa "dressed to the nines," as Mom would say, in creamy white ruffles and chiffon. Her poufy blondish-brown hair looked freshly done with the characteristic flip on one side. Her lips were, as usual, outlined with a darker shade to show off the perfect cupid-bow shape. How could someone so delicate, I wondered, have given birth to Teddy who was so big and Little Louise, so athletic-looking?

Teddy, Louise's third youngest, curled up next to her on the sofa but didn't bother to stand as we entered. Louise stayed seated, too, but held out her hand—the one that wasn't holding a cigarette. "Come in, girls," she said in her wispy voice.

Little Louise and her older siblings, Carl and Bonnie, stood over by the massive Christmas tree on which there wasn't an inch of space without a ribbon, an ornament, or a tiny white light. Bonnie, nearly twenty, smoked a cigarette. Carl, 19, held a crystal glass filled with what looked like Coke. A fire crackled in the fireplace, framed by the mantle decorated with the same garland and ribbon as the banister in the front hall.

"Your decorations are beautiful," I said softly, shaking Louise's hand.

She smiled. "Thank you."

"Ah, don't let Mom fool you," Little Louise piped in, now moving away from the mantle over to us. "Her florist comes with his crew. They do it."

"Merry Christmas!" Bonnie moved towards us, cigarette in hand. Carl, always quiet, stayed back by the mantle and I tried to remember in all the years I had been coming over to play with Little Louise, if we'd ever even said two words to each other.

"Great tree," April said. "But, my God, I've never seen so many presents." I could always count on April never to hold back.

She was right, though. There were piles of gifts in all shapes and sizes under the huge tree. So many that they fanned out on the carpet way beyond the bottom branches. The packages were all store-wrapped with little glittery things on the bows like reindeer and silver bells and I felt a pang of guilt eyeing it with glee. *I don't want them to be swayed...*

Little Louise plopped on the couch on the other side of her mother. "Mom, now that they're here, can we get to the presents?"

Teddy, who still had not said a hello, chimed in. "We've been waiting all day."

"Dinner first," Dad said. "Of course, that's after we have a drink." He turned to Louise. "The usual, darling?"

Louise nodded and lit another Kent. "Thank you, Bob."

Dad had never called Mom "darling."

Bonnie had stubbed out her cigarette and reached for another from the silver box on the coffee table.

Carl sneered at her. "Why the hell do you do that, Bonnie?"

"What?" Bonnie reached for the crystal lighter beside the box. She wasn't as dressed up as her mother, but she looked just as rich in her black skirt with the ribbon at her waist and tucked in pink cashmere sweater. She was around the same age as Sarah Stubbs and had a similar tailored style, but Bonnie's clothes looked designer, and she wore diamonds in her ears instead of pearls.

"Cigarettes," Carl answered. "You don't want to be like Mom and Bob, hooked on the things. They're bad for you."

"Now, Ca-arl, it's Christmas." Louise said, sweetly.

Carl looked away from her. "Sorry, Mom."

April wore a plain pair of black slacks with a white sweater. She could get away with anything, but when you're heavy like me, it's tough. That's why I'd been in Mom's mirrors earlier. My mother had charged my new dress a week ago at The Broadway. It was the first time she'd used Allan's Broadway charge-a-card and it went right through! She was so relieved, confessing, "I'll never get over worrying about money."

I'd been excited to wear the green velvet dress. Until tonight. Suddenly, I felt stupid in it with the babyish empire-waist. Little Louise who looked so grown up in her plaid skirt and sweater. We'd only been here ten minutes and I was ready to go home.

Dad sat next to Louise on the plush sofa. I couldn't help but think back to last year when he'd been in a casual belted jumpsuit on our worn white sectional on Christmas morning. He was relishing his new surroundings, moving about with confidence and ease as if he'd always lived this way.

Louise and Dad finished their drinks when Cecile, Louise's maid, came in to announce dinner. I remembered that she wore a black uniform at night and a grey uniform during the day. I'd asked Mom once when I'd gotten home from Louise's why Lupe never changed out of her everyday white uniform. Her reply was simple. "Cecile gets paid a lot more."

The dining room dazzled under the sparkling chandelier. Each place was set with lace-edged linen napkins, place cards, fine china, and crystal goblets. In the center, an arrangement of greens with holly berries and white flowers overflowed, separated by two large silver candelabras with white candles. The candles were not red and green, like on our table at home. I felt guilty again, that I preferred Louise's table décor.

I sat next to Big Louise, who took the head of the table. Teddy (whom, Mom claimed, was Louise's favorite) was on the other side of her. April sat between Bonnie and Carl. Little Louise was next to me, and Dad at the head of the other end of the table.

Little Louise tried to be nice, asking me about my friend, Mary Jo, school, things like that. Her mother must have given her the same speech that Dad had given us in the car.

Cecile served prime rib to us from a big silver platter. There was no buffet. No turkey like at home. Home... I thought of all of this beauty around me that money could buy—including my own father. I started to get uncomfortable. My father, meanwhile, looked so at home at the head of the table.

Louise's table.

"Do you like school, Heather?" Big Louise tried to make conversation with me.

"Kinda."

"Do you want to whisper to me what you think you might get for Christmas?"

"It doesn't really matter."

I couldn't believe what was coming from my own mouth. I was always nice and polite. Jolly, happy Heather. But, I couldn't help myself. My hatred was growing by the minute and I couldn't stand her kids even though they were trying to be nice. I didn't want to believe that my father wanted all of this more than us. That *I* had been awed by all this wealth at the beginning of the night.

Dad looked over at Little Louise. "Fred, can you pass the horse-radish sauce, please?"

He used that nickname again. I wanted to scream.

"Fred?" April asked.

"Silly, huh," Little Louise replied. But, the tone of her voice didn't sound like she thought it was so silly. It sounded like she liked being called Fred. A lot.

April went back to picking the cranberries out of her pear salad. Louise had given up on me and now turned to her beloved Teddy. I focused on my plate and jabbed my fork into the crispy Yorkshire pudding.

••

Dessert was served in the living room. The table lights had been dimmed and the tree looked magnificent. Dad started handing out the packages, leaving his from April and me under the tree, hoping, I was sure, that Louise wouldn't notice that we'd brought nothing for her.

April let out a big hooray when she opened a new state-of-the-art stereo with speakers. The gifts just kept coming. I got clothes, books, a collectable Sound of Music Doll from the fancy doll section at Bullock's Wilshire. It was like nothing I'd ever seen. Little Louise, Teddy, all of them, except Carl, tore at their packages. Carl, opened each gift at a snail's pace, saving the wrapping.

Suddenly, I couldn't stand it anymore and stood up. The two-toned pink unopened box from I. Magnin that had been on my lap fell to the floor. "I want to go home, Dad."

The room turned silent except for the soft sound of Bing Crosby's White Christmas in the background.

Everyone froze with half-opened packages in their laps. April shot me a look. It wasn't a mean one, more like, "what the heck?"

Dad smiled through clenched teeth. "Heatherbean, you still have presents to open."

"Take her home, Bob." Louise's normally wispy voice sounded harsh.

Dad mouthed an "I'm sorry" to her and told us to follow him to the car.

April slowly stood, thanking Louise for the gifts. In the awkward silence, my sister and I picked up some of our gift boxes. Carl offered to help and followed us with the rest of the gifts to Dad's car in the driveway. Teddy, Little Louise, and Bonnie stayed back with their mother.

Dad slammed the door behind me and I sunk into the buttery leather in the back seat of his car. April tried to talk to him up front. "Dad, she didn't mean it. She's just a kid. You know, the little Louise thing at camp and all."

"Nice try, April, but it's all ruined now."

I was upset but didn't cry. I had wanted to go home, and, now I was going home. I hated these people and I couldn't pretend anymore. I didn't want gifts from Louise. She'd taken everything away from me. I just wanted to go home to my mother, to Allan, and to our dumb ugly tree.

The rest of the ride was silent. When we reached our house, there was no goodbye. No Merry Christmas, just the purr of the Rolls Royce engine as he waited for us to get out of his car.

I slipped into bed. The weight of the night settled in my stomach with a dull ache. April stayed downstairs to explain to Mom and Allan why we were back so soon. Thankfully, the Stubbs kids weren't back yet and I was alone. Sarah would be back soon. I turned off the light so that I wouldn't have to talk. I lay awake in the dark. I need to face Mecca, I thought, using one of Mom's expressions. Dad picked them over us.

Chapter Twenty-Eight

Double drill and no canteen.

—Mom

"Dr. Ferguson told me what to do about Sarah," Mom said to Aunt Carolyn, who sat cross-legged on the floor of Mom's dressing room cuddling our cat, Thomasina. Aunt Carolyn listened as my mother worked to clean up the accumulation of drugstore cosmetics scattered across the counter of her dressing table. It was Carolyn's turn to listen to Mom's problems, rather than the other way around.

"Ferguson said that, Sarah was there first, and that if I wanted my marriage to work, I'd better try to get along with her."

Since Mom had married Allan, Aunt Carolyn had been over more. Allan had said that "a nice family atmosphere" would be good for her, might help her to not feel so lonely.

"It's a Catholic thing," Mom had explained. "They're big on the casseroles, taking in people, things like that."

Today, Carolyn looked good. She wore a baggy cotton blouse tucked into high-waisted jeans. There were not any spots on her shirt and her jeans were clean. She hadn't colored her hair since the wedding, so a few inches of dark roots showed, but it was combed and neatly pulled back in a ponytail. I could tell she was trying, with her orange lipstick a touch of eyeliner that kicked up a little at the corner of her eyes. Still, it didn't mask the strange, far-off look in her eyes ever since Uncle Charlie left her.

Being with Aunt Carolyn reminded me of how much I missed my cousin, Jonathan. He and his little brother, Robert, spent more time at Uncle Charlie's apartment now. And, Aunt Carolyn, alone, wasn't fun to be around. Bill and everyone made an effort to cheer her up. April tried to get her to talk about horses. Bill tried with funny jokes but couldn't get a laugh out of her. Jim kept his music down low so it wouldn't make her "nervous," and I offered to read her some of the less-secret entries in the diary she'd given me. She politely refused and insisted that I continue to write for myself. "Once you share it with someone else, it isn't yours anymore."

Nothing made her happy and her sadness frustrated and scared me. I didn't understand why she couldn't pull herself together and why we all had to suffer because of it. Wasn't it enough that Mom had a new husband and four new step-kids? She shouldn't have to worry about the burden of Aunt Carolyn, too.

Mom, meanwhile, took Ferguson's advice and gave Sarah compliments. "Sarah you look pretty today." It didn't sound genuine. And yet, Allan continued to remain oblivious to Mom and Sarah's iciness. Or, maybe feigned obliviousness was his way of dealing with his daughter and his new wife not getting along.

The night before she went back to school, Sarah asked if I wanted to come visit her at college down in San Diego. "It's much prettier than LA," she'd said. "You'd love it."

"Sure!" This was exciting. Me, visit Sarah at college? Sleep in a real dorm room? Who knew if it would ever happen, but it made me feel good that she'd asked. She wanted me around which was more than I can say for my own father, whom I hadn't heard from since that awful night on Christmas Eve.

That memory still stung. Clearly, I'd been replaced. My father had chosen Little Louise over me. So, I tried not to think about him. When I did, it hurt too much.

Soon, Sarah and John went back to school and things around the house went back to our new way of life—Allan getting up early, us going to school. Mom and Allan coming home, Mom and Allan having cocktails in the living room at night, dinner with Bill, Jim and April in the Green Room, then back into the private world of our own bedrooms at night. We were settling into a routine, after all.

That was, until that second Saturday in January.

The house was freezing that morning, and I'd slipped out of bed before eight o'clock to press the top black button on the panel in the hallway outside my bedroom door. Warm air rumbled through our big old wooden house making familiar thump-thump noises in the wall. I hoped that Mom wouldn't wake up. She'd gotten used to not turning on the heat after Dad left and now that Mom was married to Allan, I could turn on the heater without worrying that the bill wouldn't get paid.

Back in my room, I crouched in my flannel nightgown next to the heating vent on the wall. The air from the heater smelled stale and dusty from having been dormant for so long. But soon, I could feel the warmth as it reached the second floor vent.

Outside my room, I heard Allan's footsteps going past followed by the tap-tap of his K-Swiss tennis shoes on the back stairs. I was relieved. He hadn't turned the heat off.

Warmed up, I slipped back into bed and pulled out my diary.

> *Saturday, January 11ᵗʰ—Bill thinks that he owns the den next to his room. Well, he doesn't. And, I told him so yesterday. He said that it's because the den's attached to his room and that you have to go through his room to get there. So now every time I want to*

watch TV in the den, I have to get permission from Bill?
April doesn't care cuz she never watches TV, but—

Where was that marching band music coming from? I put my pen down, closed the diary and listened. When I opened the bedroom door, the music got louder, blasting from the hi-fi in the Music Room. Still in my Lanz flannel nightgown, I stepped into the hall. April cracked her bedroom door a few inches and popped her head out. Her hair, as usual, was rolled up in concentrated juice cans.

Bill came down the little hall adjoining April's room. "God," he said, "not this again."

Hurrah for the flag of free! May it wave as our standard forever.

I could barely hear him over the music. "What?"

Bill shouted above the noise, "I'd hoped that that crap would be over now that we have a maid."

"What crap?" asked April.

Bill wore only plaid pajama bottoms. His body was compact and tight and I hadn't noticed before that he had such narrow shoulders. I looked away from him, embarrassed by his half-nakedness.

"The chores," Bill said.

April and I responded in unison. "Chores?"

"And, what's with the music?" I said.

"Dad thinks that John Phillip Sousa's music motivates."

April stepped into the hallway. Her blue nylon nightgown was slightly see-through and Bill's eyes went straight to her huge breasts. April crossed her hands over her chest to hide them.

Bill turned red in the face, aware that she'd caught him staring and looked away.

My mother appeared in the doorway. Other than the day of her wedding to Allan, I'd rarely seen her out of her nightgown before ten in the morning. She was dressed in thick cotton JAX pants and a button-down blouse that was partially tucked in, showing only half of her slim waistline. She didn't have her face on, just fake eyelashes. Without the lipstick and the rouge, Mom's eyes looked more like two black spiders in a bowl of Cream of Wheat. She gripped the banister and staggered over to us near the landing. "I don't do morning."

"What's this all about?" April asked her.

"Allan wants us to start doing chores on Saturday like they used to do back on Plymouth."

April and I looked over at Bill. We were in sync again. "You used to do chores on Saturday?"

"To band music?" I added.

He shrugged and nodded yes. "Better get dressed," he said, heading back to his room.

"Mom?" April asked. "You in on this?"

"Don't make waves." Mom picked up the back of her hair with her fingers to add height. "It'll only be for a few weeks, then, he'll forget about it. Not to worry."

Mom pushed away from the banister, straightened her shoulders and tucked in the rest of her blouse. Stiff-legged, she made her way to the back stairs. "Hurry and get dressed, you guys. I've got to go down there and help him with the breakfast like I promised."

"Wait a minute," I said. "What about Lupe?"

Allan called up from below: "Pancakes are on!"

Mom sighed, debating whether to answer me right then. "Later, Heatherbean," she said, starting down the back stairs. "I need coffee."

My sister and I headed back into our rooms to get dressed. What was I supposed to wear to do chores? I never wore pants. My thighs were too fat. I slipped one of my cotton empire-waist dresses over my head and pulled on a pair of nylon pantaloons, the ones with the lace edge on the pant legs that I wore everyday under my school uniform skirt. Thank god for pantaloons. At least if I had to bend down, Jim and Bill wouldn't see my underwear, or worse, my upper thighs. Just as I was about to leave my room, I saw my diary lying on the unmade bed. Quickly, I shoved it in the back of the drawer of the nightstand.

The smell of pancakes began to waft through the house, encouraging me to speed up. I threw on my tan Keds, proud of the cool little blue label on the heel, and dashed down for breakfast.

Bill was already at the stove dishing up from a platter stacked with lopsided pancakes. He piled his plate high with lumpy pancakes. What was in them to make them bulge like that?

Allan was busy pouring another lumpy-rounded circle of batter onto the hot griddle. "Heath," he said turning around, "come get a plate of my famous corn pancakes."

Corn? "Sure," I said, and held my plate out.

Mom, leaning one hip against the counter on the opposite side of the kitchen, struggled with the manual can opener and a can of Welch's Grape Juice Concentrate. Her fingers were contorted and flexed to prevent her long fingernails from breaking. One had already been opened and dumped into one of the yellow plastic pitchers the Stubbs had brought with them in the move. We hadn't owned a plastic pitcher before the Stubbses came around. My mother had only bought concentrated orange juice for the cans April used to straighten her hair at night. We never actually made the juice; she just pushed the frozen orange tube of concentrate down the disposal.

April was already eating at the table in the Green Room wearing an old pair of navy culottes and a big sweatshirt. Her feet were bare. "How'd you get dressed so fast?" I asked her.

"I threw on the first thing that I saw," she said, smearing Mom's safflower margarine on her pancakes.

I sat down next to her and Bill wistfully thinking how I would love to be able to put on "the first thing that I saw." How freeing it must feel to not have to think about what I was going to wear, whether I'd look fat, much less, whether it would fit.

I reached for the stick of real butter and began spreading it in between pancakes on my plate. Bill passed the syrup while April eyed as I poured it over the stack of cakes. She watched me take a big bite. "Ummm, these are good!" I had no idea corn pancakes could be delicious.

April raised her eyebrows. "Pancakes are fattening."

"I know," I said, taking another bite.

Soon, Jim appeared in the Green Room, disheveled as usual, wearing the same grey Pendleton and tan thin-wale cords he wore most days. He carried a plate filled with the pancakes and a huge glass of grape juice and plopped himself in the chair next to me. Ed, the dog, followed behind him and found his way under the table, curling up by Bill's feet. Jim reached over and snatched one of my pancakes.

"Hey!"

He laughed and put it back. Then, he reached across me with his fork to Bill's plate and stabbed an extra pancake off his plate, dripping the whole mess over Mom's green tablecloth.

"Pig!" Bill said to Jim.

"Shut up, pint-size. I'm bigger than you and need to eat more."

I prayed that Jim wouldn't tease me about my being fat and not needing that pancake but he didn't.

Bill opened his mouth about to get the last word in when April interrupted. "Stop it, both of you!"

A few quiet minutes of eating passed and then the military music started up again. "Allan must have sent Marilyn to the Music Room to turn the record over," Bill said, around a mouthful of pancakes.

"What kind of chores does your Dad have in mind?" I asked Bill and Jim.

Jim cracked a ghoulish grin. "Cleaning toilets."

"Quit it, Jim," Bill said, shaking his head.

Allan called out from the kitchen, ordering us to clear the table and line up in the pantry. "Aren't they going to eat?" I asked April, gesturing at Allan and Mom.

"Guess not."

"This is like *The Sound of Music*," I whispered to her, "You know the part where the Captain whistles and makes the kids all line up."

"I hate to tell you, Heath, but we're not in Austria and Allan is no Captain Von Trapp."

We stood across the pantry, in an alcove where Mom kept every kind of liquor and mixer one could imagine was lined up against the tile backsplash like trophies on a mantle. Mom had everything, including a bottle of Pernod (whatever that was) that had sticky brown drips on the label.

Just as Allan was about to give out our list of chores, the phone rang.

"Just ignore it," Allan ordered.

It kept ringing. It was up to eight rings when Mom, more alert now, interrupted. "It might be Papa, or maybe Carolyn." A slight panic made her voice waver.

"Oh, yeah, sorry Marilyn," Allan said. "Go ahead. Take it in the other room."

My mother sped through the swinging door that led to the dining room. She must have gotten the phone in the Music Room because the music stopped, and so did the phone's ringing.

Allan began with what Mom would later refer to as: "Our marching orders."

"Bill, you're in charge of cleaning the pool. Jim, you're in charge of trash and cleaning up after Ed. Scratch that. You and Bill *both* will be responsible for cleaning up Ed's mess on the lawn. April, you're in charge of cleaning up the kitchen after meals. Heather, you are to help her, and both of you are responsible for cleaning the Orange cat's litter box."

I looked over at the piles of dirty breakfast dishes on the kitchen counter with dread. Those would take forever to wash.

April interrupted. "But...."

"No buts." Allan took a pack of Winston's out of the pocket of his navy striped t-shirt. He peeled off the foil to expose one side of the cigarette pack and tapped the opposite end to get a cigarette out.

"Every Saturday?" April asked.

"Every *day*," he said. "Chores build character."

April's hands went straight to her hips. "Are you kidding me? What about Lupe?"

Allan reached for a book of matches lying on the counter. "Lupe quit."

"What?" How could Lupe quit?

I broke away from the gathering and ran into her room. It was empty. Even the little altar was gone. On the dresser, she'd left one lone Virgin Mary statue. "Wow," I said aloud, "she really *is* gone."

Allan called after me. His voice had softened. "Heather, c'mon back in here."

I wanted to cry. Forget the chores. Lupe had been with us for three years. How could she leave without saying good-bye? It was Molly all over again.

On my way back to the pantry I heard April. "Lupe was a complainer. Doesn't surprise me."

"Well, it surprises ME!" I said, joining them. "Lupe always smiled."

219

"She wasn't smiling much lately," Allan said, trying to lighten the situation.

"After you kids went to bed, she told your mother and me that she was leaving. She said that it's too much work since we've moved in."

"Didn't you offer her more money?" April asked.

"No way. We'll get a cleaning lady twice a week instead. You kids are all capable. There's no need for live-in help."

"What'd Mom say?" April asked.

"Your mother pleaded with her to stay. But, Lupe'd made up her mind. She was already packed."

Allan held out his hand to me. "Lupe wanted me to tell you goodbye. You, specifically."

That made me feel a little better and I smiled. "Where'd she go?"

"To live with her sister back in Mexico."

The four of us kids stood quiet, absorbing the loss of Lupe and the luxury of having her around to pick up after us.

Bill broke the silence. "Knew it was too good to be true. Having a maid around day and night."

Allan lit his cigarette. "O.K. let's get started. Bill, the pool..."

Just then, Mom came back on the scene. "That was Carolyn," she sighed. "And, now no Lupe. Jesus. I wasn't wild about her. She holed up in her room too much, but she was an extra pair of hands," she said, looking at Allan.

"The kids are on scene now," he reassured. "They'll pick up the slack."

Mom reached up to twist the ends of her hair. "Just the same, I'm calling Connie now to see if her Vicky will come two days a week."

Chapter Twenty-Nine

He'd screw a snake.

—Mom

The afternoon was short, the watery winter sun setting early like it does in February. I lowered the window shade over the desk in my bedroom to shut out the approaching darkness, picked up my pencil, and tried to concentrate on the page of Pre-Algebra problems due tomorrow. I had no clue how to solve them.

I had become frustrated trying to follow the math lesson when bored in class so it was no wonder I didn't understand my homework. Besides, I was distracted. In the living room below, the steady murmur of Allan and Mom's conversation kept drawing my attention.

Allan had just gotten home after having a drink with Dad at Scandia up on the Sunset Strip.

I tapped the corner of the Pre-Algebra workbook my pencil. My worksheet became a blur.

The meeting had been arranged when Dad called Allan and asked to meet him for drinks so they could talk. He never told Allan what the meeting was about, just that it was something that should be discussed in person. Mom told me about it two days ago.

"Why does Dad want to meet Allan? He hasn't even talked to *us* since Christmas Eve."

Mom shook her head. "He just called Allan at the office and asked to meet him at 5:30 on Wednesday."

My mother's lack of insight gave no comfort. I'd spent the last two days wondering what Dad was going to say. Was he going to tattle on me about how badly I'd behaved at Christmas? Would Allan tell Dad I wasn't doing my homework?

This morning, I'd overheard Mom advising Allan to get to Scandia early. "It'll give you the upper hand," she'd said.

Why did Allan need the upper hand?

I put my pencil down and tried to picture the scene at Scandia. Dad would be sitting at the copper-topped bar, impeccably dressed in a dark suit, white-monogramed shirt and silver tie, nursing his second scotch on the rocks by the time Allan showed up. Would he grasp Allan's hand when he arrived and hold onto it as he said 'Good to see ya, buddy' as he always did with his friends?

I imagined Allan, stiff-legged, taking a seat next to him on the leather barstool. His back would be ramrod straight in his off-the-rack brown suit and short-sleeved button-down shirt. He'd order a gin, light on the tonic.

When Allan arrived home half an hour ago, I'd ditched my homework in two seconds flat. April and I ran down the stairs.

Allan had raised his hands to hold us back. "Girls, I need a few minutes." He looked serious. The lines on his forehead were etched deep under the light of the hall chandelier. He loosened his tie as my mother took his briefcase and set it down on the dining room chair. "I'll call you down and tell you everything after I have a few words with your mother," he said. Abruptly, he turned and headed straight for the living room. "Marilyn, get me a drink."

••

For the past two months, there'd been no phone calls from Dad. No letters. Nothing. I was afraid to call him. What if Little

Louise answered and I'd have to talk to her? Or worse, Big Louise might answer and hang up after she heard my voice.

That scene from Christmas Eve haunted me, Louise sitting on the puffed-up brocade sofa with the huge cushions swallowing up her delicate frame. I could still smell her Joy perfume, overpowering the natural scent of evergreen from the Christmas tree in the corner. I'd never forget the stony look on her porcelain face when she opened her pencil-lined lips. The way she spoke that night, disconnecting me. "Bob, take *her* home."

My mother had been right about the golden rule. Whoever has the gold, rules.

While I waited in my room to hear about the meeting with Dad, I wanted to ask Bill if I could listen to music on his headphones to get my mind off it, but he was already listening on them and I didn't want to bug him and then get into a whole conversation about the Dad and Allan meeting.

It was hard to distract myself from the scenarios my brain was concocting.

Would Dad explain to Allan why he hadn't contacted April or me? Maybe after telling Allan about how I'd upset Big Louise he'd tell him that he'd give me a second chance. Or what if the worst happened? Maybe Dad would say he needed a few more months without seeing us to let Big Louise cool down after I'd made such a scene. I was still sitting at my desk, my unfinished homework before me, by the time Allan finally called April and me downstairs an hour later.

My mother was seated next to Allan on the curved living room couch, not in her usual chair by the doorway. From the smudge marks on the wine glass in her hand, it looked to be her second or third. April settled herself a few feet away from them on the couch and I sat cross-legged on the living room floor, facing all three of them. There was no sign of Bill or Jim.

Allan swallowed what looked like the last bit of gin in his glass. The ice clinked as he set it down in front of him on the coffee table. He picked it up again and gave it a few shakes, rattling the ice against the crystal. He brought it to his lips and tilted his head back to get that last drop. Behind him on the sofa, a dim table light framed his silhouette. I focused on the diamond-shaped pattern of pleats on the light's shade, each section, separated by a fabric-covered button.

"As you know, your father and I met tonight for drinks," he began. I counted the diamond-shaped pleats. One, two....

He paused. I shifted my gaze from the lampshade to study Allan's face for some hint at what he was going to say. His thick eyebrows drooped heavy on his forehead. My mother reached for another cigarette to light off the end of the one in her mouth.

Allan looked back and forth between April and me. And then, like ripping a Band Aid off a wound, he just said it.

"Your father is disowning you."

The room grew silent. Melting ice cubes shifted in Allan's glass. I was stunned and looked over at April who seemed deep in thought as if deliberating how to react. Outside, a car drove by.

Allan handed Mom his glass. "Marilyn, get me another drink."

I finally spoke. "You mean, like, get rid of us?"

"From the sound of it, Heath," April said, her voice so matter-of-fact, as if she was expecting this.

Mom was stone-faced as she took her wine glass, along with Allan's glass and slipped away to the bar in the butler's pantry without saying a word.

"Look, this is hard for me to be so blunt, but I don't know how else to tell you." He paused. "I suggested that he speak to you girls about this himself."

I wasn't sure if I was more worried about how bad Allan felt telling us this, or how bad I felt hearing it. I had thought up lots of scenarios over the past hour. But, this bad? I tried to understand. I wasn't even sure what his words meant.

"So, is he going to call us?" I asked. I'd had visions of Dad taking just April and me to Perino's for dinner on Wednesday nights. Wasn't that the night divorced dad's saw their kids? Divorced parents saw their kids. That's what they did, right? They didn't just give them away to the next available father.

"No," Allan replied. He reached for a cigarette from the packet of Winston's in the breast pocket of his short-sleeve shirt, shook one out, and held it in his hand.

"Why isn't he going to call us and tell us himself?" I asked calmly, amazed at my own self-possession.

"Your father said that he's finished."

"Finished with what?" I asked.

Allan reached for the lighter on the table with his free hand and lit his cigarette then put it in the ashtray. He placed both hands on his thighs and looked down at the floor. He took a deep inhale, then exhaled slowly as if he needed to steady himself for what he had to say next. He straightened and looked at both of us.

I asked again. "Finished with *what*?"

"Finished with being your father."

I parted my lips to speak, but no words came out. Everything stopped.

He held the burning cigarette in between his thumb and forefinger. "'They're yours now,' is what he said to me."

"Just like that?" April asked, her voice frosty. "Over a goddamn drink at Scandia he's getting rid of his kids?" She shook her head. "Doesn't surprise me, though. Hell, he left Mom over a roast beef dinner, so what's to stop him from getting rid of his daughters over a cocktail at Scandia?"

I looked down at my lap, tracing the plaid pattern of my wool uniform skirt. It was all sinking in now. Dad's words *"Disowned... Finished... They're yours."* He'd chosen Little Louise over me.

I felt heavy, as if it would take a crane to lift me from the floor, a weightiness I'd never felt before. Not the heaviness from being fat, or even like a block of cement. This was different, like someone was pushing down on my shoulders. Weighting me down hard against the carpeted floor. I fought to sit upright and hold back the tears that welled. But when I looked up at Allan and saw the pain in his own face, they spilled over, burning my skin.

Mom had returned with her refilled wine glass and Allan's drink. I looked at her.

"He hates me because I was bad." I bent my face down to dry my cheeks with my shirtsleeve. She reached over and patted my head before she sat down on the couch. That was all? A pat on the head? Was she actually happy now? That he wouldn't be in our lives and complicate things?

"It's my fault," I sobbed, trying hard to suck in air between the sobs to get my words out. "I was mean to Big Louise at Christmas. If I'd just have gotten along with Little Louise and..."

April cut me off. "It is not your fault, Heath." Her voice was soothing, motherly, exactly what I needed.

"Damn right!" Mom's voice grating and angry, which I did not need. "It's not your fault. It's that idiot, Louise!"

"Mar-i-lyn," Allan said calmly, stubbing out his cigarette in the ashtray. "Let's be careful here and stay on course."

Allan looked at me, deliberately softening his tone. "April and your mother are right. It's not your fault, Heather. Your father never said that it was. It's just that he thinks life would be a lot simpler now if I took over as your father."

I nodded, tightening my lips, and waited for Allan to say more, but he was silent. "What do I tell my friends? That my Dad doesn't like us anymore? Or, that my dad thinks that it's *simpler* for him not to be my dad anymore?"

April turned to Allan. "Dad didn't tell you everything." Her eyes were red. "I called him."

"What?" Mom asked.

April took a big breath. "I didn't want to tell you, Mom, but I was upset because Allan makes us do chores and stuff. I called Dad to tell him to order Allan to stop making us work around the house."

My crying came to an abrupt halt. "You did?" I couldn't believe she'd do that and not tell me. I had to hand it to her, though. Calling Dad like that took guts.

"Jesus Christ!" Mom said. "You went behind my back?"

April shot back. "Mom, I have a right to call my own father, you know."

Allan sipped his fresh gin.

"What did he say?" I turned to April.

"He told me that Allan's in charge now and that I need to follow his rules."

This got a reaction from Allan. "Really? Hmmm."

"Yep. And that he didn't want to disrupt our new home life."

My eyes stung and my nose was stuffy. "So, you knew this was coming April?"

My sister shook her head. Her long honey-colored hair whipped around her face, stray strands catching the wetness on her cheeks. When she spoke again, her voice was throatier. "Not the part that he was disowning us."

I looked up at Mom. "He just wants us out of the way so that Big Louise will be happy. I'm right, aren't I?"

Mom turned to Allan. "Tell 'em what you said to Bob."

He put his drink back down. "I was getting to that."

The strain on Allan's face suddenly lifted. The lines on his forehead seemed to smooth out and the shadows disappeared. "I want you girls to know that I am proud and happy to have you as my daughters. I would like you to consider me your father."

"Did you tell Dad—I mean, *him*—that?" April asked.

"I did."

"What did he say?" I asked Allan.

"He said, 'great.'"

"That's it? 'Great?'"

"That's it," Allan nodded slowly.

"April. Heather. I love your mother. And I love you girls. Your father wants to be out of the picture. And," he added, staring back and forth between my sister and me, "I *am* in the picture and want to be a part of your lives."

"Isn't he wonderful?" Mom said, reaching for Allan's hand.

He moved his hand away. "Marilyn, now's not the time to, as you would say, 'water my plant.'"

April stood with a weak smile, her cheeks now dry. "Thanks, Allan. You did what you had to do and, well, it was nice of you."

"No, April," he replied. "I didn't *have to do* anything. I am not a man who would give up my children. A man who would give up his children is not a real man."

Just then, Jim appeared at the entrance to the living room.

"Oh, shit," April said, looking over at him. "Does this mean that he's my brother for real?"

Allan opened his mouth, probably to scold her for her language when I busted out laughing. The tension finally broke.

Mom and Allan stifled their laughs. Poor Jim looked puzzled.

I picked myself off the living room floor. My crying had stopped, but the heaviness was still there. It was over. Dad was out of my life. Just like that, over a drink at Scandia.

Chapter Thirty

First you abhor, then you tolerate, then you embrace.

—Mom

It took me forever to fall asleep later that night. On my way upstairs, I'd overheard Mom. "I feel awful, Allan. That son-of-a-bitch dumped the girls like they were nothing."

I wish I hadn't heard that, but I had. I couldn't let go of the heaviness in my chest. Was that my heart aching? I kept repeating over in my head what might have happened if I'd played along with Little Louise becoming my stepsister and Big Louise becoming my stepmother. If I'd been nicer or more polite, maybe I'd still have my dad. But it would have hurt Mom. I couldn't hurt Mom. Kiss up to the woman who had hurt and betrayed my mother? Never.

I woke to the familiar sound of Allan's footsteps down the hall-way leading to the back stairs. My mother would tell me later that he had been blown away by what Dad had said to him at Scandia. "Allan doesn't know from evil."

April seemed to be able to slough everything off and just concentrate on her boyfriends. How did she do that? I would never have boyfriends to make me forget bad stuff. What boy wants a fat girl? Heck, what boy wants a fat girl whose father doesn't even want her? Over the past few months, Dad had become a phantom in my life. The previous night had sealed it.

I'd tossed and turned so much during the night that my flannel nightgown was wrapped around my body like a mummy. But, the heaviness I'd felt the night before was gone. I slipped out of bed, feeling the chill of the house, and pulled the shades up on all four big windows in my room to let in the morning light. The muted winter sun seemed to be telling me that all was not lost. At least Allan wanted me. I would not be fatherless.

I went to the hallway heating panel to push the top black button and turn on the heat when April appeared outside her bedroom door ready for school in her navy uniform with a stack of books in her hands.

"You're up early," she said, lifting a forearm to adjust her glasses.

"Shhh...don't tell that it's me turning on the heat," I whispered.

"Ah I think Allan already suspects it's you."

"Maybe," I replied. "Hey, you forgot to put in your contacts."

"No time. I'm late this morning. Gotta go," she said, rushing to the back stairs. "Traffic's a bitch on Western if I don't leave by seven."

I pressed the button and the heat began the familiar rumble through the thick walls. My sister and I hadn't said a word to each other about Dad. What was there to say?

••

In June, Mom and Allan had been married eight months, and I was grateful for the busy, sometimes-chaotic cadence that had become our household with the Stubbs. The news had been bad this past spring with the assassination of Martin Luther King, Jr. and, recently, Robert F. Kennedy. There wasn't time to mope around about the news or my father not wanting me when there was constant action around the house.

My mother, however, was not as grateful. She had been without household help since Lupe quit back in February. "Clean house" topped the list each day in her tiny spiral tablet and it was never crossed off. The honeymoon was over.

Mom complained on the phone to Charlotte. "No paid help is the way they keep house in the god-damn Midwest where he's from. His mother still hangs wash out on a line for chrissakes."

Since marrying, she hadn't had much of a social life, either. "I feel like I don't have any more friends to entertain," she told Connie on her morning call. "It's all about the kids with Allan. They come first. And, you know me," she added, "I'm hardly a kiddy person."

••

Summer vacation with all the kids underfoot ratcheted Mom's workload up a notch. Plus, Mom was also keeping an eye on Aunt Carolyn whose depression was getting worse despite seeing Dr. Ferguson on a regular basis. Mom complained to Papa that she'd been operating on all four burners. "Papa, I'm living on Valium by day and wine by night."

John was home only for a few days that June before he shipped out with the Navy. Sarah, using any excuse to get away, had signed up for summer classes at her college in San Diego. Still, the rest of us teenagers around the house all day was a recipe for chaos.

It started with the animals. Ed, the shepherd-mix mutt who'd arrived with the Stubbs, discovered the fun of chasing April's new dachshund, Shatzi, also known as Hot Dog. Ed barked non-stop hunting the little dog from hiding places under side tables, chairs or anything else where she could hide, terrorizing her. Thomasina, the cat, was traumatized when Jim cut the hair on its tail, shaping it to look like a Christmas tree. April accused him of animal cruelty.

That same day, Jim called up to April's open bedroom window from the backyard. "Oh, Aaaa-prrrr-illl," he taunted in a sickeningly sweet voice.

My sister leaned out of her window to find her Shatzi, trembling on top of an upside-down metal trash can lid, floating in the middle of the pool. Panicked, she tore downstairs out to the pool. She stopped at the edge and leaned down, frantically raking the pool, stopped at the edge. "Be still, Shatzi, Momma's going to help you."

Nearby, Jim stretched out on a chaise, placing his hands behind his head and crossing his legs, a smug, smug grin on his face as he watched.

Shatzi, eager to get closer to April, tried to move forward on the lid and lost her balance. She and the lid dunked under water. Just the lid popped up. No Shatzi. April shrieked then jumped in to save her as Mom came rushing outside.

Up from the water like Venus from her shell, April rose holding Shatzi who was drenched but alive. Sopping wet in what had been a bright yellow shift, now muted and plastered to her shapely body, April stepped out of the pool. She let go of Shatzi who ran straight to Jim on the chaise. The dog planted herself right next to him, and shook wildly to dry her coat.

Jim sprung from the chaise. "Jesus! You little Hot Dog! What the hell?!"

My sister, ringing out her hair in a thick twist, hollered back. "You are fucking nuts, Jim! How do you think up this shit?"

He laughed. "What? It's funny. I would'a gone in to get the dumb dog. I wasn't going to let it drown."

"Oh, really? You just sat there on your fat ass!"

Mom, standing over near the covered porch, was mad. "Enough you two! I don't need this!"

"April started it."

"The hell I did!"

"Didn't I tell you both? I don't need this," Mom shouted. Then, looking around, "Where are my cigarettes? I need a cigarette."

As they argued, the phone was ringing off the hook.

After the pool incident, Ed had escaped the house and wandered unleashed around Fremont. Hank, the patrolman, found him near the Olympic Boulevard gate and managed to lure him into the patrol car with a half-eaten bologna sandwich from his lunch. He returned Ed to our front door with a firm warning to my mother: "Mrs. Stubbs, keep an eye on your dog. If he escapes again, I'm calling the dog catcher!"

I counted the weeks until school started again. It was going to be one long, hot summer.

••

By the end of the summer, Vicky, a new maid, came to Mom's rescue. Mom had gotten her from Connie Rossi. Vicky worked at the Rossi's three days a week, so she was free to work for us two days a week, which, according to my mother, "wasn't chopped liver," and it beat the alternative, which was no help at all.

I wasn't prepared for Vicky. She wasn't like the maids on our street who wore white cotton button-down dresses with aprons and white sneakers with nylons.

Vicky wore what she called "her own little uniform" which consisted of tight spandex pants in wild prints that were glued to her long legs, topped with tight t-shirts in matching bright colors, accentuating her ample bosom. Patent leather slip-on heels (like the ones my old Barbie's wore) showed off her red-painted toenails.

Vicky's skin was caramel-colored and her cheeks glowed when she smiled, which was most of the time. At least, initially. She wore her wavy black hair pulled so that just a ripple of wave showed from the crown of her head to her ponytail.

The first day she arrived, I recognized her from the Rossi's. But now, seeing her coming up our front path, she was larger than life.

"Hi, sweetie," she said when I stepped out to greet her. "remember me?"

Her oversized gold-toned hoop earrings caught the sun peaking through the old sycamore with a sparkle as she made her way up the brick stairs to the porch.

"Yeah," I answered. "Kinda." I looked beyond her to the curb where she'd parked her metallic pink old-model Cadillac.

She noticed. "Like my car? Pink's my favorite color."

"Mine, too."

Vicky winked at me. "Then, we'll get along just fine, child."

I opened the door wider and led her in.

Mom came running down the stairs. "Vicky, I saw you pull up. Thank god, you're here!"

Vicky laughed. "You're scaring me, honey."

Mom extended a hand to her. "Vicky. You're going to save my ass."

••

On July 20th, Neil Armstrong walked on the moon. It was Bill's fourteenth birthday and he'd invited his friend Phil over. There we were, Mom, Allan, Jim, April, Bill, Phil, and me watching in Mom and Allan's room sprawled out on the big bed and on the floor beside the TV stand watching the grainy figure of Neil Armstrong as he placed his foot on the surface of the moon. "One small step for mankind…"

I thought about Dad. Was he watching this?

No sooner were my thoughts about Dad interrupted. "By god, Bill," Allan beamed. "Man landed on the moon on your fourteenth birthday!"

••

In August, Aunt Carolyn came to stay the weekend. Papa and Virginia had needed a break from watching over her.

A heat wave pummeled us; every window that hadn't been painted shut by Moe the painter was open. The air felt thick. Especially upstairs.

One Saturday night, Aunt Carolyn, normally not a big drinker, drank too much vodka at our house and ended up getting sick in the bathroom. Her retching woke me. It was so loud, it probably woke up the Fowlers next door, too. I slipped out of bed and cracked the bathroom door to check. Aunt Carolyn wore a loose-fitting white nightgown and her hair draped forward as she knelt over the toilet bowl. I quickly and quietly shut the door and ran back into my bed. I pulled my pillow over my head to muffle the sound and prayed that her sickness would be over soon.

The door on April's side opened. It was my mother.

"Oh, you poor little thing," she said to her sister. "You, ok?"

My mother was not the soothing type. Rarely had I heard her voice so comforting and soft.

"I just need to get some sleep now," Carolyn answered, dryly.

Chapter Thirty-One

The knots have come to the comb.

—Mom

I started eighth grade in the fall. Anne Woodward, who'd not been as fat as me but plump enough to be in the same social group, had lost weight over the summer. And because the weight had come off while she was away at their beach house in Del Mar, now Anne was beautiful, tan, *and* thin.

I sat silent in the crowd around her the first day back at school. Pasty white and still fat, I stared in awe at the waistband of Anne's new uniform skirt, two sizes down from the year before. The one-inch band lay flat against a stomach that no longer stuck out. There were no permanent creases in her new waistband like there were in mine. We'd always had a bond with our shared chubbiness.

"How'd you do it? I mean, lose the weight?" I asked her in the girl's bathroom when I got her alone.

"I got a boyfriend," she whispered, "Suddenly, I didn't feel like pigging out anymore."

My best friend, Anne, got thin and had a real boyfriend that I didn't know about until now. I was envious. What would we now have in common?

She turned the conversation to me. "Wow, your hair's grown so long in three months. It looks great."

Standing next to her, both of us looking in the bathroom mirror, I felt huge and disgusting next to her. She was right about my hair. It was no longer stringy. I'd taken care of it and trimmed it regularly. It had grown longer and thicker and swayed all in one long piece when I moved. "Well, Annie, good hair's about all I have."

She looked at me with those soft blue eyes and smiled. "Not true, Heath. You've got a lot more than good hair, my friend."

Anne was so kind. And I hated myself for being envious of someone so good. But I was.

••

My father held to his deal with Allan. Christmas came and went without a word from him. No call. No letter. No present. It was strange, but I didn't really miss him that much. When he'd given April and me away that night at Scandia, I'd tried to adjust by blocking him out of my mind, along with any chance of seeing him in the future. I remembered the coldness of his words to Allan: "They're yours now." The chill of that scene replaced any warm memories I had of him.

From that night on, Allan had become my father. And the Stubbes had become my family. Allan didn't have a nickname for me like "Smiley," but he cared about me and drilled me daily about trying hard in school. "You must learn your arithmetic, your geography, all of your subjects," he'd say. "It'll be important when you grow up." His comments annoyed me because schoolwork was hard. School bored me, and my C's reflected it. But, I liked that Allan didn't give up on me. Like Anne, he saw something in me besides what had become my pretty long hair.

The only thing I'd heard about Dad and Louise was that he and Louise had thrown a lavish Christmas party upstairs in a private room at The Bistro in Beverly Hills. I read about it, together with

Mom, in the social section of *The Los Angeles Times*. "A Winter Wonderland" was the caption, which of course, made Mom furious. "Son-of-a-bitch," she said. "No one can stand them. I'll bet their only guests were the hired help," Mom said, slapping the morning paper down on her unmade bed, toppling her cup of morning coffee.

In the meantime, Allan had his hands full. His mother back in Raytown, Kansas, had taken seriously ill and he'd flown back to visit her. Mom stayed home to "watch the store," meaning us. Thankfully, Vicky turned out to be a godsend.

Meanwhile, Aunt Carolyn's depression lingered and seemed to get worse. Lost to me was the aunt who had loved to write. She loved her children and yet recently let them stay long-term with Charlie and Sherry because she couldn't handle them. That's when Mom got really worried. "Letting go of her kids is not good," she'd told me. "I'm afraid she's given up."

In January, Papa felt that she needed to be on a twenty-four-hour watch. There was concern about suicide. This meant some-one—Mom or Papa and Virginia—needed to keep watch on her around the clock. At least that's what I overheard Mom say to Allan. Aunt Carolyn saw Dr. Ferguson almost every day.

So she came to stay with us. It felt creepy. I couldn't stand to look at her, and truthfully, the thought of her wanting to kill herself scared me.

From the top of the front stairs, I watched her on the chair in the downstairs hallway with her head in her hands. Her hair was all stringy and clumpy. Her face was pale, her eyes sunken. Once, to distract her, I showed her my diary, the one she'd given me.

"You wanna read it?" I asked, putting it in her hands, trying to get her to engage.

She smiled weakly. "Not now, Heatherbean."

All hell might break around Aunt Carolyn with Ed chasing Thomasina or Jim and Bill arguing, or "Hot Dog" barking at the mailman. But nothing got a reaction, except an occasional sigh, followed by her sinking her face deeper into her hands.

"What's with your aunt?" Bill asked me one day when I was watching him sift through his record albums.

"Mom says she's depressed. Papa says she needs to be watched. Besides, your dad thinks that if she's around a family, she'll feel better."

"*This* family?" he laughed. "That'll make her feel worse!"

Jim, on the other hand, felt sorry for her. "Man," he said, "she's messed up. I feel her pain." It surprised me. I didn't think Jim felt anything.

When Mom had to leave to go on errands, April was in charge of Aunt Carolyn. April was just a kid, but she was strong and getting stronger. My mother deferred to her way too much, like when she asked April to call Mrs. Woodward to tell her to stop feeding me sweets at their house, but I kept my mouth shut. As long as she didn't ask me to watch Aunt Carolyn, who cared?

••

At the beginning of February, Aunt Carolyn seemed better. She was showering every day, dressing in her old favorites, even putting on a little make-up. She was well enough to go off the hourly watch, and she convinced Dr. Ferguson and Mom and Papa that she was fine to go back to her own home. She'd been back at the house less than a week when she learned Sherry and Uncle Charlie were expecting a baby.

I hadn't talked on the phone or seen Jonathan since he'd moved in with Uncle Charlie and Sherry, so I had no idea how he felt about the new baby. Mom and April were furious about the news. "This isn't good," Mom said, shaking her head.

"Jesus," April replied, shaking her head. "Poor Aunt Carolyn."

••

"Heather, it's for you," Mrs. Woodward said that Sunday morning, handing the black phone to me in their kitchen. I'd spent the night at Anne's, and Mrs. Woodward was making waffles for breakfast. Virginia was on the line for me. "Heather, honey, you need to come home. Aunt Carolyn is very sick."

Virginia's voice sounded weird. Anne walked me back around the block to my house. She left me at the corner. "Call me." She looked me in the eye. We both knew something was wrong.

Mom's eyes were puffy from crying as she paced the floor of the Music Room. It was only nine-thirty in the morning and she already had a cigarette in her hand, never a good sign. Jim and Bill sat stone-faced on the Music Room couch facing the front lawn. They were following my mother with their eyes and never looked at me as I entered the room.

"This, over Charlie?" Mom asked, talking to the ceiling. She looked down at the boys as if they held the answer. "Now Cary Grant, I could understand," she said, her voice cracking, "but Charlie? Charlie from Needles?!"

I didn't understand what was happening. "What's going on?" I asked. "Virginia said that Aunt Carolyn's real sick." I stood at the entrance to the room.

April was seated opposite the boys on the other couch. She was the one to tell me. "She not sick, Heath. Aunt Carolyn killed herself."

••

Papa had found her that morning. He and Virginia had gone over to the house to check on her after having rung Aunt Carolyn's

241

phone off the hook with no answer. When they got there, no one came to the door. Papa smelled gas fumes and ran to the small garage. Virginia was right behind him when he found Aunt Carolyn inside her beige Dodge Dart. She was slumped over the wheel of the driver's seat with her left hand on the driver's side door. The engine was still running and the car door was half-opened as if she had changed her mind.

Fighting the fumes, Papa hurried over to her. He thought he might save her. Desperately, he attempted mouth-to-mouth to bring her back to life. But it was too late. Rigor mortis had already set in. On the seat beside her lay an empty bottle of vodka and an empty bottle of sleeping pills.

Aunt Carolyn had wanted to be sure.

Late that Sunday afternoon, Mom went to the airport to pick Allan up. He was returning home from his mother's funeral in the Midwest.

"Keep your blue suit on," Mom said as he exited the "Arrivals" gate at LAX. "Carolyn finally got what she wanted."

••

Since Aunt Carolyn didn't believe in God, we didn't plan a church funeral, just a nondenominational service in the small chapel of the Hollywood Mortuary. My mother was distraught and spent two days going through her sister's things, trying to find the right outfit for Aunt Carolyn to wear in the casket. She decided on the white dress with the blue sash at the waist that Carolyn had worn after she'd given birth to Robert five years before. I'd loved that dress. I remembered when she wore it. It was so pretty and lacey and Aunt Carolyn had seemed so happy then, so proud of her new baby.

My mother was the first to enter the tiny chapel. "Jesus," she said, holding us back with her arms, "they've got her propped up."

I could still see into the chapel. There she was, in a casket up on a dais. It was open from the waist up with her body bolstered slightly so that you could see the profile of her corpse though a gauzy tulle canopy of fabric that had been draped over her body. It cast a ghostly effect.

My eyes fixed on her angular face, her eyelids lined with black liner and dusted with blue eye shadow. Familiar orange lipstick grazed her thin lips. It was eerie.

The rest of the service was a blur. Virginia, pink and puffy, donning a dark suit and blubbering; Papa, with deep bags under his eyes, my mother clutching Allan for dear life, April, stoic. I looked around. Uncle Charlie was to our right. Jonathan, ten years old, and Robert, five, were nowhere to be seen, thank God. For them to have this lasting impression of their mother would be haunting.

That night, I sat alone in the Music Room and dialed my cousin Jonathan on the yellow phone. I twirled the spiral cord around and around in my fingers, nervously waiting for someone to pick up. It took seven rings until Uncle Charlie answered. I had nothing to say to the man who'd caused my aunt so much pain. "May I please speak to Jonathan?"

Silence, and then, "Sure, Heatherbean."

My cousin's voice was little. "Hello?"

"Hi, Jonathan, I'm calling to—to tell you that I'm sorry that your mom died."

We talked for an hour. I tried to reassure him that she was in a better place. That she loved him. And we talked about her. "She was so smart, Jonathan."

"I know. She wrote all the time."

We remembered the good times, like Halloween. "Boy, did she do it up on Halloween. Remember the spaghetti she made and said it was brains that time at Halloween?"

And the time in Westlake Park when we rode those little paddleboats. "Remember when you almost drowned in the lake and I was mad because your mom was holding my popcorn and dropped it when she dove in to save you?"

He gave a small chuckle. "Forget you were drowning," I added. "I was more worried about my popcorn!"

Then my voice turned serious. "Jonathan, she loved you."

"I know," he replied, his voice still little.

"How about all the times she took you to Disneyland?"

"Yeah."

"Yeah, your Mom loved you."

He didn't cry. "I know," he answered.

He was only ten. Did he really understand? How could he? I sure didn't.

Five months later, Aunt Carolyn's old house on Longwood, where she'd first lived with Charlie, burned to the ground. Supposedly, it caught fire due to some old wires or something.

Years later, the small garage attached to the house on Lillian Way also caught fire. It was the garage in which she'd died. Aunt Carolyn had not rested in peace.

Chapter Thirty-Two

Pointing with pride—viewing with alarm.

—Mom

It was March and the air was clear and sunny. There'd been rain earlier in the week that had given Los Angeles a good clean scrub. I'd been waiting for the mail to come that Saturday afternoon and had been sitting on the front steps just as the mailman walked up. He greeted me wordlessly, tipping his postal pith helmet as he handed me the pile. I sifted through the stack quickly. It was there.

I made my way over to the white wrought iron bench that Mom had placed at the edge of the front lawn by the side yard next to the Fowler's house. It was an odd place to put a bench, but then, most of my mother's decorating was a little odd. The bench was cold and the raised ornate leafy iron filigree would surely leave an impression on the back of my fat-cushioned thighs. Still, it was a quiet place to be.

I put the mail on my lap and held the envelope in my hands. *Notre Dame High School for Girls* was printed on the left-hand corner. I ripped it open and read the first line. "Congratulations." I let out a sigh of relief. I'd gotten in. I didn't have to go to public school! No one in my neighborhood went to public school.

The idea of sending me to Notre Dame had come from Mom's friend, Ti Biscayart, whose daughter, Michelle, was the same age as me. Michelle wasn't dumb, but Notre Dame was cheaper than most of the private schools in the area and her parents didn't have a lot of money. Mom wrangled a deal with Michelle's parents to carpool, driving out of their way from their duplex near Cathedral Chapel to Fremont then taking the Santa Monica Freeway to this Westside high school every morning. If we both got in, the arrangement was that the Biscayart's would drive in the morning and Mom would pick us up in the afternoon. She'd rarely picked me up from Cathedral Chapel, only ten minutes away. Notre Dame was a thirty-minute drive, part of it on the Santa Monica Freeway, which she hated. I had my doubts about her end of the bargain. But I had done my part. I had been accepted!

I lifted my legs from the suction-like hold on the wrought iron and shifted to the right side of the bench. To my left I noticed that the loose bricks on the edge of the driveway had been repaired since Allan had moved in and that the Birds of Paradise and the scraggly roses in the flowerbed next to the driveway were blooming despite pretty much zero care from Jim who was supposed to look after them.

Anne Woodward had gotten into Immaculate Heart High School for Girls, where April went, but I could never have gotten in. Besides, Allan said that the nuns there were too liberal. The elite Marlborough School for Girls was out of the question, too. I took the test, but didn't get in. Even if I had, it was too expensive. I liked the uniforms that the Marlborough girls wore—shirt maker dresses in Easter egg colors and the white one with the lavender Marlborough crest. Their uniforms looked crisp. Smart. Rich.

I'd be wearing a drab brown-and-white cotton checked skirt with a pale yellow over-blouse finished with a cuffed bottom edge and riding to school in Mr. Biscayart's bastardized VW bug that had no rear hood to show off a souped-up engine that could be heard blocks away. I had no reason to complain, though. I hadn't studied for the entrance exam. I hadn't paid attention in school so Notre Dame was the best I could get. I reread the first word in the letter. *Congratulations.* Notre Dame was easier academically and had a reputation for accepting anyone. If they took me, I knew that reputation must be true.

I folded the letter and stuck it back in the stack of unopened mail. My mother would be relieved. Allan would certainly give me a speech about how important it was to study hard there. He'd offer to help me if I needed it. My sister would shrug it off. I don't think that she cared where I went. Jim would undoubtedly sneer and Bill would probably say that Notre Dame's not that bad. They were both at Daniel Murphy High School for Boys, which like Notre Dame for Girls, had a reputation for being second fiddle.

I had wondered if I should call my cousin Jonathan and tell him. I hadn't talked to him since the night of his mother's funeral three months ago. I'd asked Mom about Jonathan a few nights ago. "I don't have time to deal with him and Robert," she said. "I've got six kids to worry about, Heather. Jonathan and Robert are Charlie and Sherry's responsibility."

Mom was still mad at Aunt Carolyn for killing herself and leaving her boys. It was easier for her, I supposed, to just cut them off. I did wonder how my cousin was doing, though. And I missed him.

I stood up, smoothed the back of my skirt over the leafy impressions on the back of my thighs and headed inside with the mail.

A week later Papa had a stroke.

••

Virginia hovered over Papa as Mom and I entered his den.

After weeks in the hospital, he was now in a special bed, the hospital kind. The prognosis wasn't good, but Virginia had the

247

rental people put the bed downstairs in the den with the hope that if Papa got better he would be able to see out the big sliding glass door to the pool and the Hawaiian-landscaped garden with its over-sized ferns and the yellow hibiscus that he adored.

Virginia leaned over the side rails of the bed to whisper in Papa's ear. "Goodwin, Marilyn and Heather are here to see you."

His eyes stayed shut. The only response was the sound of his shallow breathing.

Mom furrowed her penciled brows, moving closer to his bed and reaching for her father's limp hand on top of the blanket. My mother had lost her sister only three months before. Now, she was losing him, too.

"How is he today?" she asked, not taking her eyes off him.

Virginia squared her shoulders as if she was bearing the world on them, which, to her, she was, and in a dramatic stage whisper, she replied, "The same."

My mother edged closer to the bed. "Papa. Papa," her voice was low. "It's me. Marilyn."

No response.

Mom brought her face closer. "Papa? Do you hear me? I love you, Papa..."

"I just keep saying my prayers," Virginia said, continuing to pat Papa's other hand yet still looking at Mom. "Prayer is very power-ful, you know." Virginia looked back at Papa as if for reassurance. "Isn't it, Goodwin?"

Still, no response.

I stepped back away from the bed toward the sliding glass door, afraid to see Papa up close.

"Heather. Heather," Virginia coaxed. "Come closer. Your grandfather doesn't talk but he knows that you're here."

Tentatively, I moved forward to the other side of the bed oppo-site Mom and Virginia. The thin white blanket had been pulled up to Papa's chin. His hair appeared less grey, whiter now, and had been parted on the side and combed, I assumed, by the nurse sitting in the chair just outside the den. The skin on Papa's hands and face was pale and translucent, each vein traceable. Those hands had once been strong, had once held a gavel in a courtroom that decided people's fates, and had once been responsible for the entire State of California.

I studied his blank face taking in features that I'd never seen without expression. His nose and ears looked bigger than I'd remembered. And his mouth was slightly open where the sound of his breathing came through, labored and hissing.

I stood rigid by the side of the bed with my arms glued to my side. The only thing moving was my lips. "Hi, Papa," I said. "I hope that you get better soon. OK?"

More breathing and the sound from the Danish coo-coo clock from the kitchen marked time.

I looked up to find Virginia dabbing away tears on her puffy cheek with a lace-edged handkerchief.

Mom's eyes were still on her father. "Papa, Allan will be by later. Sarah the bitch, is coming home from college and he had to pick her up at the train station downtown." She looked over at Virginia, then to me. "I say it like it is," she said, defending her profanity. "Papa expects that."

My throat felt dry. I licked my lips and swallowed to get some moisture going.

"I hope you're better soon so that you can come to my eighth-grade graduation next month. OK, Papa?"

I looked up at Virginia with desperate eyes. "He doesn't react to us? Is he ever going to wake up?" I asked.

Virginia tried to soothe me. "It's all right. He knows that you're here."

Mom offered me an out. "You can go sit down over there, honey," she said, motioning to the two leather chairs at the far end of the room, the same chairs where Jonathan and I had spent countless hours looking through Virginia's prized scrapbooks of her and Papa's days in Sacramento while both sets of parents, still alive in the case of Aunt Carolyn, and married to each other, had cocktails by the bamboo bar outside in the pool area. It was only five years ago. But, really, it was a lifetime ago.

Virginia and Mom turned their attention back to Papa while I sat quiet surrounded by my grandfather's achievements. Mounted and framed brass plaques, awards, certificates, letters with gold seals' and photographs of Papa doing important things like cutting the ribbon to open Disneyland and launching a Naval submarine, covered the grass-cloth den walls, familiar fixtures that I had seen many times before but had never paid much attention to.

In the corner, at the other end of the room near the head of Papa's hospital bed, was the official flag of California edged in gold fringe on Papa's eagle-topped brass flagpole that reached almost to the ceiling.

Papa had been a lawyer. A judge. The Lieutenant Governor of California, then the 31st Governor. But, I didn't know Papa as those things. I only knew him as my grandfather who ate catsup on a spoon, who wore Converse high-top tennis shoes, who had a hearty laugh, and who could break into an Irish jig on Larchmont Boulevard on a command from me.

Papa never got better. I was the last grandchild to see him alive.

••

A row of black limousines lined the curb in front of Virginia's house. The plan had been to meet there and then go together as a family to the service. Everyone from our group was in attendance except my stepbrother, John, who was training overseas with the Navy to fly jets off aircraft carriers in Vietnam.

As we got closer to the house, I saw Jonathan getting into the second limousine with his father and his little brother, Robert. I didn't see Sherry, or maybe, she was already inside the car. Virginia was standing beside the first limousine dressed in black from head to toe, complete with a veiled hat. "So Norma Desmond," Mom murmured.

Papa's funeral was held at St. James Episcopal Church on Wilshire, several blocks east of Perino's. The church was massive and packed with mourners. Governor Reagan sat in the front pew opposite us. He was tall and had a handsome profile. Nancy, his wife, was not there. Mom leaned down to me and whispered that Papa hadn't been wild about him and his politics. "Your grandfather," she whispered, "was one of the last of the moderates."

Two rows behind Governor Reagan sat Jimmy Durante, Papa's good friend. His famous long big nose was hard to miss.

After the service, outside the church, I tried to catch Jonathan's eye before he got into the car. But no luck. Our car was second in the line-up. The hearse that would carry Papa's casket to the cemetery was now first in line.

From the car window, I looked up at the office buildings across the street. People were hanging out of the windows to get a glimpse.

"Look," Virginia said, weeping. "Everybody loved Goodwin."

My mother's eyes were somber as she scanned the floor of the limousine. She slid her gaze up and out the window to the crowds. She whispered softly to herself one of Papa's campaign slogans. "Good. Good. Goody. Goodnight."

"You say something, Marilyn?" Allan asked.

Mom was paralyzed with grief and made no move to answer.

The driver pulled away from the church following the hearse.

"Sir," Virginia said, loudly so that the driver could hear her. "Will we be going down Larchmont before the cemetery?" she asked.

The driver nodded, never taking his eyes off of the road. "Yes, Mrs. Knight. Just as you had requested."

"Thank you," she said, sniffing into her handkerchief, "Goodwin loved Larchmont and I want him to go down the boulevard one last time."

Chapter Thirty-Three

Fall 1980

Never take a dancer out after the show.
—Mom

Eleven years passed since that Christmas Eve in 1969, the night I'd wanted to go home from Louise's. I hadn't heard from my father since. At twenty-four, my once long light brown hair was shoulder length and highlighted blonde. I'd grown into a young woman, bearing little resemblance to my chubby childhood self. Would he even recognize me if he passed me on the street?

I'd seen him once since then while driving in Beverly Hills. I'd been driving east through the intersection of Beverly Drive where it curves onto Olympic Boulevard in a Chevy LUV pickup branded with Allan's company, WCS, on the side. He was heading west in a Silver Cloud Rolls Royce. It had been a fleeting glance, but I was sure that it was him.

There was a time when I held out hope that Dad would feel bad about pawning us off on Allan. That he might call or make an overture. That he might want to let me know that he still cared. But once I heard he'd adopted Teddy and Little Louise, I knew that that wasn't going to happen. I had just started high school then and my life was and would be moving forward without him. Outwardly, I'd shrugged the grief off, owing it to my father's selfish greed to please Louise who held the purse strings.

Inside me though, the loss was corrosive. I believed that to him, I hadn't been worth it.

I was nothing to my own father.

••

At fifteen, though, I finally lost the extra weight I'd been carrying. My mother, desperate to find a solution, had taken me to Weight Watcher's.

"Heather? Where are you?" Mom had called out from the entry hall. "It's time to go to your first meeting!"

"I'll be right there," I called back from my hiding spot crouched under the table in the breakfast room off the kitchen. I'd taken a hurried bite of my BLT sandwich. Mayonnaise oozed outside the crust as I'd bitten into it, licking it up all around the edges.

"Heather! What the hell are you doing?"

"I'm coming!" I'd held the rest of my sandwich, looking at it, debating. Then, stuffed the rest of it into my mouth, taking in the flavor of the bacon, the rich texture of the mayonnaise, the soft white bread.

The meeting was held at a Synagogue in West Hollywood. The standing scale loomed large as I took my place in line to be weighed. Sweat poured down my sides as I stepped onto it. The woman weighing me slid the bar over, and over, and over. I watched the numbers pass by, willing the bar to stop at some acceptable place. "You're 5 feet 3 inches tall and 172 ½ pounds," she said, jotting it down in a little booklet that she handed to me.

I stared down at the booklet and looked sheepishly over at my mother who ushered me into the meeting room.

"It's my fault you're heavy," Mom said, taking a seat next to me. "I fed you a cookie every time you cried as a baby. It was the only way to make you stop."

The first item on the agenda was "True Confessions." I listened in disbelief as an obese woman, who hadn't lost any weight that week, told of her midnight search for something to satisfy her craving for a snack. In a desperate effort to stick to the Weight Watcher Program, she'd devoured a box of her toy poodle's Milk Bone's.

I'd pictured the woman, all by herself, polishing off a box of dog biscuits. I often ate alone, too. But not dog biscuits!

My attention turned to a brunette woman in her late forties. She was having difficulty seating herself in one of the folding chairs. The man next to me, his protruding belly pushing against the constraint of his button down shirt, had noticed my eyeing her. "She's come a long way," he whispered in my ear, "last week she graduated from the aisle to a chair. We are so proud of her."

I knew that if I didn't get control of my eating soon, I'd end up like that woman.

"Do you eat because you are lonely or depressed?" Mimi, the meeting leader, asked the group. "If you do, you are not alone."

I was the youngest in the group, but I wasn't unique, just a fat girl who was hung up. If I polished off a can of Redi Whip in one sitting, hid candy bars in the drawer of my nightstand or Oreos in my closet, these people could relate. Unlike the Milk Bone lady, though, I hadn't learned to laugh at my own self-destruction. Food had become my only comfort in a chaotic home.

Within a week of that meeting, I lost 6 ¼ pounds and was on my way. Though I continued to be a poor student in school, barely earning C's at Notre Dame, losing 6 ¼ pounds had been my first real success. I was going to see it through.

The program was easy to follow. I learned how to weigh my food to modify our meals at home. How to choose a Pippin apple instead of an Almond Joy bar and make a satisfying, healthy lunch. Each week, I saw progress. Some weeks only ¼ of a pound, but I stuck to it, determined to meet my goal.

I'd been inspired that first meeting when Mimi had addressed me in front of the group of new members. She'd said something that I'd never heard before. She told me that I was beautiful.

"Frankly, too beautiful," she'd said, "to be hiding under all of that mascara and fat."

When I started to see the numbers on the scale go down, I'd found a discipline and a drive inside me that I hadn't known existed. For a solid year, I never broke the diet. Not once. Even after I'd reached my goal of 115 pounds, I would never eat anything with wild abandon, again.

••

I'd also gotten married and was majoring in English at UCLA.

I'd first attended community college in San Diego and then transferred to the university. I'd finally implemented what Allan had tried to drill into me. *"You're smart, Heather. All you need to do is try...."* Like keeping with the Weight Watcher Program, studying hard had paid off. Allan took out a second mortgage on 127 Fremont to pay for it all. Maybe I was smarter than I realized.

And then there was Hank. We got married last summer.

I first met him when he'd come to the apartment I shared with other students in San Diego. He was taking out my roommate, Cindy. April had been visiting that day and we'd both run to the window to catch a glimpse of him walking up to our door. Cindy had told us about him and we wanted to see the son of the H.R. Haldeman, Nixon's former Chief of Staff, who was now serving time in Lompoc Prison.

Inside our small living room, dressed in a corduroy sport coat wearing round wire-rimmed glasses, Hank seemed out of place in our beach community. He was formal and gracious. I liked that, and his brown eyes. They bore into me as if he could see inside my soul. What I *hadn't* seen in those eyes was that he was interested in me.

It turned out that Cindy and Hank were old friends from high school, nothing more. Three months later, I'd moved into an apartment I shared with April on the Westside of LA to be closer to UCLA. April, then, was already on her career path at a real estate company.

Two days after I'd moved in to start at UCLA, she answered the phone. She called to me. "Heather! *Hank Haldeman* is on the phone." She gave me a thumbs up and I'd rolled my eyes at her as I took the receiver.

"Hi, I got your number from Cindy..."

Our first date was the following weekend and I knew that night that a whole new world was opening up for me. We talked about literature and his life back in DC, his love of his alma mater, UCLA, and his desire to be his own man, not caught in the shadow of his bigger-than-life father. I shared the feeling. I knew we had something special, leaving our dinner plates half-finished, too engrossed in conversation.

On the ride back to my apartment, I thought I might be turning into my conniving mother, plotting how I could see him again. "Can I borrow your copy of the Iliad?" I asked, innocently.

"Sure," he'd smiled. "I'll bring it over on Tuesday."

The following year, we became engaged while his father, Bob, was still serving time at Lompoc. I'd met Bob on a furlough. I never visited him with Hank while he was at Lompoc; those were special times for Hank, just him and his father. I wondered at the irony of a man convicted of obstructing justice having raised a son with such integrity.

When we got engaged, I received a heartfelt letter Bob had written on prison stationary, welcoming me to the family. I placed it in my wedding scrapbook below the letter from his mother, Jo.

At our engagement party in their home a few months after Bob's release, April asked upon being introduced him: "Shall I call you Mr. Haldeman, or Bob?"

"Or, maybe prisoner number 1489-163B," he laughed.

I'd married a man who had loving parents and a father with a sense of humor.

••

All these life changes had taken place by the time I saw my father again.

That day, I tightened the drawstring on the waistband of my purple corduroy jumper and smoothed the pointed collar on the black blouse underneath. Checking myself in the massive beveled mirror over the Rossi's bar, I straightened my shoulders and studied my reflection. I was slim, confident, loved, maybe even pretty. Would he even know me? I spotted him on the other side of the Rossi's large family room. Beige walls and heavy furniture flanked the dark room with thin terra cotta-tiled floors. This room had once looked so fresh and new but now appeared dated. It hadn't been redone since the late 60s.

Many of the mourners at Connie Rossi's wake were mutual family friends who knew our story. Many knew that my sister and I had not had any communication with our father in more than a decade. And many were aware that my father, my sister, and I were all in there in the same room for the first time in years.

He looked smaller than I remembered. Or perhaps, it was just that the men standing around him were large. He'd stayed lean, but his hair, still wavy, had thinned a bit and was completely grey, hinting at white around the temples. He'd aged. A lot. That was no surprise.

Louise's son Teddy, whom along with Little Louise Dad had formally adopted not long after he'd relinquished my sister and me, had died of leukemia the year before. It was said that Big Louise had not coped well with his death; she'd contracted breast cancer soon after. I'd heard these things third-or-fourth hand and had no idea how Louise or Little Louise were really doing, much less, Louise's older children, Bonnie and Carl, whom I'd heard had sided with their father.

I looked over at the bar area to where my mother and Connie used to sit so long ago, back when Richard would make the drinks. Mom had decided not to attend Connie's service. The friendship had gone south years ago when Mom married Allan. Mom claimed that Connie liked it better when Mom's life was in shambles. "It gave her the upper hand," she'd said.

Life was no a bed of roses for Mom during those days. Allan's business, the once prosperous Western Concrete Structures, was hanging by a stem and engaged in a court battle. As the company troubles mounted, Allan began to drink more.

"A victim," Mom said, "of the Catholic virus. Dipping into the sauce."

He began taking longer lunches at The Alpine Inn, a restaurant close to Western Concrete, and returning to the office drunk where my sister, April, working as a special favor as his assistant before returning to real estate, had to cover for him, fielding calls until he sobered up.

During those years, maintenance on the Fremont house became an issue all over again. Lack of money and no kids around anymore to do "chores" exacerbated the situation. Allan had lost his enthusiasm for keeping up the house, and for my mother.

Thus, Mom's familiar pattern surfaced. Endless calls to the office and The Alpine Inn looking for him. The Bufferin and the cocktail in the evening while she waited for Allan. Her hanging onto a marriage over drinks with an unhappy husband in the living room at night, and a housekeeper (now Vicky) emptying overflowing ashtrays and picking up empty glasses in the mornings.

Plus, Allan had begun traveling regularly to San Francisco for what he told my mother was business. She grew suspicious. After years with my father and his philandering, she knew the signs. He offered her no details. "Marilyn, I've got work up there. That's all you need to know."

My mother tried to accept that. "I was wildly in love with him," she said later. "I didn't want to make any waves."

••

It was hard to study my father in the dimly lit room. The Rossi's thick-walled Mediterranean-style home had always seemed dark. It's why I never liked going over there as a kid. Dark houses gave me the creeps, which explained why I was so fanatic that my own first home in the hills of Glendale, where I was now living with Hank, needed to be bright and cheery.

April, was also married and now six months pregnant. She came to join me near the bar area. She'd married Glenn, in August of '79, six weeks after I'd married Hank. We both married in the same church and had our receptions at home in Fremont Place.

I whispered into April's ear. "Look across the room."

"I know," she said, "I saw him."

"Have you talked to him?"

"Not yet," she replied, patting her belly. "I need some food, first. Where is it?"

"Not sure," I shrugged, "Maybe in the dining room."

"Oh, right," April, laughed. "I'm asking *you* where the food is?"

This made me chuckle. My sister teased me about my discipline with food, often deprecating herself, who hadn't needed discipline when it came to eating. She'd always been able to maintain her figure without dieting. She told me many times how much she admired that about me.

"I know *you* won't be wanting any but I'm *dying*. I'll be back," she said, and made her way toward the dining room.

I turned my eyes back to my father on the other side of the room as he pulled out a cigarette and lit it with a gold lighter. He appeared distracted as an older man beside him prattled on in an animated fashion using hands to emphasize what he was saying. Dad moved back a bit to dodge the hands, reminding me of how standoffish he could be, and particular about his person. The tie was always just so, the French cuffs on his shirt, perfectly pressed. My father was nodding politely. I could tell that he had no interest in what this man was saying. My father had aged, but he hadn't changed.

He'd tried to talk to me once, or so my husband, Hank, concluded. It had been on my wedding day. Hank had been moving the last of his things into what would soon be our first apartment in Pacific Palisades when the phone rang and Hank answered.

An older male voice was at the end of the line. "Hello, is Heather Eaton there?"

Hank told him that I wasn't, and had asked if he wanted to leave a message. The caller quickly hung up.

"It had to have been him," Hank said. "I never met the guy, Heath, but there was just something about his voice."

"It's okay. I don't need him," I told my husband. "Allan was there to walk me down the aisle."

Yet, I never lost the feeling of anguish over my father's choice to adopt Louise's kids. The years had dulled the pain, but had not wiped away my contempt. If his name came up, my jaw clenched, my stomach tightened. Still, I considered myself fortunate to have had Allan around. He'd taken an interest in me, had sacrificed for me, and believed in me.

From the other side of the room near Dad, I spotted Angela Rossi and her brother Vito. They were holding strong, carrying out a conversation with one of their mother's friends. Silent, they listened while the woman spoke. Just then, I felt a hand on my shoulder.

"You fine, Hon?"

I turned around to find a face that never seemed to change, our housekeeper after Lupe who still worked for my mother. "Vicky!"

"This is so sad," she began. "Mrs. Rossi was a good woman."

I nodded.

"Your mother. It's good that she's didn't come. Your father here and all."

"You're probably right," I said.

"Child," she said in her wonderful, warm familiar way. "Everybody here knows he blew you girls off." She rubbed my shoulder.

Typical that it was Vicky who would comfort me now. Vicky, the housekeeper who made me ginger tea in high school for my menstrual cramps. Who brought me soup when I was sick at home in my room, and who had stayed working for Mom and Allan for six years without a raise.

"Ok, then," she said, "Can't trust a caterer, you know. I'm gonna find out what's happening in that kitchen. See what's taking so long to get more of the food out."

The room had gotten crowded with more guests trickling in and I lost sight of my father. Where was he?

Just then, the group of Rossi friends around me thinned, exposing a wide space on the tile floor. I looked up. It was as if

Moses had parted the sea as people moved aside to make way for my father who was heading toward me.

I stood fixed, my heart pumped wildly.

Not knowing what to do as he came near, I extended my hand for him to shake. We met each other's eyes. They didn't look as steely as I thought they should, and the warmth I saw there threw me off. He took my hand and kissed it lightly.

I let go of his hand, then, took a deep inhale through my nose. "I just want to thank you," I said.

A look of surprise came over his face as he lowered his chin and looked up at me with thick furrowed eyebrows. His face betrayed relief as he relaxed his forehead, smiled, and waited for more.

"I want to thank you for leaving Mom."

His smile became fixed and rigid. He tilted his head slightly, not sure what was coming next.

"Because when you left Mom, she met Allan Stubbs who has been the best father I could ask for."

A shadow moved across his face, but he held the tight smile. "That's...that's good," he stammered. Then, he turned back and walked away as the crowd filled in.

No one said a word to me as I stood there. Before I had a chance to tell April what had happened, I overheard someone say that my father had left without saying goodbye to anyone.

Soon after, I left too, thankful that I had driven alone. Two blocks later, waiting at that familiar long signal at Tremaine and Wilshire, the tears came, unleashing eleven years of hurt. "I did it," I said aloud through my sobs. "I did it!"

Chapter Thirty-Four

It's a long alley without an ashcan.
—Mom

Labor Day, 1982. The phone startled me out of a deep sleep. I opened my eyes. Just a hint of morning light peeked through a gap in the closed bedroom drapes. Our three-month-old baby, Allan, was not a good sleeper and had kept us up most of the night. Hank, answered the phone and passed it across the bed to me. "It's your mother."

"Mom?" She never called this early.

"He left," she said. "This time, for good."

I switched the phone to my other ear. "Okaaay." I slowly absorbed the information. Her words went straight to a pit in my stomach, but I wasn't surprised. Allan had been seeing another woman for the past year. He'd confessed it to my mother in June, right after I gave birth to Allan, whom we'd named after him.

Arlene, the other woman, had been his high school sweetheart, he'd told Mom. Her Naval officer husband had passed away, there'd been a high school reunion, and she'd contacted Allan. "It was all very innocent, really," Allan explained. "In the beginning."

"But, I love you both," he'd said to Mom. "Now, I don't know what to do."

That confession launched what Dr. Ferguson labeled my mother's card-carrying masochistic behavior, lying down like a doormat to please Allan in any way. She made his favorite Hamburger's Hawaiian and chipped beef for dinner. Ensured her make-up was on at all times and strived to "be sparkle plenty" no matter what he said or did. It was her twisted game plan to get him back. She even went so far as to allow Allan to see Arlene so that he would hopefully compare the two and realize how much more attractive and fun my mother was than her.

"As long as he keeps saying that he still loves me," Mom had said, "I still have a chance."

I pleaded with her to keep her dignity. "He says that he loves her, too, Mom. How can you live with that?"

"What choice do I have?" she replied. "I have no backup. I still have no education. No money."

As much as I hated infidelity, I wasn't angry with Allan, or sorry we'd named our son after him. I'd managed to separate his longstanding encouragement and support of me from my mother's unhappy marriage to him. I'd seen where it had been going. After all the kids left the house, they had nothing in common. Allan was a mountain man. My mother was a city girl. It had just been a matter of time.

"I'll be right over."

I handed the phone to Hank who reached over to put the receiver on its nightstand cradle and grabbed his eyeglasses, sitting up. Clumps of his short, dark brown hair shot out in every direction from a fitful night's sleep with a crying baby. "So?" he asked, bringing me close.

Resting my head in the crook of his neck, I answered. "I guess he chose Arlene."

I passed through the concrete pillar gates at the entrance to Fremont and was waved through a few yards down by Sam, the latest Fremont watchdog, standing at attention inside the new Guard Shack, an elaborate tollbooth-like structure in the center of the street. In the 80's, the need for better security had increased. The surrounding neighborhood was changing and robberies were on the rise. Gone were the days of sleepy Hank in his recycled patrol car parked at the first corner in front of the Cardinal's house.

The front door was unlocked. As I entered, my mother moaned loudly from upstairs. "Thank God you're here."

The shutters in her bedroom were closed to block the daylight and the lamp on her nightstand was on. My mother stood in a knee-length nylon sleeveless nightgown that had seen better days, a lit cigarette in her hand. It was nine am.

The bedside lamp cast an upward glow onto her long "permanent" false eyelashes shadowing puffy lids, giving her face a theatrical look.

I didn't go to her. She had never been big on hugs. Instead, I sat down at a safe distance at the foot of the bed. "Tell me about it, Mom."

Her face was wet with tears. She took everything to the extreme and indulged every emotion—something I found weak and frustrating. I felt disgust and pity. But she was my mother, and I wanted to make it better for her.

She'd been up all night, she told me. My eyes went to the full ashtray on the nightstand and the empty glass tumbler next to it, which I was sure, had held several refills of vodka. She put a hand through her bobbed and layered hair. The story unfolded.

"Last night, he started crayfish-like, slow and measured. Said he needed to work somewhere, like in a hotel, two nights a week. That he couldn't concentrate at home. It all started to make sense. The jogging to keep fit. He never jogged before. Swimming laps in the pool. Christ, he was getting in shape for *her*." She shook her head. "Worse was the sparky look he had when he'd get back from being with her." She brought the cigarette to her lips. Her crying had stopped but I braced myself, remembering her agony fourteen years ago when she'd learned about Dad and Louise.

"When I kept at him, begging to know why he needed to go somewhere else to work, he finally said: 'I'm not giving her up.'"

"Where'd he go?"

"Oh, who the hell knows? He owes money to the Jonathan Club. Maybe Seattle, where the bitch lives. Jesus, what am I going to do noooow?" she wailed. "I don't want to be alone."

Allan's business, meanwhile, had been declining. April and John had held on as long as they could, fielding calls, keeping the creditors at bay as Allan, so smart, such a great problem-solver, the man who had built Western Concrete from scratch, preceded to drink Western Concrete into the ground. Thankfully, he'd decided to protect the Fremont house by changing the deed to only list my mother's name. A year after he left my mother, the machinery at Western was put on the auction block. Each piece was sold while Allan stood by and watched. The house in Fremont, meanwhile, wasn't touched.

Allan continued to pay the mortgage, but there was no money for upkeep. The mortgage and Mom's minimal weekly spending allowance were all he could afford to give her.

Though the calendar had moved forward, Mom reverted to the woman she'd been when my father left, on her weekly alert for a check from a wayward husband. And, just like before, the white colonial in Fremont took the brunt. "It's falling apart like a dollar watch," Mom said.

In a way, 127 Fremont Place had become one of her husbands, and at fifty-seven, my mother was hanging on for dear life, like Scarlett O'Hara hanging onto Tara.

She got down to business. She was forced to let go of Vicky, her longest running housekeeper, and to ask Henry, the gardener, to only care for the front once again. This time she didn't have to hide from the paperboy. She cancelled *The Los Angeles Times* altogether.

The pool man, re-hired after Bill left for college, was scaled back to once a month. The dishwasher broke and stayed broken. Gangly weeds sprouted in the gutters as if it were springtime in the garden. The worst, though, was the maid's room, empty now except for a single bed against the wall. It reeked of cat pee that had saturated and dried on the worn carpet. Apparently, Mom had been lazy about training her two strays how to use the litter box.

"A boarder? Some stranger?" April said on the other end of the line the morning after Mom had found cockroaches. "Why not Glenn and me?"

Mom mulled it over.

"We'll pay rent, Mom," April added. "And, remember, Glenn's an ironworker and all-round handyman."

"You sure you want to move in?" my mother asked. "'Cause I saw a rat, too. Last week in the dining room. Shit, it was the size of a cat."

April's voice rose. "A rat?"

A month later, pregnant with her second child, April and her family moved in. April and Glenn made an agreement to do much-needed repairs on the house, plus pay monthly rent. That, coupled with Mom's new job as part-time sales, at The Tennis Boutique, would keep them in Fremont. At least, for the time being.

Christmas night 1985, Glenn answered the door, his 6-foot, 5-inch frame taking up most of the doorway. He broke into a wide grin, but the whites of his pale blue eyes were as red as the Christmas lights draped around the front door. "Hey, guys," he drawled. "Merry Christmas!"

Holding our six-month-old Hilary, I reached for little Allan's hand as April's kids swarmed us. "Uncle Hank! Auntie Heath!

Cousin Allan! Cousin Hi-ra-ry!" Her two-year-old Jeffrey, was the image of our father. I'd noticed it the day he was born. Even with the soft features of a newborn, he mirrored Dad right down to the shape of his eyebrows. The same black curly hair, the same dark lashes. And, now as a young toddler, his eyes had the same hazel mix of light brown and green, and his nose had taken Dad's familiar shape, straight with a slight knob at the tip. April saw my reaction. "I know," she said. "It's weird, isn't it?"

We entered the front hallway where cousin Jonathan, Carolyn's son, now 27, stood with a Scotch in one hand, a cigarette in the other. "Well, look who's here!"

It had been fifteen years since Aunt Carolyn's suicide and I was glad to see Jonathan back in the fold. While Mom's life had filled to overflow, dealing with her own two children and the Stubbs kids back then, she'd made no effort to include him in family gatherings. Always generous, Jonathan never faulted her. Still, he would tell my sister years later that it had been painful, having been cast aside for the Stubbs kids.

Mom came down the hallway wearing the red silk pants with matching low cut V-necked sweater (always, the cleavage) that she'd worn for the past three years. She reached out to Hilary, in my arms. Hilary took hold of Mom's hand and studied her long fingernails, painted red to match the season. "Pretty," Mom said to Hilary. "Nana likes pretty."

After the presents, Jonathan filled us in on Uncle Charlie, divorced now from Sherry. He reached for a Ritz cracker from the platter of hors d'oeuvres. "Yeah, Robert's doing fine," he said of his younger brother, "spending Christmas with his..." He stopped, cheese knife held in mid-air, "Wait. What's under the cheese on this plate? Marilyn, you did the hors d'oeuvre's, right?"

Mom pointed her cigarette at the platter across the room. "Oh, it's décor," she said. "You know, like the fall leaves they put under cheese. Only these are green. Christmassy, isn't it?"

Hank and I leaned in over the platter to look. Hank raised his eyes to my mother. "Marilyn, where'd you get a marijuana leaf?"

••

We learned later that April's husband was growing the crop. Though it took a while to fully see the situation, it seemed he had a drug problem. Over two years, the habit went from marijuana to cocaine to crack cocaine. His drug use had been "creep-mousy," Mom said. "Slow to show itself."

April said little to me about it, but I prodded. Glenn had become rail-thin. "What's he on?" I'd asked. I was worried about her, too.

"He's fine. Just a little slender."

"Ape, I think it's more than that."

"No," she shook her head. 'That's pretty much it."

Even if she didn't recognize Glenn's issue, she did feel the financial insecurity his addiction created closing in on her. She took job after job, working weekends and every spare moment.

"I worry about you, Ape," I'd said. "You've taken on too much."

"What else am I gonna do?" she'd said. "I can't depend on *Glenn*. That's for sure!"

She'd even stopped trusting him to watch the boys. I was glad about that. But hated to see the toll it was taking on her.

••

On a sunny but cold Saturday morning I went outside our modest suburban home in La Canada to get the newspaper. April was crouched in a ball at my back door. She was disheveled, shaking, her eyes red from crying. "I can't take it anymore," she barely lifted her head. "Glenn..."

I sat down next to her on the cement step and put my arm around her. "He's an addict, Ape."

"I know. I thought I could deal with it. Fix it somehow, but I can't." Her face was puffy.

"When did you get here?" I asked.

"About an hour ago."

"Where are the boys?"

"With Mom."

"Oh my god... Come inside."

She pulled herself together and even went to a Salvation Army luncheon honoring Barbara Bush with me that day as the guest of my mother-in-law. That evening, she went back to Fremont where Glenn promised to quit doing drugs—a promise that lasted just two weeks. That's when she kicked him out for good.

Chapter Thirty-Five

He's tall when he stands on his money.
—Mom

I sat on the edge of the Fremont house lawn, watching our two-year-old Hilary hold a running hose. She was "helping" April wash her black Taurus station wagon. April lifted a small bucket of soapy water over to the driver's side door while Hilary followed, watering everything in her wake. The sky was a blue haze and the weather was hot, typical for a late summer afternoon in Los Angeles. We'd been talking about April's, son, Justin, starting first grade, and my Allan starting soccer. We kept to easy topics now. Our relationship had become guarded since her reconciliation with Dad two years ago.

My sister's unruly blonde hair was pulled back in a tight twisted knot. A clump of stray wisps masked her ears. When she bent down to dip a sponge into the bucket, she tucked the loose strands behind her ears, revealing Mabe white pearl studs wrapped in a circle of small diamonds. They were hard to miss.

"Those new earrings?"

Keeping her eye on the sponge, she squeezed out the excess soap and began washing the driver's side door in circular motions. "Oh, they're from Dad," she said, lightly. "For my birthday, back in April."

"They're pretty," I said, realizing that things between her and Dad must have ramped up since she'd contacted him. Up until now, all she'd gotten from him was a thin gold bracelet.

I'd been helping her fold laundry on her bed two years ago when she'd told me about their reconnection. I'd just reached into the wicker laundry basket when she blurted it: "I called Dad and we had lunch."

My hand froze holding a pair of Jeffrey's wrinkled Spiderman pajamas. The air thickened. I could hear the boys playing He-man in the next room, Hilary, amusing herself with a doll on the hard-wood floor beside us. April knew how I felt about our father.

Slowly, I brought the pajamas to my lap. My heart sank. So this explained my mother's behavior that past week. She'd been avoiding me, getting off the phone quickly. She was busy when-ever I called. Normally, Mom made time for me on the telephone whenever I called; the telephone was her god. So, I suspected that something was up. But nothing prepared me for this; they both knew that I wanted nothing to do with Dad.

"That's why Mom's been weird," was all I could say.

"I don't know why she's weird about my calling Dad," April picked up a little pair of red OshKosh overalls. "It was just lunch. What's the big deal?" The buckles on the straps clinked as she folded.

I kept my eyes on the pajamas, folding them like an enlisted man makes his bed, slow and precise, creasing small blue sleeves, pulling back the red cotton ribbing on the cuffs. My mind rustled from anger to disbelief to betrayal.

"I'd been thinking about getting in touch with him ever since Jeffrey was born," she said without looking up. "He looks so much like Dad I felt that I should call him and tell him about his grandson."

I was stunned. All along, I'd thought that April felt the same way I did about Dad. I hated the self-centered, selfish S.O.B. My mother felt the way that I did. He had abandoned us. What was my sister thinking?

In the next room in our children's make-believe world one of the boys was He-Man warrior, "Thunder Punch" defending Castle Greyskull against the evil "Hordak." Hilary twisted in my arms, dropping her doll. She wanted to get back down to play, but I didn't want to let her go.

"He took me to the Bistro Garden."

I found my voice, but it came out quiet. "Did he notice his resemblance to Jeffrey?"

"He didn't see him," she said. "He told me not to bring the boys."

"But, wasn't that the reason why you called him?"

Her tone softened. "Yeah, at first. Then, I don't know..." she trailed off. "I felt kind of sorry for him."

I lowered my chin, locking eyes with her. My words were sharp, deadpan. "You felt sorry for him?" Blood rose to my cheeks.

April shrugged. "I don't know, Louise died of lung cancer a few years ago. Then, he broke up with this woman friend. He just seemed lonely."

I started to tremble. I needed to compose myself. I took a deep breath, peaking slowly and deliberately: "April, you've seen Dad once in sixteen years." I paused, measuring the sentences to make my point. "By accident. At Connie's wake. And you felt *sorry* for him?"

"Listen, Heather, I'm not like you. I accept him for who he is. I wasn't close to Allan like you. And, well, he's my father. I was curious."

"Who he *is*, April, is an asshole!"

"You haven't given him a chance, Heath. It's not all black and white. Good or bad. He said he tried to reach out to you before the wedding."

"One lousy phone call, *and he didn't even leave a message!* I'm supposed to erase the past over one phone call? I've got to get out of here." I clutched Hilary closer and called out to Allan that it was time to leave.

April carried Hilary's doll as we headed down the hallway to the stairs. "I think it was more than that, Heath. He said something about a letter he'd written to you."

We reached the landing where little Allan met us with two He-Men figures in one hand. "A letter? I never saw a letter from him."

I started down the stairs with Hilary in my arms. My sister was behind me, holding Hilary's walker. I turned to her. "April, he *had* his chance."

"And now you have one, too, Heath. You can forgive him. I have."

That night my mother called me. She was worried about what this would do to my relationship with my sister. "There's nothing I can do about it," she told me. "I can't stop her from seeing him."

"Neither can I," I sighed.

I lay awake in the darkness that night while Hank slept soundly beside me. Accept who he is? How could *anyone* accept who he is?

Whatever had led April to connect with our father was her business, but it ate me up inside. In a way, I was jealous. We'd been cast out as a pair, and now she was the special one, the one let back in. She'd gotten him to give her the one thing I'd spent my entire life pining for: his attention. Was it too late for me? Might he still have some attention to give my way?

These "night thoughts" as Mom used to call them continued to swirl in my head. Maybe April wanted to repair the hurt with Dad and mend the original wound of Dad's rejection. Now that she was back in the fold, back in his good graces, she could reverse that rejection and make it go away.

My stomach churned. I was tormented. Was my wound repairable? Was there any way to clean up the past? He'd abandoned us! Was it possible that he was a better man now? Maybe he *had* changed. Maybe he realized that he'd done wrong by his own children and repented. My sister had forgiven him. *Could I?*

A month after seeing the earrings, I told my sister about my conflicted feelings. She suggested that I join them for one of their lunches. "I'll ask Dad if you can come next time," she said. "See for yourself. Then, decide."

"Sure," I replied.

Wait, I thought. "*If*" I can come?

••

My father agreed to have me join them at Scandia on the Sunset Strip. I arrived ten minutes late, rushed and nervous. I'd changed my outfit multiple times. I had no idea what to expect and had slept little the night before, conceiving all sorts of scenarios in my head, both good and bad, finally falling asleep around four only to be woken at six by Hank getting ready for work and wishing me luck.

Pulling up to the parking valet, my thoughts were swirling. Would my father still be mad that I'd embarrassed him four years ago at Connie's wake? For that, I had no regret. What I said to him that day had been the truth. Yet, as the attendant handed me a ticket, I realized that for as mad as I was at Dad, I still longed for the magical world of an expensive restaurant, for the muffled sound of plates on linen, pumpernickel toast, and for a father who called me Smiley.

I still longed for my father's love.

Scandia was dimly lit and I had to adjust my eyes from the bright sunlight outside on Sunset Boulevard. I was greeted by the maître'd who led the way to where Dad and April waited, passing shiny copper and brass fixtures sparkling on the wood-paneled walls to Dad and April's table under a Danish Coat of Arms.

"Hi, Dad," I managed a shy smile.

My father's eyes, still so familiar, looked up at me, hazel and heavy-lidded. He pushed back his chair and stood. He held his napkin close to his chest like a shield and nodded for me to sit. He played it safe this time with no attempt to kiss my hand. "I was in the middle of a story," he said, taking his seat.

The maître'd placed a linen napkin in my lap. "A drink for you, madam?"

"Coffee, please." I looked over at my sister for support. My mouth was as dry as cotton.

She gave me a "Hi, Heath," then turned her attention back to Dad. Her hair was down around her shoulders with a slight flip at the ends, a puffier version of how she'd worn it as a teenager. She had make-up on—eyeliner, mascara, shadow, the works. I hadn't seen her made up since she'd separated from Glenn eight months ago. I could tell from how she dressed that her noontime breaks of watching *All My Children* had rubbed off. Large doorknocker earrings hung from her ears and she sported a white billowy blouse, buttoned to show no cleavage. She looked every bit the sophisticated woman in the mythical Pine Valley and every bit the rich man's daughter. My father had given her a lunchtime escape into his world of ease and opulence, a respite far from her nonstop tedious jobs, the drama of my mother, and the falling-down house in Fremont.

It didn't take long to see that my sister and my father had their own rhythm. Dad nursed a double Scotch, chain-smoked, lighting my sister's cigarettes one after the other. April hung on his every word, interrupting only to add some bit of humor or a witty comment. I was the interloper, feeling strangely competitive with my own sister. She had all his attention. I was the outcast and I wanted back in. She had the entrée back into his life. She had not insulted him in a room full of people. Would I have to wait on her to let me know if I was granted back in?

Neither looked my way as he continued to tell some long tale about a card game against his "old buddy" Fred Astaire. Mom always claimed that Dad was a pathological liar. I wondered if this story was true.

Dad made no attempt to engage me. He looked my way only when the waiter refilled my coffee, peering at me through the corners of his eyes. I studied his profile like I had at Connie's wake. Nothing much had changed except that the white hairs outnumbered the grey ones and the lines were a bit deeper around his mouth. My mind wandered back to those dinners years ago and the father who loved me, the father who'd given me a conspiratorial wink, patting my chubby hand on the linen tabletop after Mom had scolded me for sneaking another Parmesan cheese toast. I focused on his hands, willing them back to the kind gestures he used to make. I missed the expressions of softness that he'd had back then, now gone from his face.

As I sat and watched him, studying his every move and shifts in the timbre of his voice, the truth sliced through me like a blade: I could never make him love me again. I'd stopped being Smiley that Christmas I'd walked out on him and Louise. And I'd sealed my banishment by insulting him at Connie's wake.

The subject of their conversation moved to his cufflinks. "New," he told April, twisting his wrist near the candle on the center of the table to show off the gold.

His mouth moved, words came out shallow and vacuous. He puffed on his cigarette, sipping his cocktail. He smoothed his thick brows with manicured hands. He talked only to April as though I was not at the table.

I looked at my watch. We'd been sitting there for an hour and a half with the menus still closed. He'd yet to ask a single question about my life.

In that moment, my curiosity turned to disdain. He was all about the trappings, the Silver Cloud Rolls Royce, the custom suits, the home on Cherokee Drive in Beverly Hills, all of which had come his way at a cost that he'd been willing to pay. He had no relationship with Louise's children anymore. No relationship with me. The only person who cared about him outside of my sister and a local priest (notorious for sucking up to the rich to feed his coffers) was his houseboy, Ernie.

And Ernie was paid to care.

I sipped my coffee pretending to listen. Decades had passed since I'd had regular contact with my father. Back then, he'd been my only link to the lives of rich and fancy people, to expensive restaurants and the ease they promised. But time had passed. Through Hank, I'd learned that the world was a lot bigger out there. Literature, music, art. Through him, I'd met impressive people, men and women who spoke of politics, business, and world affairs. People with passion and drive and interests in the world at large. A world that was larger than the one my father presented.

Perino's with my father seemed like another lifetime now. And gradually, like my father's cigarette, smoldering throughout lunch, I realized that I was no longer dazzled by the fancy life he represented. I no longer needed him to be my passport.

What I wanted was much simpler, and I already had it. I didn't live in a grand home or on a grand street. We had a ranch-style home with a picket fence on a cul-de-sac in Pasadena. "Cozy. Warm." That's what people said about my home. *That,* I realized, had been my goal.

I managed to get through the meal and beg my leave as soon as I'd finished my salad. "I need to get back to the babysitter. Thank you, Dad, for lunch."

He'd waved his cigarette, an absent goodbye as I stood and left.

••

Several lunches later, Dad asked my sister about my children, their names, and the dates of their birth. "Why do you want to know?" she asked him.

"So that I can make sure they're not part of my will."

April blew the comment off when she told me about it. "He says stuff like that. He's always telling me he's not leaving me, or my children, anything. I don't really care, though. That's not why I see him."

Chapter Thirty-Six

January 1988

I need to go out and swing my legs on the barstool.
—Mom, in search of a man

High winds kicked up that January afternoon. Not the warm Santa Ana's that Los Angeles gets in the fall. These winds were cold, strong, and gusty. Unsettling.

I parked at the curb in front of Fremont after taking Mom to lunch. She put her key in the tarnished lock and opened the front door. The air was stale.

"Jesus," she said, stepping inside. "This house smells like a room full of old people."

A gust blew the door open wider. I closed it behind me, turning the lock after a few futile attempts to align the uneven door sash. "Mom, it's the cat smell in the maid's room. But forget that," I replied. "Let's hope these walls can hold up to the wind."

The years of Moe, the cheap painter, dangling cigarette ashes into the paint can, painting over paint and wallpapering over wallpaper, three decades of eras, had created a unique scent. Even with April and Glenn's effort to strip and repaint some of the rooms when they first moved in, the smell of age mixed with musty grit still lingered.

127 Fremont Place had progressed from tired to dilapidated. The carpet was now twenty-nine years old, its seams unraveling at the baseboards. The white window shades and shutters had morphed to a deep caramel color and several hung askew. The drapes behind the bed in my mother's room were so frayed the threads looked like a ragged fringe dusting the shabby once-powder-blue carpet. Roof leaks had spread from the balconies to the roof proper, and April had become adept at plugging the holes with a paintbrush and a can of Henry's Mastic Sealer.

My mother, meanwhile, was now back at "work" searching for another man to support her. This time, she had put together her "resume," a photo of her sitting on the edge of the backyard pool in a swimsuit holding an old Thomasina, the cat, in her lap.

"It shows I have good legs," she said, handing me the picture.

"Why the cat?"

"To confirm that I'm a loving person and like animals." She took the picture back and put it in her wallet. "But, mainly, the cat hides my belly."

"You're serious? You're going to show that photo to some guy to get a date?"

"Any port in a storm."

"You mean, you would?"

"Hell, yes. I've got to sell myself."

I closed my eyes to take in her desperation. Her determination. "Mom..."

"I know," she replied, reading my mind. "Don't be like me, Heatherbean."

I didn't need to say anything. I'd decided that long ago.

••

My mother had a goal in mind: an Italian man. She'd always been obsessed with them, claiming that they were romantic, swarthy, and sexy. Now whenever I came for a visit, I checked the latest addition to her "inspiration table" in her bedroom. It was crammed with folded maps of Italy and pictures of Italian landmarks, all propped up on display.

"My god, Mom, all you need is a candle," I teased, picking up a picture of The Spanish Steps. "This reminds me of Lupe's old room!"

"Don't laugh," she replied. "I'm working on getting to Italy for my sixtieth. I just asked Lou if she wants to go with me. Everyone else is too poor or has a husband."

"Lou's broke, too, Mom," I knew Lou, had an ex- husband who'd left her high and dry. "How's she going to pay for it?"

"Like I said," Mom told me. "I'm working on it."

The latest ode to Italy was a picture postcard of Venice's Grand Canal. I wondered if she'd intentionally propped it up in front of the tarnished sterling toast rack filled with bills marked "Past Due" to block the view of her make-shift filing system and the reality that lay stuffed between six slats of silver.

The house's dilapidation, meanwhile, had turned dangerous that winter when the bathtub in my old bathroom above the living room began to leak. Everyone kept an eye on the small brown water stain on the living room ceiling that was growing bigger by the day.

"That damn bathtub's about to fall right through the ceiling onto the coffee table," Mom told me, pointing to the mark. "If the chickens come home to roost and I haven't found anyone, I'm not even sure I can afford an apartment in Lou's building on Wilcox."

Looking back from the ceiling stain to me, she said: "I need to find a winner, Heatherbean. And, fast."

••

When I next came to visit, my mother launched right in. "I've figured out how I'm going to get to Italy with Lou!"

"How?"

"Follow me." She led me up the front stairs into her dressing room. "I've already told your sister the plan."

"What plan?" I asked, catching sight of myself in the mirrored doors of her dressing room.

"You'll see." She moved over to the jewelry box on top of the counter of the built-in dresser.

I couldn't help running my eyes up and down my body in those three-way mirrors, my mind registering disbelief at the slim figure reflecting back at me. Those mirrors had reflected a fat girl for too many years. Would I ever be able to see my adult self in them?

Mom opened the jewelry box and began shuffling through a tangle of costume pearls clicking with fake gold necklaces. "Ah, ha!" she pulled out a small Chinese satin jewelry pouch, unknotted the drawstring, and extracted the 3.15-carat emerald-cut diamond engagement ring my father had given her. "I've been saving it." She held the ring out to me in the palm of her hand. "It's my silver bullet. When all else has failed."

"What about all the bills in the toast rack, Mom? Why not use the ring to pay those off? This is all you have that's worth anything. What did April say?"

"That it's my ring and to do what I want," Mom extended her hand, bringing it to the dressing room window to catch the light. "Damn, the Sycamore is blocking the sun. You should see the it sparkle when it's lit just right."

"April's ok with selling it?"

"Yes. She said that the house was too far gone for anything this ring could fix."

Mom turned her hand in a royal wave. "It's a flawless blue-white diamond, Heatherbean. Top drawer."

"Well, if Ape's ok with it, I am."

With her hand still extended, she looked back at me, meeting my skeptical eyes. "Listen, I don't want to be alone, broke and single in LA on my sixtieth birthday. Okay?" Her eyes widened, the tips of her false eyelashes reaching almost to her arched eyebrows. "And, who knows, I may find a man in Italy."

"Mom," I sighed, "don't tell me that you're selling the ring to find a man in Italy. What happened to Sundays at The Beach Club?" She had been cooking up a plan with her friend Marge to hit up The Beach Club in Santa Monica looking for men. Marge was a member and could bring Mom as a guest.

"I've gone the last two Sundays. The lake was dry."

••

Hank woke me in the night with a tap on my shoulder. "Does your mom have health insurance?"

The room was dark and I groped for the clock on the nightstand. The clock read two in the morning. I mumbled for him to go back to sleep.

He sat up and switched on the light. "Heath, she's going to Italy tomorrow and I'm not sure she even *has* health insurance."

I turned on my side away from the light. "It's too late, now, Hank," I muttered in a sleepy haze. "Go back to sleep."

"What about her driver's license?" he pressed. "Did she get it renewed?"

I squinted against the harsh light. "Hank, it's the middle of the night."

He put his hand through his hair, a signal that he had more to say. "Check on that before you take her to the airport tomorrow, okay? She's got to have health insurance and she can't be driving around without a license."

"Hank, she's not renting a car in Italy. Go back to sleep."

"I know, but this stuff is important." He reached to turn off the light.

Wide-awake now, I stared at the dark ceiling. Mom had sold the ring. The trip was on.

••

Four days after her return from Italy, Mom sat in her dining room at the head of the table talking on the phone that had been stretched from the butler's pantry through the swinging door to the dining room table. The water stain on the ceiling in the living room had spread.

She gestured with her hand for me to take a seat. "Oh, Heather just walked in. I'll dig you later." Silence, then, "And don't say a word!"—her stock telephone sign off.

I got right down to business, following up a bit late on the items Hank had asked me to look into. Turns out, her driver's license had been expired for two years. "I owe four hundred dollars in traffic tickets," she said. "That's why I haven't registered the car, either."

When I asked about her health insurance, she drew a blank. "You know me and papers."

"We need to check on that, Mom."

"I know Hank's worried about my insurance and the car registration. He looks out for me," she said. "Such a straight shooter, he is. Lucky you. With him you'll never worry about this crap."

She was right. Hank was my rock. "It's not 'luck,' Mom," I said. "I chose the right guy."

"You did," she'd nodded and handed me a small paper bag with Italian writing. "Open it. It's your present."

I opened the tightly wrapped tissue to find a rosary made up of clear blue plastic beads.

"It's not blessed by the Pope and all that, but I got it near the Spanish Steps."

"Thanks, Mom." I put the tissue aside. "I'd better start praying with this thing. Did you notice that the brown stain on the living room ceiling has doubled in size?"

"Why do you think I also got one for April and me."

I looked down at the rosary in my hand and fingered the little beads. "Mom, was your trip really worth selling your ring even though you didn't find an Italian man to bring home?"

"Worth every lire. Lou and I had a ball," she replied. "But, now it's back to work."

She reached for her tablet and scribbled, "Call Marge (Beach Club)."

••

A week later, the phone was ringing as I came through my back door after visiting the doctor. It was confirmed. I was having another baby, due the beginning of January. Five-year-old Allan and two-year-old Hilary would welcome a new sibling. Hank and I had been thinking about having another child, and in fact, had scheduled a genetic counseling appointment to make the final decision. Our middle child, Hilary, had been born missing a bone in her hand. It had not been an impediment and two surgeries later, her hand looked graceful and her agility was remarkable with just three fingers. But now we wouldn't need that appointment. I knew this baby would be fine. The pregnancy was a surprise gift.

I answered the wall phone in the kitchen, clutching my purse and the appointment card next month for the obstetrician.

It was Mom. "Your father's sick."

It took a minute for her words to register.

"Your sister found out yesterday. She's going to call you today."

"Sick like the flu? Or, sick like, cancer sick."

She was blunt. "Cancer sick."

I sat at the kitchen table beside the phone. I had cottonmouth,

289

and my tongue felt thick. "April told me he'd been having trouble eating when they went to lunch. Like not being able to swallow well."

"The chickens have come home to roost," she said.

I paused and tried to find a way to describe how I was feeling. "It's weird, Mom."

"Your sister seems to think that he can beat it."

"What kind?"

"A bad one. Esophageal."

I wasn't sure if it was morning sickness, or the news about Dad. I suddenly felt nauseated.

"You still there?" Mom asked.

"Still here."

"Where have you been? I've been trying to reach you all morning."

"At the doctor's."

"Well?"

"Yep, due in January."

"Aww. What did Hank say?"

"I called him from the phone in the doctor's lobby. We're both excited. It's just that hearing about Dad and all throws me off."

"It always happens this way."

"What way?" I asked.

"When someone is on the way out, another one is on the way in."

••

A few days later, Mom's daily call brought brighter news. Her voice echoed over the line. "I landed one!"

I extended the cord on the wall phone to the stove and reached for a potholder to check the vegetables. "Mom, I'm in the middle of cooking dinner—"

In the background, I could hear Allan running back and forth in the family room mimicking the baseball players in the game Hank was watching on TV. I watched Hilary rolling her dolly in the toy stroller over the brick kitchen floor. This would have been Mom's version of Dante's hell, but I loved being a wife and mother in a stable home.

"Pay attention!" Mom barked into the phone. "I'm serious. I found a winner!"

I put the lid back on the green beans. Marge had invited Mom to The Beach Club both Sunday and Monday for Memorial Day Weekend a few days ago. That must be where she landed her guy.

"No way!" I became excited, but hesitant. "Really, Mom?"

"Swear to Buddha," she said. "It only took me four trips to the club to jump in the lake and come up with a fish!"

I covered the receiver with my hand and called to Hank over in the family room. "Mom found a winner!"

Six-year-old Allan came running into the kitchen. "Did he win a race?"

"He's about to, Allan." I laughed. "Tell me quick, Mom. I can't put off dinner for too long."

"Well," she began. "I was standing in the middle of the lobby at The Beach Club. Oh, and I was wearing this yellow jumpsuit, you know the one, it's tight. Really cute. I was tapping my foot to the piped-in music while I was waiting for Marge in the locker room."

"I can just see you," I laughed.

"So, this guy is sitting on a chair right there in the lobby and he calls over to me."

"How old, do you think?"

"Upper sixties, I'd guess. Anyway, he asks, 'Are you single?' and I say, 'Yes,' and he said, 'Well, come on over here and sit next to me.'"

"No!"

"Yes!" her voice rippled with excitement. "So, I go over there and sit in the chair next to him and he starts in with his repertoire."

"Like what?"

"He spoke with this hurried staccato voice as if he was trying to get it all out fast. 'Name's Allan MacDougall...My friends call me Dougie...I'm single...Been married four times, same one twice, so really three...I have five grown children, all good kids...I live in Bel Air, belong to The LA Country Club, and The Beach Club. I'm a retired investment guy, but I still keep a hand in it.'"

"Sounds like his resume. This guy's a crackup."

"Then, he points to my feet. I guess I was still tapping to the beat, and he said: 'You look like fun. You like music?' I told him that I did, and he asked for my phone number."

"Wow, Mom."

"He wrote it down on one of his cards and put it in his pocket just as his date walked out of the ladies room."

"Uh oh."

"Nope. She's too Gucci-Pucci. Had the face done and all. She's uptight. Not his type. I can tell. She gave me a look when he said, 'Nice to meet you, Marilyn.' Like daggers."

"Then, what?" I asked.

"I ignored her, batted the baby blues, and said, 'Pleasure.'"

"So," Mom continued, "he opens the front door of the club for Gucci-Pucci and as soon as she passes through with her designer scarf waving in the breeze, he turns back around to me and pats the pocket of his sport coat where he'd put my phone number."

She took a pause for effect. "That's when I knew that I had him."

Chapter Thirty-Seven

There's snow on the roof and fire in the furnace.
                                      —Mom about Dougie

Lighting from the church rafters bounced off of the Presbyterian pastor's forehead as he faced the audience. He opened his arms to welcome the three-hundred guests sitting in pews before him and gently pressed his hands together in prayer. "A miracle has brought us together here today."

Laughter broke out. The pastor stood bewildered, his hands frozen in prayer. This was not been the reaction he'd expected.

Little did this pastor know that he had hit the nail on the head with his stock greeting at *this* wedding ceremony.

••

Mom and Dougie's first date had been for cocktails on a Tuesday night at The Los Angeles Country Club. Mom had charged a new outfit at Robinson's, the only store left where she still had credit. It was a sailor-type suit with a red tie, white lapels, and a navy skirt. "I don't know if he likes the Junior League type or sexy," she told me. "I'd heard that he was in the army during World War II, so I'm opting for military."

Mom splurged to have her hair combed out for the occasion and drove her twelve year-old Mustang to meet Allan MacDougall.

"We spent two hours drinking wine and eating a handful of cardboard hors d'ouevres," Mom said the next morning.

As the date progressed and she became comfortable calling him by his nickname, she'd asked Dougie: "Do they feed people at this place?"

She must have passed muster during cocktails as he led her into the club's dining room.

After dinner, Dougie walked her to her car. "This yours?" he asked, obviously aware of the car's age. Mom proudly told him that it was paid for. When he closed the door and leaned down to say goodbye, he used the side mirror on the old Ford Mustang as an anchor, which promptly fell off in his hand.

"You should have seen him," Mom said. "He kept fumbling around with the side mirror in disbelief."

"Then what happened?" I asked.

"He asked me out for Thursday!"

Dougie had been born into wealth and raised on the east coast. He was to the manor born, complete with an authentic MacDougall family crest on the wall in his den. He'd settled in Pittsburgh after serving in WWII, married, and produced three children. After receiving his MBA in finance at the University of Pittsburgh, he'd decided that he was finished living where it's so cold.

His wife was not. "I was born in Pittsburgh and I'll die in Pittsburgh," she'd said. Which she did, years later, with Dougie, returning to serve as one of her pallbearers.

When he was thirty-four, he settled out west in Los Angeles where he remarried and had two more children in a second marriage that lasted eight years.

A year after his third wife died of lung cancer, when he was sixty-nine and widowed, he married my mother.

Even with all the marriages and divorces, Dougie maintained a good relationship with his children, who, as adults, still called him "Daddy." For me, that said it all. He was a man who hadn't given them away.

The lighting had dimmed in the church, highlighting Mom and Dougie before the altar. Standing next to my sister as Mom's bridesmaids, I remembered Mom telling me about the proposal. "Can you believe it? I'm sixty years old, twenty pounds overweight, haven't had a facelift, never finished college, have no money, and I still got one?"

My sister, dressed in pale pink lace, her blonde hair full and tousled in an up-do at Mom's insistence, gave me a knowing glance. There we were, once again, enveloped into a new family. "Can you believe this whole thing?" I whispered to April, glancing at the five adult MacDougall children on the other side of us.

"I know," she whispered back. "Another whole group."

"I like them, though."

"Hey, listen," she whispered, "it's easy this time. We don't have to live with them."

It had been years since I'd had contact with any of my step-siblings, Little Louise, Carl, or Bonnie. As for the Stubbs, I hadn't seen Sarah or Jim since Christmas dinner 1982. Bill and John I'd kept up with, but had not seen in four years. And, now, here I was looking across at a new cast of characters—Polly, Lanny, Lorain, Randy, and Sandy—bringing the total stepsibling count to thirteen, less Teddy (Louise's son), who had died of cancer.

"It'll never be dull," Hank had said about of the ever-changing cast of characters.

••

Their courtship had been a whirlwind. After a few dates, Dougie began asking my mother to travel with him. The first trip had been a group golf outing in Oklahoma. Mom hated golf and planned to spend the days lounging by the hotel pool. Dougie had wanted to make sure that she would be able to use the rental car in case she wanted to go out and explore. When the rental agent asked for my mother's driver's license, she crossed her fingers and handed the Hertz agent her expired license that she'd jerry-rigged.

"Ma'am," he said, smoothing his hand across her license. "Looks like some liquid paper, or something, is covering the expiration date."

"Oh," Mom said, brushing the air with her hand, "don't mind that."

"But, Ma'am..."

Dougie, who knew what was going on, rolled his eyes and told Mom to put her license back in her wallet.

"He never got mad," Mom told me later, "or scolded me. He laughed it off and simply said that we need to fix it."

"'We,'" I replied. "That means he's invested, Mom."

"Sure is," she said. "He's paying all the back tickets for me."

She'd finally met a man who looked out for her without demeaning her.

••

When Hank and I met him for dinner, I liked him right away. It was clear that the scotch in his hand was not the center of Dougie's attention as it had been with my father, or with Allan. My mother was the center.

I had never seen her like this with a man. She didn't jump to, as she always had with Dad and Allan. There was no desperate need to amuse or to jolly him up. It was the first time I'd seen my mother *relax* and enjoy herself around a man.

By the end of the evening, I knew she'd found her winner. "We have fun together," Mom told me, "Other than the golf, we like the same things."

They'd only been dating a few months when Dougie asked my mother to move in with him. Mom had been over at his home in Bel Air. It was four in the morning, and they were both drinking Tuaca.

"No," had been my mother's answer. She'd had the candles going, the music on, and was wearing a sexy outfit.

"Then, I'll buy you an apartment," he offered.

"No."

"Then, what?" Dougie asked.

"I just need four words."

Without skipping a beat, Dougie knew what to do. "Will you marry me?"

When they woke later that morning, the sun was up. "It was all bright and shiny," Mom told me. "I wanted to make sure he wasn't all talk, so I said to him: 'I guess I'll call the girls to tell them.' He agreed and handed me the phone and I thought, 'Bingo!'"

••

There was no nervous shaking of baby's breath and roses in Mom's bouquet of scented white gardenias during this ceremony. My mother extended her hand as Dougie placed a sapphire and diamond wedding band on her finger and slid it next to her engagement ring, a flawless five-karat Ceylon Sapphire. Her long pale pink nails (painted to match her dress) complemented the ring's dazzle.

The pastor stood before Mom and Dougie. He crossed his hands at the waist. "By the power invested in me, I now pronounce you man and wife. You may kiss the bride."

After dining and dancing at Mom and Dougie's wedding reception at The Beach Club, their adult children and spouses headed north Friday morning to the Alisol Guest Ranch in the Santa Ynez

Valley to join the newlyweds on their weekend honeymoon. It was Dougie's idea. "Everyone will be in town for the wedding," he'd told my mother. "This way they'll get to know each other. I'll pay."

Mom thought it was a good idea, too. "A honeymoon's a little different," she told April and me, "when you're on your third and he's on his fourth."

Hank and I were the last to arrive, having dropped Allan and Hilary with Hank's parents at their home in Santa Barbara on the way up. At check-in, we were given the room next to the newlyweds amidst a barrage of jokes and jeering from the rest of the clan: "Last to arrive gets the prize room!"

That night, we celebrated Dougie's seventieth birthday in a private dining room. When the cake came out, Lorain, his second oldest from New York, started a round of toasts. Raising a glass of champagne, she said: "Happy Birthday, Daddy. You've found the perfect mate."

"And," added Lanny, the oldest son, but the youngest of the Eastern contingent, "she's not greedy!"

Prior to the nuptials, Mom had made it clear to Dougie and his children that she was not interested in what she called his "trappings" during the negotiation of the prenuptial agreement. "I just want security."

Now Lanny looked over at Mom. "Marilyn, what was that Gershwin song you told us you used to sing?"

"The one I sang in piano bars when I was on the hunt for a man?" Mom asked.

"That's the one," he said. "Something about a lamb lost in the woods?"

"Was I *ever* lost in the woods," Mom laughed.

"Then," she said, taking Dougie's hand, "I found your father."

Dougie turned to face her. "Hey, you got that wrong. *I* found *you.*"

Mom stood up and backed away from the dinner table. Dressed in a blue pants suit with a sparkly top, she fluffed up the back of her frosted bouffant with her long pink-lacquered fingernails and cleared her throat. "My pipes are rusty, but I'll give it a go."

"Oh, god," I cringed to Hank. "Here comes the singing."

"C'mon," Hank laughed, "she enjoys herself."

"Do you think she's any good?"

"Like I said," he smiled, "she enjoys herself."

All eyes were on Mom as she began in a low B flat: *"There's an old saying that love is blind...Still, we're often told 'seek and ye shall find."*

Hank dipped his chin and leaned in to me. "Check out the shepherd."

I looked over at Dougie. Behind his glasses, his eyes were filled with tears.

"I was a little lamb who's lost in the wood...I know I could always be good...to the one who'll watch over me."

"Look," Dougie's youngest son, Sandy, said. "Daddy's puddling up."

"Won't you tell him please to put on some speed...Follow my lead....Oh"—Mom belted these lyrics out for effect—*"Oh, how I need....Someone to watch over meeee."*

A loud applause broke out. Mom, grinning ear-to-ear, curtsied, the heart-shaped sequins on her top sparkling with her every move.

"He loves it when I sing." She sat next to Dougie who was dabbing at his eyes with his pocket-handkerchief. "He tips the guys at the piano to let me accompany them."

The MacDougall's egged her on. "C'mon, Marilyn. More! More!"

"Another one?" Mom asked, more an announcement than a question. "Guess I'll get back out there and trot the boards."

April and I both laughed. "Oh no, they're encouraging her."

On Saturday, everyone went horseback riding and played tennis. At seven months pregnant, I stuck with croquet and the organized walks. In the late afternoon, a few gathered to watch the UCLA football game on TV in the resort's library. I sat with Hank as he, Randy, and Sandy (all of us UCLA fans) watched our favorite lose to Washington State. While they shouted insults at the referees, my mind was elsewhere, trying to hold on to the good feeling of being with these people who treated us as if we'd been family for years. My alma mater Bruins may have lost but, at that moment, I felt as if I'd won. I'd finally been blessed with a happy extended family.

On Sunday morning, April and I headed for the pay telephone just outside the dining room area. My sister wanted to call our father to see how he was doing after surgery to remove the cancer. I wanted to check in again on our children at Hank's parents' house.

Hank's parents, Bob and Jo Haldeman, were the quintessential grandparents, doting on our children and babysitting them whenever they could. I had no worries when they were in their care. Bob and Jo's life now was all about their grandchildren, their church, and the quiet life in Santa Barbara. They were solid, dependable, and loving to Hank and me and our children. The so-called "Nixon's son-of-a-bitch," the man with the severe flattop on the cover of *Time Magazine*, was anything but that in his personal life. I loved to watch him play with his grandchildren, whom he adored. Or, to spend time with Hank and me. He was solid, like the son whom I'd married. I'd envied Hank's childhood. Growing up with parents who paid the bills on time and were devoted to their children. Even with Watergate, their family had held together.

As expected, when I called, Allan and Hilary were great, living it up at Grandpa and Grandmother's with horseback rides in the ring at the back of their property, picking avocados in the garden, swimming in their pool, all the while Grandmother was making home videos of it all.

April made her call next and I could tell by the look on her face that Dad, lying in a hospital bed at Cedar's Sinai, was not good.

I'd stepped to the side to give my sister some privacy. After she hung up, I moved forward.

"It wasn't successful," she said.

There was a long pause. Then she sighed. "They were unable to operate. Closed him back up. The cancer's too far gone."

My features gave nothing away. No sadness at hearing of a father who was gravely ill or a joyous revenge that my father who had disowned me, rejected me to please Louise, was now terminal.

I knew that I should have felt something, but I didn't. My first thought was to console April.

My mother had once told me that feeling nothing is worse than feeling hate. "If you hate someone," she'd said, "they still matter to you."

"Don't tell Mom," April said, cocking her head and twisting a piece of her shoulder-length blonde hair. "It'll spoil her honeymoon."

"I doubt that," I said. "But don't worry I won't."

"You, ok?" I asked. I *did* care about her.

"I'm all right," she said, letting go of the spiral of hair. "He might pull through."

"He could," I said, knowing he wouldn't. April was an optimist. In this situation, I was not.

Chapter Thirty-Eight

Even houses on even streets.

—Mom

Mom agreed that it was time to sell the Fremont house. Dougie, a retired financial analyst, felt that the inflated housing market was about to burst and there was no reason to hold onto it. April had been looking at homes an hour's drive north of Los Angeles in the Conejo Valley. She'd reconciled with Glenn who was now making enough income as an iron worker to pay a modest mortgage.

Allan Stubbs, who with Arlene had moved from San Diego to a home in Prescott, Arizona, had signed off on the Fremont home long ago.

After a walk-through of 127 Fremont Place with the realtor, John Woodward (brother of my childhood friend, Anne), he, my mother, and my sister sat down with him at the scratched dining room table on stained and worn upholstered chairs and set up the terms of the deal.

The 4,500 square feet of now-tired bones would go on the market for $1.4 million. It would be an "as is" sale, meaning that the buyer would receive the property in the exact condition it was when the sale papers were signed.

My mother called me later that afternoon. "Well," she said, "it's official. The candle has flickered and dimmed."

"How do you feel?" I asked.

"I don't look back."

••

"Can you believe that people live like this?"

It was the Broker's Open House, the day where the agents preview newly listed homes for a potential buyer. Our family home teamed with realtors determined to pick it apart like crows on a carcass.

A younger agent nodded in agreement as she handed her colleague the information sheet listing the details. As they made their way toward the living room, the older agent stumbled slightly and grabbed onto the arm of the younger one. The heel of her sensible black pump had caught in one of the holes in the carpet. Unfazed, she straightened and adjusted her suit jacket with a swift tug at the hem. She raised her eyebrows: "My dear, *this* is one where you have to watch for hazards."

Noticing the cracks in the ceiling near the piano by the window she gasped. "Un-be-*lieve*-able."

"Look over here," the younger one said, eyeing the huge water stain from the bathroom above.

"Good god!"

"A leak for sure."

"More like a gush, my dear."

The younger one nodded, pointing to the yellowed shutters missing some of its slats. She rolled her eyes. "This place is a shambles."

"Honey, that's why it's listed 'as is.'"

My sister, a few feet away, heard every word. "I was mortified," she told me later, recounting the details. "I should have never stuck around to watch."

Despite its loss of luster, 127 Fremont Place had been my home from childhood through adolescence. I cringed to hear it so disparaged.

Outside, every crack on the sidewalk lining the street from our house to the big cement entrance gates on Wilshire Boulevard was embedded in my mind. I knew exactly where the hardwood floors creaked, was intimately familiar with the groan from the tired furnace as it cranked up. I could still smell the stale blast of the warm musty air that came through the vents after a long period of no use. In the maid's room, Molly had had pictures of her native Ireland on the walls and lace doilies on the dresser. Later they were replaced with Lupe's collection of religious candles that surrounded her twelve-inch resin statue of the Blessed Virgin. Most recently, the empty room had been a refuge for my mother's cats. Though April and Glenn had stripped the carpet to the hardwood, the smell of cat urine remained in the room that had once been a refuge for two housekeepers during turbulent times.

I could feel the itchy brown sofa that had once been in my father's den off of the once-named "Hong-Kong Room." I could see Allan's no-nonsense wooden desk that had replaced it, a desk lacking accents or ornamentation except brushed brass handles on six drawers. I could see him sitting there, paying bills with his slim silver Cross pen and the familiar yellow-colored checks from Crocker Bank. In the corner was Allan's leather chair where I'd listened to Jethro Tull through Bill's big white earphones. I'd looked out that window at holiday time and been mesmerized by the Christmas tree lit up on top of the Farmer's Insurance building blocks away on Rimpau and Wilshire.

Out front was where I'd snuck my first kiss in the eighth grade from a boy named Brian. I'd been wearing an orange shift. I'd stood on the sidewalk. He was on his bike. It had been awkward. When he reached for my waist, I'd been glad I'd worn one of Mom's girdles to hide my bulges.

My first friend, Mary Jo, had lived down the street at 122 Fremont Place. Around the block, at 76 Fremont was where my best friend, Anne, had lived.

The Green Room was where my first boyfriend, Mike, gave me a small sapphire ring on my seventeenth birthday. It was also where Allan Stubbs had played solitaire each morning with his finished breakfast plate nearby.

That backyard was where the big round light from the pool's deep end cast a shaft of light the night Hank asked Allan Stubbs for my hand in marriage. My wedding reception, held there, was where my mother, holding a microphone, sang "I Can't Give You Anything But Love" with the band in front of the garage. I'd seen her from April's old bedroom window upstairs while I was dressing to leave on my honeymoon. She'd still been singing as Hank and I dashed down the familiar brick-lined front walk under a shower of rice.

127 Fremont Place was where I'd once hid in my bedroom closet as a child, the safe place where I could cry when I was sad. My father had thrown his scotch against the wall along the front stairs, the brown liquid dripping down on the floral wallpaper. I could still trace the faded stain. I'd seen the fat me in my mother's three-sided dressing room before Weight Watcher's, each angle confirming big thighs, chubby arms, and a large rear.

April's boyfriends had dubbed me "Hot Dog Heather" on that front porch because I looked like I ate a lot of hot dogs. I'd kept Van de Kamp's chocolate cookies hidden in the white bread box in the kitchen, the Reddi-Wip nearby in the refrigerator to spray into my mouth when no one was looking. In the drawer beside my bed, I'd stored my candy stash and hid Dad's check before I ripped it up.

I'd last seen Aunt Carolyn, a thin figure with her head in her hands, in the straight-backed chair in the Music Room before she committed suicide with a combination of pills, booze, and carbon monoxide.

I'd listened to the record player from the Music Room below until the early hours of dawn when my mother dated different men. April sang Leslie Gore for endless hours in her room, setting her hair in orange juice cans in front of the dresser mirror.

Drunken fights had started with my mother and father in that living room, and later between my mother and Allan Stubbs. She'd begged both husbands not to leave from her blue bedroom as they'd hurriedly packed their bags.

127 Fremont was where, at eleven, I'd told my desperate mother, in bed with the covers over her head, that she needed to get up and face what lay ahead after my father's departure. It's where I had lived with two different fathers and two different families—and all that went with it.

There would be no pulling the For Sale sign out of the lawn this time. I was ready to let it go.

••

Within the first week there were offers. When counter offers were figured in, the best was a buyer offering $1,150,000, cash.

"Take it," the realtor advised. "Before it's 'two bathroom's upstairs and 'two down' instead of the one."

April laughed. "Before the bathroom above the living room falls through?"

"Exactly.

••

And then a couple weeks later, on a late Saturday afternoon in May, I got the call. I picked up the wall phone in the kitchen. It was my mother.

"Your father died."

Chapter Thirty-Nine

The mills of the gods grind slowly, but oh, so exceedingly fine.
—Mom, quoting the ancient pagans

The microwave dinged, signaling that Joseph's cereal was ready. The conversation with my mother had ended, but I stood paralyzed, staring out of the kitchen window at the San Gabriel Mountains in the distance, my hand frozen on the receiver of the wall phone. Everything had stopped.

Joseph cooed in his infant seat. The sound of Hank typing on the computer close by in the sunroom brought me back. I slipped my hand off the receiver and started to reach for the cereal in the microwave. Each movement was slow and deliberate, as if I was walking underwater.

"Hank?"

The tap-tap stopped. "Yeah."

"Can you come here?"

The legs of his desk chair slid on the hard wood. "What's up?"

I turned from the microwave, holding the steaming bowl of cereal. "I just need to let this cool down." My face must have given me away.

"Heath, you alright?"

"Dad died."

"Ooooo—kaaay," Hank took a breath. He knew the history. Knew how I felt. Knew that the hate had turned to some strange form of disinterest, but the man who had just died was still my father. "You knew from April that he was near the end."

"That's true." I picked up the baby spoon with its soft plastic tip. "But somehow, you know..." My voice trailed off. Tears pooled.

"Here, let me feed Joe." He gently took the warm bowl out of my hand.

"I haven't talked to April, yet." I swiped at tears with the back of my hand.

"Don't call your sister yet. Give yourself a minute."

"I know." I left to go to our bedroom.

"I'll come when I finish here," he called out as I headed down the hallway.

The air was still in the bedroom and I opened a window to get a breeze. I could hear Allan and Hilary playing in the yard. Allan was pretending to be a football star, mimicking the roar of the crowds as he raced around with his ball. Hilary was on the swing set. The methodical squeal of the chain-on-steel hook back and forth, back and forth, was like the ticking of a clock. Kid sounds.

I sat at the foot of the bed not knowing, really, what to do with myself. I stretched out on my right side, propping my head up with a bent elbow and stared at the lines of the late afternoon sun slicing through the plantation shutters. I'd stopped crying.

Hank came in the room just as the phone rang. "I put Joe in his playpen," he said, reaching for the phone. It was Glenn.

"Yes," she knows." Hank nodded, listening to the details. My father had passed away that morning at his home on Cherokee Lane in Beverly Hills. His houseman, Ernie, was there. Cancer had been the cause.

Before Hank could finish the conversation, I sat up. "Ask him if he left everything to April."

Hank furrowed his brow. "Now?" he mouthed.

"I need to know," I whispered.

"Heather wants to know if he left everything to April."

Silence. Hank stared at me. His brown eyes: I could always read them. "I see," he said, looking me head-on, nodding.

I felt as if someone had dropped one of those thick dental X-ray aprons on top of me. The heaviness. My shoulders. My chest. My arms felt detached as if they didn't belong to me. This was the final rejection. He'd had the last word.

"Thanks for calling, Glenn. I'll let Heather know." Hank hung up. He leaned over to me as I hunched down on my side of the bed and studied the carefree maiden with her basket of fruit on the toile bedding. A little bird, above her, carried a piece of ribbon in its beak.

"Heath, look at me," Hank said, leaning closer.

I noticed the soft lines on his face, so close to mine, as he lay there with me. "Would you want his money?"

I remembered the check from my father that had arrived in the mail on my twelfth birthday, his signature, then, so familiar on the pale blue bank paper. I'd kept it in my nightstand drawer for days, hidden next to the candy wrappers, eventually ripping it up in tiny little pieces. At twelve, I knew that money wasn't going to fix his leaving us.

My eyes glided back down to the soothing pastoral scene. Hank was right. I'd never wanted Dad's money.

Still, I wondered. What would it be like not to have to rely upon Hank for every dime? We were on a tight budget. There was no room for frills with two children in private schools, now a third baby, a mortgage, car payments, insurance, taxes. Money was tight. And I had a love for beautiful things. What would it feel like to buy something extra without having to worry about where the money would come from?

I smoothed my hand back over the maiden. I, too, wanted to be carefree with my own basket of fruit. I wanted financial independence. I wanted to have some wealth of my own.

Still, Hank was right. I'd never wanted Dad's money.

Joseph began crying in his playpen and Hank dashed off to check on him. The heaviness started to lift as I went for my address book. I needed to hear his voice. To reaffirm what I felt, to speak to the father who'd been there for me through my childhood, up to, and including, my wedding.

I dialed the number and waited. On the fourth ring, Allan Stubbs answered. It had been months since we last spoke.

"Allan, it's Heather."

"Hi doll! You sound funny. You ok?"

"No, not really."

"What?" His strong yet soothing voice made me start to cry again, filling that parental need I hadn't realized I was seeking.

"Dad died today. And, I guess…I guess, I just wanted to tell you that I love you. That's all."

"I love you, too, Heather."

"I just needed to hear your voice."

"You can call me anytime."

"I know."

••

April never told me the amount of money she inherited and I didn't ask. It was her inheritance. Not mine. She'd loved him. She could get over his abandonment. I couldn't.

I was jealous of her newfound wealth. It was hard not to be bitter. Our father had chosen her over me, leaving his message loud and clear. He'd wanted nothing to do with me. Especially after I'd embarrassed him in front of everyone at Connie's wake when I thanked him for leaving us. In the end, he'd had the final word in a legal document, gifting all his worldly wealth to his more deserving daughter. It was a "fuck-you," Mom said.

••

The first time April and I were together after Dad had died, I visited her new house in Agoura. Dad's large-scale furniture crowded the small living room like an antique showroom on Robertson Boulevard. Dad's imprint was everywhere. There was even a framed picture of him perched on a side table.

"So, you really had no idea Dad was leaving everything to you?" I sat across from her on a delicate French mint-colored loveseat.

"It was a complete surprise." She curled her shapely legs under her on the matching side chair.

I reached for my coffee cup among the menagerie of *objet d'arts* that littered the glass-topped coffee table. "Remember, I told you that Dad said he wasn't leaving anything to me. That's what I always thought."

"I know," I looked down at the coffee cup I held for comfort in both hands. "It's just that..." My voice trailed off, "I don't know..."

"I've always been totally upfront with you about my relationship with Dad." April unfolded her legs and stood up from the chair. "C'mon into the kitchen and let's eat lunch."

I followed her, rehashing our former conversations. It was true. She had told me that her relationship with Dad wasn't about the money. "He told me a million times that I wasn't in his will. That he was leaving it all to Jean, his ex-girlfriend," April added. "They were still close."

She took out a big wooden bowl. "Look, I got you green apples." She began to chop them. "And, carrots, too. Your fave."

"Cottage cheese?"

"Of course. It's Heather food," she laughed. "Can you grab the plates?"

I reached up in the cabinet. "How could you have cared about a man like him, Ape?"

"We've been over it, Heath," she sighed, loading my plate.

"I just hated it when Justin and Jeffrey called him Grandpa Bob. You, yourself: You said he had no real desire to be around them, that if you brought them over they'd have to hang out with Ernie, the houseman."

She was matter-of-fact. "They loved Ernie's special hamburgers. It was a big deal for them."

My anger boiled under the surface. "Didn't that bother you? That he pawned them off on Ernie? Forget that he pawned *us* off on Allan over a scotch on the rocks at Scandia!"

Without looking up from her salad, April replied: "It's the way he was, Heather. And, I accepted that."

I stabbed at my salad, my fork making an angry sound. I had not been able to accept that about him and it was eating me up that she had.

••

Months later, I was still struggling. And Mom was furious that my father had left me out completely. "So typical, the bastard," she'd said. "I could kill him, but he's already dead."

Despite Mom and Hank's empathy, I couldn't seem to pick myself up. Both worried about how my father's death, and his final dig was affecting me.

He and Mom agreed. "Go see Bill."

Bill, Mom's therapist who'd seen her through the Allan-leaving debacle, had recently retired but remained "on call" for my mother. He agreed to see me for an appointment at his apartment in West Hollywood.

••

314

Dried-up fall leaves from the maple tree above crunched under the wheels of my Volvo wagon as I maneuvered back and forth into a tight spot in front of Bill's apartment building. Traffic had been heavy that morning, giving me time to think. Six months had elapsed since my father's death and I couldn't seem to sort through my feelings about my sister; I was all over the map.

Now, seated across from Bill on a worn leather sofa, I told him the story. He looked at me through black-framed glasses, his tall stature and shoulders erect in the plaid wingback chair. He coughed before picking up the burning cigarette in an already full ashtray to take another puff.

"How do you want to handle this?"

I searched for an answer among the framed English hunting scenes mounted on the wall above his chair. Finding none, I glanced out the window to his terrace to the wall of bamboo that was the backdrop in the shaded garden of potted plants.

"I thought I was alright," I told Bill. "I've got a happy marriage, three healthy, beautiful children. We own a home and Hank is building his business," I paused. My mouth became dry and my stomach started to ache at the core. "But, I'm not all right. He left everything to my sister, leaving me out completely. I mean, I didn't even *like* him and had written him off years ago, but it was...I don't know...the nail in the coffin. And, Bill," I added, "I hate to admit it, but I'm jealous and hurt and basically feel like shit."

"What are you looking for?"

My eyes slid over to the terrace and the wall of bamboo. Without thinking, I blurted out: "I love my sister more than the money."

Bill nodded.

"I love her and I'm not going to let my father ruin that."

"Then," he said, "there's your answer."

••

315

A few days later, navigating the tight curves and narrow lanes of the Pasadena Freeway, it dawned on me. Maybe my sister had been so influenced by my mother's first two failed marriages that she felt that she couldn't depend on a man.

Her marriage to Glenn was on the rocks again. Was this inheritance her way out?

Heading home up Orange Grove Avenue, the traffic was heavy. Something was going on at the Tournament of Roses House. As I crept up in the line of cars, I saw a group of well-dressed men and women making their way down the long driveway adjacent to the massive front lawn of the Wrigley Mansion. It was fall. Preparations for the New Year's Day Rose Parade must be in full swing.

Maybe the money was a way for her to ensure that she'd be able to take care of herself and her boys financially on her own? Maybe Dad knew that. Maybe he was protecting her?

I didn't need what he had to offer. Still, I had resentment. I loved my sister. She loved me. It was my problem and I'd get over it.

But, it would take time.

••

At the end of June, the escrow closed on 127 Fremont Place. The new owner, a Korean fellow, had it razed to the ground. By August, a foundation had been laid, ready for a new home to be built. But not before my cousin Jonathan paid a visit, salvaging out of the rubble, a balustrade from one of the balconies. Tara had become the Titanic.

As for the sale, an agreement had been made and my mother paid Allan Stubbs $75,000, after he threatened litigation, feeling that he deserved a part of the profit. The rest, my mother put into an investment account that Dougie set up for her in her name.

For the first time in her life, my mother had money of her own. "And," she boasted, "I earned every goddamn dime of it."

Chapter Forty

Don't foreclose.

—Mom

Mom thrived in her new life with Dougie, and we, their adult children, went along for the ride. We enjoyed numerous family trips similar to the honeymoon, all expenses paid by Mom and Dougie. It was a new family life for April and me. April, now divorced from Glenn, was happily married to Dennis, a realtor in the Conejo Valley. They'd teamed up together and were selling real estate side-by-side. Like my mother now, April was respected and loved, in the type of healthy and enriching relationship I'd sought out and found twenty-two years earlier. I was glad I'd decided as a kid that there'd be no drinks flying against the walls of *my* home.

But Dougie had begun to have sporadic dizzy spells. He was 82. He'd seen a doctor, started medication, and continued his active life of golf, travel, and following the stock market. But Mom was worried. "The wheels are starting to come off," she told me. "And, it scares me."

What if Dougie died? During one particular health scare in Hawaii, she smoked a cigarette, got into the "sauce," and started making lists. Instead of mundane things like "Clean house" and "Call Heather" she noted what she'd have to do for her survival if something happened to Dougie.

Between sips of Sauvignon Blanc and drags off of her Virginia Slim Menthols, she listed all the people on whom she could rely on so that she would never be alone. She hated to be alone. She'd never stopped carrying the weight of her previous marriages. Always on the ready, she needed a back-up, and added some strategies for yet another man:

1. *Facelift (optional—maybe I'm too old)*
2. *Lose weight—no problem because I'll be a wreck.*

Later, the news was good. The procedure had gone well. Dougie would be fine and could even fly back to Los Angeles in a week's time.

Mom sighed into the phone. "We dodged a bullet, Heather, thank God…"

I could tell from her voice that she was still on edge. "You ok, Mom?"

"I really dig Dougie," she said into the phone. She lowered her voice. "This time, I finally got it right."

••

For the next year and a half, Dougie's pacemaker seemed to do the trick and my mother lapsed into the familiar lull of happiness that had been her life before the dizziness started.

In December 2003, Dougie and Mom took us on another family trip, this time to The Bellagio Hotel in Las Vegas to celebrate my stepsister Lorain's sixtieth birthday. While Hank and the rest of the family slept late one morning, I wandered down to Mom and Dougie's suite.

My mother, dressed in a Chinese silk knee-length bathrobe that she'd gotten on a trip to China in the early days of their courtship, welcomed me. Her once slim waist had expanded ("I eat when I'm happy"), allowing for little overlap of the robe, exposing a thin line of her purple nylon nightgown. She held a croissant in one hand and a powder-puff in the other.

Mom gestured to a table set for two. A large red rose sprung from a slim silver vase in the center. The linen covering the croissants lay beside the overfilled basket of breads. "C'mon in. We just ordered room service."

Dougie was stretched out on a club chair in the living area reading *The New York Times*, his wavy hair topping the edge of the newspaper like vanilla icing on a cake. He collapsed one side of the paper, showing his face to greet me, his over-sized wire-rimmed glasses slipping down his nose.

"Hi Heath! What happened? No good sex with Hank this morning? That why you're here?"

"Oh, God, Dougie. You're the worst," I laughed.

My sister and I had concluded not long after the wedding, that even though Dougie had been educated at St. Paul's and Princeton, he had, after all, married Mom who was hardly "Lady Grace." There had to be a bit of the raunchy about him. And we were right. He couldn't resist an off-color remark.

He tipped his coffee cup to me. "Cheers! Grab some coffee." He turned back to his newspaper.

"Is it all right if I just hang out here 'till the rest get up?" I asked.

"Sure," they said in unison, Mom adding: "TV's in the bedroom. I'm going to go put on my face."

My mother went into the bathroom still eating the croissant, leaving a trail of pastry flakes in her wake. In the bedroom, I pulled up the bedspread and plopped down on the bed, placing a couple pillows against the headboard and leaned back. I reached for the remote on the nightstand and clicked on the set. I flipped around Sunday news programs and settled on an old episode of *I Love Lucy*, my favorite.

The door to the bathroom was open and I watched my mother picking through the plethora of makeup strewn all over the counter. She reached for her coffee cup, took a sip then added a splash of water from the tap to cool it off. It was as if I was transformed back to a child of eight watching her in her dressing room in Fremont. I studied her as she leaned into the mirror to apply more eye shadow. Her movements were the same, but the setting was so different.

I turned back to the television. Lucy was arguing with Ricky about her allowance. "I can't live on this, Ricky!" she shrilled.

A knock at the door of the suite brought me back. "Maid service."

"Dougie, can you deal with that?" Mom called out.

"Yep," he replied, moving over to the door. "You want service, now?" he asked Mom.

Mom reached for the Duo Eyelash glue, expertly lining the rim of a fake lash. "No. Tell her much later."

She was telling *him* what to do.

I'd never witnessed my mother calling the shots with a husband, much less observed her in a calm domestic scene. I followed her back and forth from her open suitcase on the folding rack, her clothes spilling over the side, to the bathroom, where she aimlessly rifled through her overstuffed make-up bag and back to the closet, looking for a blouse. There was no tension, no twisting of the hair.

Dougie called out to her with a newsy headline. She responded with a "Wow." Aimless chatter. Easy banter. Mom wasn't stilted, or overly alert, or trying to please a husband who'd stopped caring.

I leaned back into the softness of the stacked pillows. Lucy and Ricky were at the kitchen table. Toast popped from the toaster. Lucy grabbed it mid-air and plopped it on Ricky's plate to the roar of canned laughter.

Mom slipped into her day clothes and buttoned her blouse in the bathroom mirror. She tilted her head to inspect, then, unbuttoned the blouse one more notch to show a hint of now-creped cleavage. I smiled. Some things never change.

"You want me to order you breakfast?" she asked me.

I crossed my ankles and settled in, clicking the sound up on the TV. "No, Mom. Thanks. I'll wait to eat with Hank."

This must be what it feels like when your parents are happy. To be this secure, this cared for. To feel relaxed with your parents and not on-edge waiting for the fight. All my childhood, I'd been looking for this, a mother who cared if I ate breakfast, who was relaxed, whose bedroom was not a battleground and a place where the men packed their bags. It had taken me 44 years to get here, but I was going to hang onto this moment.

Then, I thought of my own three children. This must be what they feel. Or, do they even realize such a feeling, not knowing any other?

Chapter Forty-One

January 2018

In God's waiting room.
—Mom, referring to the "old people's home"

Fluorescent lighting bounces off the pale blue walls of Mom's private room at the Jewish Home for the Aging in Reseda, a mere 11 miles northwest from the home she shared with Dougie in Bel Air and 19 from where she raised me in Fremont Place. "It's East Jesus," Mom would say—if she actually knew where she was on the map.

I pull my chair closer to Mom in her wheelchair. She wants to tell me something but her words are mumbled and low. She's now 90. Her hands, nails painted fire engine red, begin to shake, a by-product of the Parkinson's.

I lean closer. "Mom, you've got to speak up. I know it's hard but just try."

"Your father..." She brings a shaking hand up to swipe her now grey bangs out of her eyes.

I straighten in my chair, bracing. She hasn't mentioned my father in decades. He's been dead 29 years. We don't usually talk about him, but it's clear she has something important to tell me.

She strings out the words. "Love, your father."

"Love my father? Mom, what?"

She crushes her eyes shut. Long gone are the false eyelashes. A faint line of sparse lashes is all that remains at the edge of her eyelid.

"A letter," she tells me, opening her eyes. "Love, your father."

She needs to unburden herself and I'm having trouble following. But there's definitely a comma in her voice between "love" and "your father." My heart beats faster and my mouth goes dry. "What letter?"

Her hands shake even more. "Don't be mad."

I lean forward and place my hands on top of hers, to steady her. To steady me. My voice is low and slow to reassure her. "Mom? A letter from Dad?"

"Yes. He signed it: 'Love, your father.'"

"When?"

The words take a long time. "Please don't be mad. *Please* Heatherbean."

"I'm not mad. Just tell me."

"He wrote to you. A letter. Before your wedding."

That would have been 38 years ago. "What? I didn't get a letter."

She nods, closing her eyes again. "I know. I hid it."

"What?"

Her eyes stay shut. "In the garage in Fremont."

"So," I try to grasp what she's telling me. "A letter from Dad arrived for me and you read it?"

She opens her eyes and looks at me. Really looks at me, her pale blue eyes fixed on mine. "Yes."

"And in that letter," my voice cracks saying the words, "he wrote that he loved me?"

"Yes," she replies, never taking her eyes away.

"And you hid it because...?"

"I didn't want him to mess up the wedding and your relationship with Allan."

"You thought that I might ask Dad to walk me down the aisle instead of Allan?"

"Yes."

I release her hands and sit back in the chair. "Oh. My. God."

"Don't be mad." She reaches for me with frail arms. Her head is lightly rattling back and forth.

I take her hands and gently place them back in her lap. "Mom, I'm not mad. I just don't know whether to laugh or cry."

I give her a kiss goodbye on her cheek and then, in a daze I walk out to my car, taking in what my mother has confessed.

Heading home to Pasadena, the 134 Freeway is at a standstill on this late afternoon. In the rearview mirror, I catch sight of palm trees radiant in the slanting light. As the sun dips further, the buildings take on a boxy silhouette.

My face feels hot and my hands are sweaty on the steering wheel. I turn the air conditioning to high and tilt the vents toward me. In the attic of my mind, I try to make sense of it all. For years, I believed that I was worth nothing. That if I was not worthy of my own father's love, than I must not be lovable.

When I was nine, I'd awoken at midnight to the noise of one of my parent's party in full swing in the living room below. I'd slipped out of bed and padded barefoot down the hallway to the front stairs, settling on a high-low carpeted step, and leaned my forehead against the spindle of the banister.

"April's smashing," Mom had been bragging to one of the party-goers. "The boys can't keep their eyes off of her."

I didn't hear the response from the party guest, none of the back and forth of their conversation, but I did hear clearly Mom's reply: "Yes, April *really* is my favorite."

I'd pressed my forehead hard against the banister in an effort to push away what I'd overheard, and in doing so, had made a red mark, branded myself as the child who was an embarrassment. Fat, foul-mouthed, a poor student. Worthless.

All along I'd been wrong about me. I cast my thoughts back across the months, the seasons, the years. I'd been wrong about myself in so many situations. And yet, despite it all, I'd made good decisions. Despite parents who made me feel worthless, I'd created a stable home and family, the most lasting prize in life. I'd chosen a way of living that didn't glitter, wasn't shiny, or to be applauded. I'd rejected the chaos, glitz, and glamour of my mother's choosing. And my father's.

In doing so, I'd chosen to go the opposite direction, to make an effort to nurture and love my children so completely they'd never know the pain I'd felt, nor feel the neglect. And it had worked. They were wonderful adults now, and I was so proud of them and pleased with the life I'd built with Hank.

Ours was a quieter life. One I loved.

My face starts to cool as dusk descends and I lower the air conditioning as I merge to the left where the 5 Freeway South splits off to the right.

I think of Allan Stubbs, and the gift he gave me, believing that I "could do it," whatever "it" was. "You're smart," he said all those years ago in the Green Room in Fremont, me holding that book basket in the doorway. "You just need to try."

Maybe, I think, feeling the sting of my mother's neglect and my father's abandonment honed my focus on the importance of my own family? Maybe the pain was actually a gift, every bit as valuable as Allan Stubbs' words to me. It taught me what I really valued.

It's dark now as the traffic crawls toward Pasadena. Out of nowhere, I recall the slogan for my grandfather's 1958 campaign when he ran for Governor of California. His name was Goodwin

J. Knight and the slogan was a play on his name. "Good, Good, Goodie, Goodnight."

Is it Papa up above telling me to put it all to rest?

When the traffic comes to another standstill at Pacific Avenue in Glendale, I tap "favorites" on my phone to HH mobile.

"Hi Heath, what's up?" Hank's voice is clipped. I can hear him tapping away on the computer. He's still at work.

"I could wait 'till we both get home, but my mind is swirling and I need to talk."

The tapping stops. "Sure. You ok?"

"Mom just told me that she hid a letter to me from Dad." I pause waiting for his response.

"Wow. When?"

"Back in Fremont. Just before our wedding. She hid it somewhere in the garage."

"Somehow that doesn't surprise me."

"Same here, the mom-hiding-it part," I laugh. "You know Mom."

The traffic begins to let up. I'm silent on the other end of the phone.

"Heath, you still there?"

"I'm here."

"Do you know what it said?"

"Hank, my father loved me."

His voice softens. "He loved you? Of course he loved you. Look at you. Even if he was a total asshole, how could he not?"

I smile to myself as we hang up the call. In this moment, I have everything I ever wanted. Maybe I didn't get it all the way I would have chosen, but my life with Hank is the grand prize. And I created it, despite everything.

The slogan from my grandfather's campaign plays on a loop in my head as I turn up the street to our home.

"Good, Good, Goodie, Goodnight."

Acknowledgements

KIDS AND COCKTAILS DON'T MIX: A MEMOIR started with a balustrade that my cousin, Jonathan, salvaged from 127 Fremont Place. He'd gotten wind that the buyer of Mom's house was going to raze the old colonial. An historian by nature, Jonathan dashed over to Fremont looking for tangible evidence of where we came from—an actual "thing," he told me later, "that you can hold in your hand."

In the pile of debris in the driveway, the balustrade was sticking up like a sword in battle along with the lantern that had hung on the front porch and a cheap crystal chandelier from the dining room.

The balustrade was my prize. "Here," he'd laughed, handing it to me. "This and a couple of crystals from the chandelier in the dining room is all we've got left of Fremont."

I'd held it in my hand, the layers of Moe's bad paint jobs now chipped away in places to reveal raw mildewed wood. I went home, placed it in front of me at my desk and wrote an essay. Bernadette Murphy, my writing mentor, looked me in the eye after I finished reading it to her. "Heather, this is a book."

••

Many people helped make this book come to fruition and I'd like to thank them all.

Our three children, Allan, Hilary, and Joseph, are now grown and married. Mom called them "winners." Their support while writing this meant the world to me. Allan, for his encouragement, looking out for me and my work. Hilary, after reading the first few chapters, told me to stop writing essays and to concentrate on my book. Joseph, for being at the other end of the line as I was going through the publishing process. His expert eye was invaluable. Their three spouses, Anna, Oliver, and Shannon, whom I love as if they were my own children. I thank all of them deeply for believing in me, in this manuscript. And, to my granddaughters, Grace and India, who are babies now but will one day read this and know their "Baba's" story.

Hank and I just celebrated our forty-first anniversary. Dr. Ferguson had been right. I have never stopped loving or trusting him. This is the guy who came home from work and surprised me all those years ago with what was then a bulky laptop. "Heath, I thought you might want this." Before that, I'd been working on an old IBM Selectric. It was the best gift he's ever given me. It was the gift of support.

Ted Walch, our children's former teacher, my husband's former teacher, and long-time friend, supported my work, and without my knowing it, put this manuscript in the hands of author Caitlin Flanagan, whose work I so admire. Thank you both for encouraging me and supporting me. You both got the ball rolling and kept it rolling for me. Caitlin, your emails. They lifted me up when I felt like giving up.

Alexandra Shelley, my independent editor in New York, pushed me hard. Jo Haldeman, my mother-in-law, understood the need to tell one's story; I'm grateful for all the sharing and writing we did together. Wendy Siciliano and Kate Westlake, my closest friends, championed every word I wrote. Cindy Salcido, Martha Brown, Joan West, Betsy Nathane, Randi Schwimer, Sally Howell, Lise Davis, Libby Baney, Ann and Bob Sargent, and Mary Lynn Roj for cheering me on from start to finish. Anne Woodward Cassolato, my first best friend from childhood, still in my life. I cherish her kindness in those challenging years and beyond.

I will forever be grateful to my Aunt Carolyn who introduced me to the world of writing with that diary. I still have it.

To Allan Stubbs, my stepfather, who believed in me. That morning, standing there in the "Green Room" with my book basket.

Thank you to Bernadette Murphy. My right arm in every step of the manuscript. She was a phone call away when I needed her. Bernadette, I will forever be grateful for your professional guidance and foresight, telling me back then, "this is a book."

Thank you to Apprentice House Press. Thank you to Kevin Atticks at the helm. To those who chose this manuscript to publish. To Danielle Como, Sarah Thompson, and Peyton Skeels whom I have worked with to complete this project. I'll so miss our Zoom meetings. I am deeply grateful to you all.

••

As I finished writing each chapter in this manuscript, I called my mother to read it to her. She'd stop everything for me and listen. My mother, then, a transformed woman, and more of a mother to me later in life without the distraction of battling a wayward husband or dwindling finances, would often stop me mid-sentence while I was reading a chapter to her ("If I don't interrupt you, I'll forget!") with a quip or an anecdote that helped me craft a scene. Sometimes, her response was "Jesus, I was that bad?" We'd laugh. "Yep, Mom!"

She often told me to hurry up and write the next chapter. "I need to find out what happens next!"

I am so thankful that she was alive and well when I completed the first draft. That I had gotten it all down before she could no longer shoot me her one-liners, give me her take on what happened, and be that person on the other end of the line to read it to. Without her sharp wit and keen memory, would I have captured so much of her flavor? A character that, many have told me "couldn't be made up."

My sister, April, supported me enthusiastically the entire time I worked on this manuscript. She never inserted her own experiences, ideas, or take on our lives in Fremont and beyond. On occasion, I'd ask about dates, details, and sequences with which she was more familiar. That's it.

"It's your story, Heath," she said.

She encouraged me, championed me, and as a smart business woman, guided me as a writer. "Don't be afraid. Get it out there!"

When Mom's health declined, we became even closer. We were in it together, and no one out there could feel or understand the conflicts, the feelings, the enormity of taking care of, and slowly losing, our larger-than-life mother. Often, it was her strength and words that got me through that challenging time.

No inheritance, no favoritism—nothing in our past usurped the bond between us. Mom had always said when April and I were in a fight, "You better get along with your sister! When I'm gone, it'll be just you and April."

I couldn't see it then. "Are you kidding?!"

I see it now. We are devoted to each other.

Thank you to John Stubbs who helped me through my stepfather, Allan's, illness and passing. He and his wife, Joan, were so good to Mom.

After Dougie died, the MacDougall stepchildren visited Mom frequently. And, when she got sick, they continued to check in on her. Visit her, send cards, flowers, and make phone calls to her when she was at the Jewish Home for The Aging.

"They didn't drop me," Mom had said. "They care!"

The MacDougalls are like that. They care.

Jonathan and his husband, Raymundo, live four miles from me. I owe Jonathan a debt of gratitude for his help and connections to get Mom into the Jewish Home for the Aging. It was an incredible facility for her. Caring, professional, and "top-drawer," Mom'd said.

She loved it and embraced her new world, attending the weekly Friday night Shabbat. "Bernie goes!"

"Always about a man," April and I laughed. "With mom, it was always about a man."

Last summer, on Jonathan's sixtieth birthday, there was a party in their home. As Hank and I were leaving, I paused in his dining room. Frank Sinatra was crooning from the speakers as my eyes scanned the room which held so much memorabilia from our grandfather's home on Arden and a few things from Fremont. "Hold on a minute," I'd said to Hank. "I need to feel this. It's my childhood all over again."

"And, strangely," I'd added, "it's comforting."

••

My mother died a month after I completed the final draft. I miss her every day.

About the Author

Heather Haldeman lives in Pasadena, California. She has a loving husband, three grown children, and two granddaughters. Her work has been published in *The Christian Science Monitor*, *Chicken Soup for the Soul*, *From Freckles to Wrinkles*, *Grandmother Earth*, *The Mom Egg Review* and numerous online journals. She has received first, second, and third prizes for her essays. Visit her blog at Heatherhaldeman.blogspot.com.

Apprentice House is the country's only campus-based, student-staffed book publishing company. Directed by professors and industry professionals, it is a nonprofit activity of the Communication Department at Loyola University Maryland.

Using state-of-the-art technology and an experiential learning model of education, Apprentice House publishes books in untraditional ways. This dual responsibility as publishers and educators creates an unprecedented collaborative environment among faculty and students, while teaching tomorrow's editors, designers, and marketers.

Outside of class, progress on book projects is carried forth by the AH Book Publishing Club, a co-curricular campus organization supported by Loyola University Maryland's Office of Student Activities.

Eclectic and provocative, Apprentice House titles intend to entertain as well as spark dialogue on a variety of topics. Financial contributions to sustain the press's work are welcomed. Contributions are tax deductible to the fullest extent allowed by the IRS.

To learn more about Apprentice House books or to obtain submission guidelines, please visit www.apprenticehouse.com.

Apprentice House
Communication Department
Loyola University Maryland
4501 N. Charles Street
Baltimore, MD 21210
Ph: 410-617-5265
info@apprenticehouse.com • www.apprenticehouse.com

CPSIA information can be obtained
at www.ICGtesting.com
Printed in the USA
JSHW031505260521
15168JS00001B/3